MW00436633

Jesus' Sermon on the Mount

And His Confrontation with the World

Jesus' Sermon on the Mount

And His Confrontation with the World

An Exposition of Matthew 5–10

—Two Books in One—

D. A. Carson

BakerBooks
Grand Rapids, Michigan

© 1978, 1987 by D. A. Carson

Published by Baker Books
a division of Baker Book House Company
P.O. Box 6287, Grand Rapids, MI 49516-6287
www.bakerbooks.com

Paperback edition published 1999

Fourth printing, November 2005

The Sermon on the Mount: An Evangelical Exposition of Matthew 5–7 © 1978

When Jesus Confronted the World: An Exposition of Matthew 8–10 © 1987

Printed in the United States of America

All rights reserved. No part of this publication may be reproduced, stored in a retrieval system, or transmitted in any form or by any means—for example, electronic, photocopy, recording—without the prior written permission of the publisher. The only exception is brief quotations in printed reviews.

ISBN 0-8010-6531-3

Contents

PART ONE

Jesus' Sermon on the Mount

Preface

EARLY IN 1974 I was asked to give six addresses on the Sermon on the Mount to the Cambridge Inter-Collegiate Christian Union (CICCU). These addresses, slated for the Easter term of 1975, consumed a large part of my time and energy for the six weeks over which they were spread. I do not think I have ever enjoyed teaching people the Scriptures as much as I enjoyed speaking to the four or five hundred students who gathered every Saturday night. Unusually receptive, they challenged me by their genuine attentiveness to the Word of God.

Since then I have repeated the series two or three times, in churches located in British Columbia. As time has permitted, I have revised the series, writing it in a form more congenial to the printed page than a sermon or Bible reading usually is. However, I have deliberately not removed all traces of the earlier form. I have added two appendixes, largely elicited by questions that have been put to me. Some of the material in the first appendix was interwoven into the original series, but I have thought it best in this book to separate it.

How does this volume differ from those now in circulation which deal with the same passage? Why offer another study on the Sermon on the Mount? Several reasons spring to mind. This exposition is shorter than most others designed for the general reader; but that is because it is more condensed. I have tried hard to be freer from the categories of systematic theology than some of my predecessors, though I want my work to be informed by the most significant theological points of view. The material in the two appendixes is not usually included in popular expositions, but it may help the interested reader to view the interpretation of the Sermon on the Mount with a more balanced vision and with deeper understanding. But more than any other reason, I am offering these studies to a larger circle because I am deeply convinced that the church of Christ needs to study the Sermon on the Mount again and again.

I take pleasure in recording here my deep gratitude to many scores of writers. I have read some of the popular expositions, but apart from the sacred text itself I have made it a point above all to read the best commentaries I could secure. W. S. Kissinger's *The Sermon on the Mount: A History of Interpretation and Bibliography* has been an invaluable tool in the later stages of study. A gold mine of information, it introduced me to some serious works of which I was quite unaware. Informed readers will also sense my indebtedness to Robert Banks' *Jesus and the Law in the Synoptic Tradition.* I want to record my thanks to Tyndale House, Cambridge, which afforded me the opportunity to read a copy of Banks' doctoral dissertation before his published revision put in an appearance. I have read only a few foreign–language works on the Sermon on the Mount. This I regret, just as I regret that I could not canvass more of the enormous body of secondary literature. Even in the journals that have crossed my desk during the past quarter there has not been any shortage of studies on these three chapters of Matthew's Gospel.

My sincere gratitude is also extended to Eileen Appleby, who transcribed the tapes of the original addresses; and to Sue Wonnacott, and especially to Diane Smith, who transformed an excessively messy manuscript into neat and near-flawless typescript.

Soli Deo Gloria.

D. A. Carson
Northwest Baptist Theological Seminary
Vancouver, Canada

1

The Kingdom of Heaven

Its Norms and Witness *(5:3–16)*

Introduction

THE MORE I read these three chapters—Matthew 5, 6, and 7—the more I am both drawn to them and shamed by them. Their brilliant light draws me like a moth to a spotlight; but the light is so bright that it sears and burns. No room is left for forms of piety which are nothing more than veneer and sham. Perfection is demanded. Jesus says, "Be perfect . . . as your heavenly Father is perfect" (5:48).

The great theme of these three chapters is the kingdom of heaven. "The kingdom of heaven" is Matthew's customary expression for what other New Testament writers preferred to call "the kingdom of God." Matthew was like many Jews of his day who would avoid using the word "God." They felt it was too holy, too exalted; therefore euphemisms like "heaven" were adopted. In meaning, kingdom of heaven is identical to kingdom of God (cf. Matt. 19:23f.; Mark 10:23f.; etc.).

Four preliminary observations may help to clarify these expressions. First, the idea of "kingdom" in both the Old and New Testaments is primarily dynamic rather than spatial. It is not so much a kingdom with geographical borders as it is a "kingdominion," or reign. In the Scriptures, the spatial meaning of kingdom is second-ary and derivative.

Second, although the kingdom of God can refer to the totality of God's sovereignty, that is not what is in view in the Sermon on the Mount. Indeed, in the universal sense, God's kingdom—his reign—is eternal and all-embracing. No one and nothing can escape from it. From the time of Jesus' resurrection and exaltation onward, all of this divine sovereignty is mediated through Christ. Jesus himself taught this: "All authority in heaven and on earth has been given to me" (Matt. 28:18). This universal authority is what Paul refers to when he says that Christ must reign until God has put all his ene-mies under his feet (1 Cor. 15:25). Some refer to this "kingdom" as the mediatorial kingdom of God, because God's authority, his reign, is mediated through Christ.

But this cannot be the kingdom of God most frequently in view in the New Testament. In the Sermon on the Mount, not everyone enters the kingdom of heaven, but only those who are poor in spirit (5:3), obedient (7:21), and surpassingly righteous (5:20). Similarly, in John's Gospel, only he who is born from above can see or enter the kingdom of God (John 3:3, 5). Since the universal kingdom by definition must include everyone whether he likes it or not, we see that the kingdom in these passages cannot be universal. There are conditions to be met before entrance is possible. The kingdom with which I am concerned in these essays, the kingdom preached by Jesus, is a *subset* of the uni-versal kingdom.

We get an idea what is meant when we compare Mark 9:45 and Mark 9:47. The first verse reads: "And if your foot causes you to sin, cut it off. It is better for you to *enter life* crippled, than to have two feet and be thrown into hell." The second reads: "And if your eye causes you to sin, pluck it out. It is better for you to *enter the king-dom of God* with one eye, than to have two eyes and be thrown into hell." To enter the kingdom of God, then, is to enter life. That is char-acteristically the language of John's Gospel; however, it is found in the Sermon on the Mount itself. These three chapters of Matthew are concerned with entering the kingdom (Matt. 5:3, 10; 7:21), which is equivalent to entering into life (7:13f.; cf. 19:14, 16).

Thus the kingdom of heaven in this narrower sense is that exer-cise of God's sovereignty which bears directly on his saving pur-poses. All who are in the kingdom have life; all who are not in the kingdom do not have life. We might schematize these conclusions as follows:

Figure 1

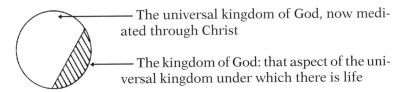

The universal kingdom of God, now mediated through Christ

The kingdom of God: that aspect of the universal kingdom under which there is life

Or, if God's saving purposes lie at the heart of his sovereignty, the scheme might be improved thus:

Figure 2

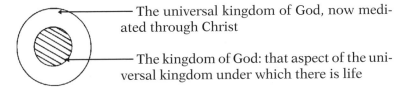

The universal kingdom of God, now mediated through Christ

The kingdom of God: that aspect of the universal kingdom under which there is life

Of course, this diagram overschematizes the evidence. The word "kingdom," having primary reference to the dynamic, can be used in the more extended sense or the special salvific sense. For example, Jesus elsewhere tells a parable in which he likens the kingdom to a man who sowed good seed in his field, yet discovered weeds sprouting up, sown by an enemy (Matt. 13:24–29, 36–43). It appears as if the kingdom at this point embraces both wheat and weeds; in nonmetaphorical terms, the kingdom embraces both men with life and men without life. In terms of the circular diagram above, the line between the inner circle and the outer becomes very thin. The emphasis seems to be on the universal kingdom, even though the sowing of good seed is its central purpose. Indeed, as a result of that purpose, the present mixed crop one day gets sorted out: at harvest time, the weeds are tied into bundles and burned, and the wheat is gathered into the master's barn (Matt. 13:30).

This ambiguity helps us to understand Matthew 8:10–12, where Jesus says, "I tell you the truth, I have not found anyone in Israel with such great faith. I say to you that many will come from the east and the west, and will take their places at the feast with Abraham, Isaac and Jacob in the kingdom of heaven. But the subjects of the kingdom will be thrown outside, into the darkness, where there will be weeping and grinding of teeth." The Jews, privileged as they were to be the inheritors of the Old Testament revelation, were the expected "subjects of the kingdom"; but Jesus indicates that in fact many from all over the world will join the patriarchs in the kingdom. He also warns that many expected subjects will be excluded from the delights of God's saving reign.

Third, the expression "kingdom of God," in the saving sense (the only way I will use it from now on), applies to both present and future. Taken together, the books of the New Testament insist that the kingdom of God has already arrived; a person may enter the kingdom and receive life now, life "to the full" (John 10:10). Jesus himself argues that if he drives out demons by the Spirit of God—and he does—then the kingdom of God *has come* (Matt. 12:28). Nevertheless, the books of the New Testament insist that the kingdom will be inherited only in the future, when Christ comes again. Eternal life, though experienced now, is consummated then, in conjunction with such a renovation of the universe that the only adequate description is "a new heaven and a new earth" (Isa. 65:17; 66:22; 2 Peter 3:13; Rev. 21:1; cf. Rom. 8:21ff.).

Jesus tells several parables with the specific purpose of removing misconceptions among his followers, misconceptions to the effect that the full arrival of the kingdom would be achieved without any delay. He wanted them to think otherwise: the coming of the kingdom in its fullness might well require significant delay. For example, in one parable in Luke's Gospel (Luke 19:11ff.), Jesus pictures a man of noble birth who goes to a distant country and then returns; and he receives full authority of a kingdom only after he has returned. Jesus is that nobleman, and the consummation of the kingdom awaits his return.

Another diagram might help to explain these truths:

Figure 3

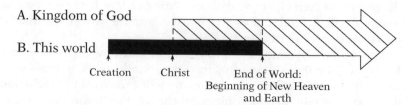

A. Kingdom of God

B. This world

Creation   Christ   End of World:
Beginning of New Heaven
and Earth

All men live on the plane of "this world"; but from the time of Christ's coming to the end of the world, the inheritors of the kingdom (and they alone) also live on the plane of the kingdom. Thus, from the circular diagrams it is clear that a man may or may not be in the kingdom of God; from the linear sketch it is clear that if he is in it now, he may yet look forward to its consummation at the end of the world, when Christ returns. There is an "already" aspect of the kingdom, and a "not yet" aspect: the kingdom has already come, but it has not yet arrived.

Fourth, although entering into life and entering the kingdom are synonymous, they are not always strictly interchangeable. The very idea of "kingdom" as "dynamic reign" brings with it overtones of authority and submission not normally conjured up when we speak of "life." The kingdom of God speaks of God's authority, mediated through Christ; therefore it speaks equally of our whole-hearted allegiance to that authority. That is why Matthew 7:21–23 so stresses obedience: "Not everyone who says to me, 'Lord, Lord,' will enter the Kingdom of heaven, but only he who does the will of my Father who is in heaven. Many will say to me in that day, 'Lord, Lord, did we not prophesy in your name, and in your name drive out demons and perform many miracles?' Then I will tell them plainly, 'I never knew you. Away from me, you evil-doers!'"

It is the kingdom of heaven, then, that is the great theme of the Sermon on the Mount. At the end of Matthew 4 we learn that Jesus went throughout Galilee "preaching the good news of the kingdom" (4:23). Both his preaching and his miracles of healing attracted large crowds to him. Accordingly Matthew 5 opens with the words, "Now when he saw the crowds, he went up on a mountainside and sat down. His disciples came to him, and he began to teach them." Some have urged that Jesus' response to the crowds was to withdraw and train his disciples. By training them Jesus would be multiplying his own ministry. This probably reads too much into the text, for in Matthew's Gospel "disciple" is not necessarily a reference to the twelve apostles, nor even to committed believers and followers; it can refer to someone who is merely following and learning at that moment—without reference to his level of commitment (see, for instance, Matt. 8:21; or the example of Judas Iscariot). Moreover, if "disciples" are sometimes distinguished from "the crowds" (as in Matt. 23:1), we may be sure that crowds often pressed in close to hear the teaching primarily designed for those most concerned to learn. From the huge crowds assembling from all over northern Palestine, perhaps a smaller crowd of "disciples" followed Jesus to the quiet hill country west of Galilee in order to receive more extended teaching; and perhaps more and more joined the class, partly because of Jesus' rising reputation and partly because a crowd attracts a crowd. This way of understanding the text is confirmed by Matthew's conclusion to the Sermon on the Mount: "When Jesus had finished saying these things, *the crowds* were amazed at his teaching" (7:28). It is confirmed, too, by the fact that Jesus presses these "disciples" to enter the kingdom, to enter into life (7:13f.; 7:21–23).

Jesus arrived at his chosen theater and "sat down." In his day, this was the traditional position for a teacher in a synagogue or school. Some English versions then say: "He opened his mouth and taught them, saying. . . ." We might ask ourselves wryly how he could have taught them without opening his mouth, until we recognize that the expression is a semitic idiom, a traditional formula. It seems to add deliberateness and sobriety to what follows.

The Norms of the Kingdom
Matthew 5:3–12

The Beatitudes, 5:3–10

There are some general observations to make about these beatitudes before examining them individually. First, the word "beatitude" is a rough transliteration of the Latin *beatus*. Some Christians call these beatitudes "macarisms." This is a rough transliteration of the Greek word *makarios*. Both "beatitude" and "macarism" are transliterations of foreign words which can best be translated "blessed."

Although some modern translations prefer "happy" to "blessed," it is a poor exchange. Those who are blessed will generally be profoundly happy; but blessedness cannot be reduced to happiness. In the Scriptures, man can bless God and God can bless man. This duality gives us a clue just what is meant. To be "blessed" means, fundamentally, to be approved, to find approval. When man blesses God, he is approving God. Of course, he is not doing this in some condescending manner, but rather he is eulogizing God, praising God. When God blesses man, he is approving man; and that is always an act of condescension.

Since this is God's universe there can be no higher "blessing" than to be approved by God. We must ask ourselves whose blessing we diligently seek. If God's blessing means more to us than the approval of loved ones no matter how cherished, or of colleagues no matter how influential, then the beatitudes will speak to us very personally and deeply.

Another observation is that the kind of blessing is not arbitrary in any of these eight beatitudes. The thing promised in each case grows naturally (or rather, supernaturally) out of the character described. For example, in verse 6 the person who hungers and thirsts for righteousness is filled (with righteousness); in verse 7 the merciful are shown mercy. The blessing is always correlated with the condition, as we shall see.

Finally, we need to notice that two of the beatitudes promise the same reward. The first beatitude reads, "Blessed are the poor in spirit, for theirs is the kingdom of heaven" (5:3). The last one says, "Blessed are those who are persecuted because of righteousness, for theirs is the kingdom of heaven" (5:10). To begin and end with the same expression is a stylistic device called an "inclusio." This means that everything bracketed between the two can really be included under the one theme, in this case, the kingdom of heaven. That is why I have called the beatitudes, collectively, "The Norms of the Kingdom."

> *First*: "Blessed are the poor in spirit, for theirs is the kingdom of heaven" (5:3).

What is poverty of spirit? It is surely not financial destitution, or material poverty. Nor is it poverty of spiritual awareness. Still less is it poor-spiritedness, that is, a deficiency of vitality or courage. And certainly the expression does not denote poverty of Holy Spirit.

The expression seems to have developed in Old Testament times. God's people were often referred to as "the poor" or "the poor of the Lord," owing to their extreme economic distress. This distress often came about because of oppression. Some of the various Hebrew words for "poor" can also mean "lowly," or "humble": the association of the two ideas is natural enough. For example, in Proverbs 16:19 we read, "It is better to be of a humble spirit with the lowly, than to divide the spoil with the proud." The word translated "lowly" is elsewhere rendered "poor"; and both "poor" and "lowly" fit the context. Two verses in Isaiah stand close in meaning to the poverty of spirit of which Jesus speaks: "Thus says the high and lofty One who inhabits eternity, whose name is Holy: I dwell in the high and holy place, and with him also who is of a contrite and humble spirit" (Isa. 57:15). Again: "To this man will I look, namely to him who is poor and of a contrite spirit, and who trembles at my word" (Isa. 66:2).

Poverty of spirit is the personal acknowledgment of spiritual bankruptcy. It is the conscious confession of unworth before God. As such, it is the deepest form of repentance. It is exemplified by the guilty publican in the corner of the Temple: "God, be merciful to me, a sinner!" It is not a man's confession that he is ontologically insignificant, or personally without value, for such would be untrue; it is, rather, a confession that he is sinful and rebellious and utterly without moral virtues adequate to commend him to God. From within such a framework, poverty of spirit becomes a general confession of a man's need for God, a humble admission of impotence without him. Poverty of spirit many *end* in a Gideon vanquishing the enemy hosts; but it *begins* with a Gideon who first affirms he is incapable of the task, and who insists that if the Lord does not go with him he would much prefer to stay home and thresh grain.

Poverty of spirit cannot be artificially induced by self-hatred. Still less does it have in common with showy humility. It cannot be aped successfully by the spiritually haughty who covet its qualities. Such efforts may achieve token success before peers; they never deceive God. Indeed, most of us are repulsed by sham humility, whether our own or that of others.

I suspect that there is no pride more deadly than that which finds its roots in great learning, great external piety, or a showy defense of orthodoxy. My suspicion does not call into question the value of learning, piety, or orthodoxy; rather, it exposes professing believers to the full glare of this beatitude. Pride based on genuine virtues has the greatest potential for self-deception; but our Lord will allow none of it. Poverty of spirit he insists on—a full, honest, factual, conscious, and conscientious recognition before God of personal moral unworth. It is, as I have said, the deepest form of repentance.

It is not surprising, then, that the kingdom of heaven belongs to the poor in spirit. At the very outset of the Sermon on the Mount, we learn that we do not have the spiritual resources to put any of the Sermon's precepts into practice. We cannot fulfill God's standards ourselves. We must come to him and acknowledge our spiritual bankruptcy, emptying ourselves of our self-righteousness, moral self-esteem, and personal vainglory. Emptied of these things we are ready for him to fill us. Much of the rest of the Sermon on the Mount is designed to remove these self-delusions from us, and foster within us a genuine poverty of spirit. The genuineness and depth of this repentance is a prime requirement for entering into life.

> *Second*: "Blessed are those who mourn, for they will be comforted" (5:4).

This verse follows naturally from the one which precedes it. Mournfulness can be understood as the emotional counterpart to poverty of spirit.

The world in which we live likes to laugh. Pleasure dispensers sell cheers and chuckles, all for a neat profit. The *summum bonum* of life becomes a good time, and the immediate goal is the next high. The world does not like mourners; mourners are wet blankets.

Yet the Son of God insists, "Blessed are those who mourn, for they will be comforted." This does not mean the Christian is to be perpetually morose, forever weepy. The Christian must not fit the stereotype in the mind of the little girl who exclaimed, "That horse must be a Christian; it's got such a long face!" Still less is the verse a defense of that grief which arises out of groveling self-pity.

What is it, then? At the individual level, this mourning is a personal grief over personal sin. This is the mourning experienced by a man who begins to recognize the blackness of his sin, the more he is exposed to the purity of God. Isaiah was one such, as he was accorded a vision of the Deity, in which even the very angels of heaven covered their faces and cried in solemn worship, "Holy! Holy! Holy!" Isaiah's reaction was utter devastation (Isa. 6:5). It is the cry of a man who goes after purity in his own strength and finds he cannot achieve it, and cries, "What a wretched man I am! Who will rescue me from this body of death?" (Rom. 7:24).

But there can also be a mourning stimulated by broader considerations. Sometimes the sin of this world, the lack of integrity, the injustice, the cruelty, the cheapness, the selfishness, all pile onto the consciousness of a sensitive man and make him weep. Most of us would prefer merely to condemn. We are prepared to walk with Jesus through Matthew 23 and repeat his pronouncements of doom; but we stop before we get to the end of the chapter and join him in weeping over the city. The great lights in church history learned to weep—men of the caliber of Calvin, Whitefield, Wesley, Shaftesbury, and Wilberforce.

The Christian is to be the truest realist. He reasons that death is there, and must be faced. God is there, and will be known by all as Savior or Judge. Sin is there, and it is unspeakably ugly and black in the light of God's purity. Eternity is there, and every living human being is rushing toward it. God's revelation is there, and the alternatives it presents will come to pass: life or death, pardon or condemnation, heaven or hell. These are realities which will not go away. The man who lives in the light of them, and rightly assesses himself and his world in the light of them, cannot but mourn. He mourns for the sins and blasphemies of his nation. He mourns for the erosion of the very concept of truth. He mourns over the greed, the cynicism, the lack of integrity. He mourns that there are so few mourners.

But he will be comforted! And what comfort. There is no comfort or joy that can compare with what God gives to those who mourn. These people exchange the sackcloth of mourning for a garment of praise, the ashes of grief for the oil of gladness. At the individual level, the mourner grieves over his sin because he sees how great is the offense before God; but he learns to trust Jesus as the one who has paid sin's ransom (Mark 10:45). He luxuriates in deep joy as he discovers in his own experience that Jesus came to save his people from their sins (Matt. 1:21). And as he weeps for other men, he finds to his delight that God is answering his prayers, very often even working through him to untangle sins' knots and provide others with new birth, new righteousness. But even this great comfort will be surpassed: one day in a new heaven and new earth, the kingdom of God will be consummated, and God himself will wipe away all tears from the eyes of those who once mourned. There will be no more death or mourning or crying or pain, for the old order of things will have passed away (Rev. 21:4).

Third: "Blessed are the meek, for they will inherit the earth" (5:5).

How does meekness differ from poverty of spirit? In this way, I think: Poverty of spirit has to do with a person's assessment of himself, especially with respect to God, while meekness has more to do with his relationship with God and with men.

Meekness is not, as many people imagine, a weakness. It must not be confused with being wishy-washy. A meek person is not necessarily indecisive or timid. He is not so unsure of himself that he could be pushed over by a hard slap from a wet noodle. Still less is meekness to be confused with mere affability. Some people are just naturally nice and easy-going; but then again, so are some dogs. Meekness goes much deeper.

Meekness is a controlled desire to see the other's interests advance ahead of one's own. Think of Abraham's deference to Lot: that was meekness. According to Numbers 12:3, Moses was the meekest man who ever lived, and his meekness is supremely demonstrated in that chapter by his refusal to defend himself, by his controlled self-commitment to the Lord when his person and privilege were under attack. But it is Jesus himself who is the only one who could ever say with integrity, "Come to me, all you who are weary and burdened, and I will give you rest. Take my yoke upon you and learn from me, for I am meek and humble in heart, and you will find rest for your souls" (Matt. 11:28f.).

Dr. D. Martyn Lloyd-Jones puts it this way:

> The man who is truly meek is the one who is amazed that God and man can think of him as well as they do and treat him as well as they do. . . . Finally, I would put it like this. We are to leave everything—ourselves, our rights, our cause, our whole future—in the hands of God, and especially so if we feel we are suffering unjustly.[1]

The Scriptures make much of meekness (see 2 Cor. 10:1; Gal. 5:22f.; Col. 3:12; 1 Peter 3:15f.; James 1:19–21), and so it is the more appalling that meekness does not characterize more of us who claim to be Christians. Both at the personal level, where we are too often concerned with justifying ourselves rather than with edifying our brother, and at the corporate level, where we are more successful at organizing rallies, institutions, and pressure groups than at extending the kingdom of God, meekness has not been the mark of most Christians for a long time.

To the extent that meekness is practiced among us—to that extent, we may be sure—a crassly materialistic world will oppose it. Materialism argues, "Grab what you can; the strong man comes first and the devil take the hindmost." This is true whether one is on the right or the left of the political spectrum. Individually, each man tends to assume, without thinking, that he is at the center of the universe; therefore he relates poorly to the four billion others who are laboring under a similar delusion. But the meek man sees himself and all the others under God. Since he is poor in spirit, he does not think more highly of himself than he ought to. Therefore he is able to relate well to others.

And the meek shall inherit the earth! These words, cited from Psalm 37:11, constitute a devastating contradiction to the philosophical materialism so prevalent in our own day. But this blessing of inheritance is true in at least two ways. First, only the genuine meek man will be content; his ego is not so inflated that he thinks he must always have more. Besides, in Christ he already sees himself "possessing everything" (2 Cor. 6:10; cf. 1 Cor. 3:21–23). With this eternal perspective in view he can afford to be meek. Moreover, one day he will come into the fullness of his inheritance, when he will find the beatitude fulfilled most literally. Fifty billion trillion years into eternity (if I may speak in terms of time) God's people will still be rejoicing that this beatitude is literally true. In a new heaven *and earth*, they will be grateful that by grace they learned to be meek during their initial threescore years and ten.

> *Fourth*: "Blessed are those who hunger and thirst for righteousness, for they will be filled" (5:6)

Thorough righteousness is often parodied as some form of obsolete Victorian prudishness, or narrow-minded and vehement legalism. The pursuit of righteousness is not popular even among professing Christians. Many today are prepared to seek other things: spiritual maturity, real happiness, the Spirit's power, effective witnessing skills. Other people chase from preacher to preacher and conference to conference seeking some vague "blessing" from on high. They hunger for spiritual experience, they thirst for the conscience of God.

But how many hunger and thirst for righteousness?

This is not to argue that the other things are not desirable, but rather that they are not as basic as righteousness. It is with good reason that this is the fourth beatitude. The man marked by poverty of spirit (5:3), who grieves over sin personal and social (5:4), and approaches God and man with meekness (5:5), must also be characterized as hungry and thirsty for righteousness (5:6). It is not that he wants to be a little bit better, still less that he thinks of righteousness as an optional luxury to add to his other graces; rather, he *hungers* and *thirsts* for it. He cannot get along without righteousness; it is as important to him as food and drink.

Most people who read these lines have experienced very little hunger and thirst. I myself am not old enough to have undergone the privations many experienced during the Great Depression or the last world war. However, two or three times during the sixties, when I was a student first at university and then at seminary, I ran out of money and food at the same time. Too proud to ask for help, and wanting to see if God would really supply what I needed, I drank water to keep my stomach from rumbling and carried on as usual. After two or three days I *began* to understand what it is to be hungry.

The norms of the kingdom require that men and women be hungry and thirsty for righteousness. This is so basic to Christian living that Dr. D. Martyn Lloyd-Jones says:

> I do not know of a better test that anyone can apply to himself or herself in this whole matter of the Christian profession than a verse like this. If this verse is to you one of the most blessed statements of the whole of Scripture, you can be quite certain you are a Christian; if it is not, then you had better examine the foundations again.[2]

What is this righteousness which we must thus pursue? In Paul's epistles, "righteousness" can refer to the righteousness of Christ which God reckons to the believer's account, even as God reckons the believer's sin to Jesus Christ. If that were the righteousness here in view, Jesus would be inviting unbelievers to pursue the righteousness God bestows by virtue of Christ's substitutionary death. Some have thought that "righteousness" in Matthew's Gospel refers to the vindication of the downtrodden and the afflicted. Now, however, those who have studied Matthew's use of the term increasingly recognize that "righteousness" here (and also in verses 10 and 20) means a pattern of life in conformity to God's will. Righteousness thus includes within its semantic range all the derivative or specialized meanings, but cannot be reduced to any one of them.

The person who hungers and thirsts for righteousness, then, hungers and thirsts for conformity to God's will. He is not drifting aimlessly in a sea of empty religiosity; still less is he puttering about distracted by inconsequential trivia. Rather, his whole being echoes the prayer of a certain Scottish saint who cried, "O God, make me just as holy as a pardoned sinner can be!" His delight is the Word of God, for where else is God's will, to which he hungers to be conformed, so clearly set forth? He wants to be righteous, not simply because he fears God, but because righteousness has become for him the most eminently desirable thing in the world.

And the result? Those who hunger and thirst for righteousness will be filled. The context demands that we understand the blessing to mean "will be filled *with righteousness.*" The Lord gives this famished person the desires of his heart.

This does not mean that the person is now so satisfied with the righteousness given him that his hunger and thirst for righteousness are forever vanquished. Elsewhere, Jesus does in fact argue along such lines: "Whoever drinks the water I give him will never thirst. . . . I am the bread of life. He who comes to me will never go hungry, and he who believes in me will never be thirsty" (John 4:14; 6:35). So there is a sense in which we are satisfied with Jesus and all he is and provides. Nevertheless, there is a sense in which we continue to be unsatisfied.

An example from Paul makes this paradox understandable. Paul can testify, "I *know* whom I have believed, and am convinced that he is able to guard what I have entrusted to him for that day" (2 Tim. 1:12); but he can also say, "I *want to know* Christ and the power of his resurrection and the fellowship of sharing in his sufferings, becoming like him in his death . . ." (Phil. 3:10). In other words, Paul has come to know Christ, but knowing him, he wants to know him better.

In a similar way, the person who hungers and thirsts for righteousness is blessed by God, and filled; but the righteousness with which he is filled is so wonderful that he hungers and thirsts for more of it. This built-in cycle of growth is easy to understand as soon as we remember that righteousness in this text refers not to obeying some rules, but to conformity to all of God's will. The more a person pursues conformity to God's will, the more attractive the goal becomes, and the greater the advances made.

> *Fifth*: "Blessed are the merciful, for they will be shown mercy" (5:7).

Some try to interpret this verse legalistically, as if to say that the only way to obtain mercy from God is by showing mercy to others: God's mercy thus becomes essentially contingent to our own. They point to Matthew 6:14f. (which we shall consider in the third chapter): "For if you forgive men when they sin against you, your heavenly Father will also forgive you. But if you do not forgive men their sins, your Father will not forgive your sins." But whenever a tit-for-tat interpretation of such verses prevails, I think there is a failure to understand both the context and the nature of mercy.

What is mercy? How does it differ from grace? The two terms are frequently synonymous; but where there is a distinction between the two, it appears that grace is a loving response when love is undeserved, and mercy is a loving response prompted by the misery and helplessness of the one on whom the love is to be showered. Grace answers to the undeserving; mercy answers to the miserable.

Jesus says in this beatitude that we are to be merciful. We are to be compassionate and gentle, especially toward the miserable and helpless. If we are not merciful, we will not be shown mercy. But how could the unmerciful man receive mercy? The one who is not merciful is inevitably so unaware of his own state that he thinks he needs no mercy. He cannot picture himself as miserable and wretched; so how shall God be merciful toward him? He is like the Pharisee in the temple who was unmerciful toward the wretched tax collector in the corner (Luke 18:10ff.). By contrast, the person whose experience reflects these beatitudes is conscious of his spiritual bankruptcy (Matt. 5:3), grieves over it (5:4), and hungers for righteousness (5:6). He is merciful toward the wretched because he recognizes himself to be wretched; in being merciful he is also shown mercy.

The Christian, moreover, is at a midpoint. He is to forgive others because in the past Christ has already forgiven him (cf. Eph. 4:32; Col. 3:13). Simultaneously he recognizes his constant need for more forgiveness, and becomes forgiving as a result of this perspective as well (cf. Matt. 6:14; and especially 18:21–35). The Christian forgives because he has been forgiven; he forgives because he needs forgiveness. In precisely the same way, and for the same kind of reasons, the disciple of Jesus Christ is merciful.

It is sometimes said that an alcoholic who won't admit he's an alcoholic hates all other alcoholics. Similarly, it is generally true that the sinner who won't face up to his sin hates all other sinners. But the person who has recognized his own helplessness and wretchedness is grateful for whatever mercy is shown him; and he learns to be merciful toward others.

This macarism forces the professing disciple of Jesus Christ to ask himself some hard questions. Am I merciful or supercilious to the wretched? Am I gentle or hard-nosed toward the downtrodden? Am I helpful or callous toward the backslidden? Am I compassionate or impatient with the fallen?

I am persuaded that, should the Spirit of God usher in another period of refreshing revival in the Western world, one of the earliest signs of it will be that admission of spiritual bankruptcy which finds its satisfaction in God and his righteousness, and goes on to be richly merciful toward others.

Sixth: "Blessed are the pure in heart, for they will see God" (5:8).

In this beatitude, our Lord confers special blessing not on the intellectually keen, nor on the emotionally pious, but on the pure in heart. In biblical imagery, the heart is the center of the entire personality. Jesus' assessment of the natural heart, however, is not very encouraging. Elsewhere in Matthew's Gospel he says, "For out of the heart come evil thoughts, murder, adultery, sexual immorality, theft, false testimony, slander" (15:19; cf. Jer. 17:9; Rom. 1:21; 2:5).

Despite this horrible diagnosis, the sixth beatitude insists that purity of heart is the indispensable prerequisite for fellowship with God—for "seeing" God. "Who shall ascend into the hill of the Lord? Who shall stand in his holy place? He who has clean hands *and a pure heart,* who has not lifted up his soul to vanity, nor sworn deceitfully" (Ps. 24:3f; cf. Ps. 73:1). God is holy; therefore the writer of the epistle to the Hebrews insists, "Make every effort . . . to be holy; without holiness no one will see the Lord" (Heb. 12:14).

Purity of heart must never be confused with outward conformity to rules. Because it is the heart which must be pure, this beatitude interrogates us with awkward questions like these: What do you think about when your mind slips into neutral? How much sympathy do you have for deception, no matter how skillful? For shady humor, no matter how funny? To what do you pay consistent allegiance? What do you want more than anything else? What and whom do you love? To what extent are your actions and words accurate reflections of what is in your heart? To what extent do your actions and words constitute a cover-up for what is in your heart? Our hearts must be pure, clean, unstained.

One day, when the kingdom of heaven is consummated, when there is a new heaven and a new earth in which only righteousness dwells, when Jesus Christ himself appears, we shall be like him (1 John 3:2). That is our long-range expectation, our hope. On this basis John argues, "Everyone who has hope in him [that is, in Christ] purifies himself, just as he is pure" (1 John 3:3). In other words, according to John, the Christian purifies himself now because pure is what he will ultimately be. His present efforts are consistent with his future hope. The same theme is found in various forms throughout the New Testament. In one sense, of course, the demands of the kingdom do not change: perfection is always required (5:48). But from this it follows that the disciple of Jesus who looks forward to the kingdom as it will be finally perfected, is already determined to prepare for it. Knowing himself to be in the kingdom already, he is concerned with purity because he recognizes that the King is pure, and the kingdom in its perfected form will admit only purity.

The pure in heart are blessed because they will see God. Although this will not be ultimately true until the new heaven and earth, yet it is also true even now. Our perception of God and his ways, as well as our fellowship with him, depends on our purity of heart. The *visio Dei*—what an incentive to purity!

> *Seventh*: "Blessed are the peacemakers, for they will be called sons of God" (5:9).

This beatitude does not hold out a blessing to the peaceful, nor to those who yearn for peace, but to the peace*makers*.

Within the total biblical framework, the greatest peacemaker is Jesus Christ—the Prince of Peace. He makes peace between God and man by removing sin, the ground of alienation; he makes peace between man and man both by removing sin and by bringing men into a right relationship with God (see especially Eph. 2:11–22). Jesus gave the traditional Jewish greeting new depths of meaning when, *after his death and resurrection*, he greeted his disciples with the words, "Peace be with you" (Luke 24:36; John 20:19). Thus the good news of Jesus Christ is the greatest peacemaking message, and the Christian who shares his faith is, fundamentally, a harbinger of peace, a peacemaker. Small wonder Paul uses the imagery of Isaiah, who pictures messengers racing along the trails of the Judean hill country: "How beautiful on the mountains are the feet of those who bring good news, who proclaim peace, who bring good tidings, who proclaim salvation, who say to Zion, 'Your God reigns!'" (Isa. 52:7; Rom. 10:15).

Yet there is nothing in the context to argue that in Matthew 5:9 Jesus is restricting himself to gospel peacemaking. Rather, the disciple of Jesus Christ must be a peacemaker in the broadest sense of the term. The Christian's role as peacemaker extends not only to spreading the gospel, but to lessening tensions, seeking solutions, ensuring that communication is understood. Perhaps his most difficult assignments will take place on those occasions when he is personally involved. Then he will remember that "man's anger does not bring about the righteous life that God desires" (James 1:20), and that "a soft answer turns away wrath" (Prov. 15:1). He will not confuse issues, even important issues, with his own ego-image; and fearful lest he be guilty of generating more heat than light, he will learn to lower his voice and smile more broadly in proportion to the intensity of the argument.

Peacemakers are blessed because they will be called "sons of God"—not "children of God," as in the King James Version. The difference is slight, but significant. In Jewish thought, "son" often bears the meaning "partaker of the character of," or the like. If someone calls you the "son of a dog," this is not an aspersion on your parents, but on you: you partake of the character of a dog. Thus, "son of God" may have a different connotation than "child of God." Both expressions can refer to some sort of filial relationship; but the former has more emphasis on character than position.

The peacemaker's reward, then, is that he will be called a son of God. He reflects his heavenly Father's wonderful peacemaking character. Even now there is a sense in which Christians intuitively recognize this divine dimension in the character of the peacemaker. For example, when Christians at some convention or church business meeting enter into heated debate, the brother who keeps calm, respectfully listens to each viewpoint with fairness and courtesy, and spreads oil on the troubled waters is silently regarded by his peers as spiritual. But such conduct ought to be considered normal among disciples of Jesus Christ, for Jesus Christ himself has made it normative. It is part and parcel of being a son of God.

> *Eighth*: "Blessed are those who are persecuted because of right-
> eousness, for theirs is the kingdom of heaven" (5:10).

This final beatitude does not say, "Blessed are those who are persecuted because they are objectionable, or because they rave like wild-eyed fanatics, or because they pursue some religio-political cause." The blessing is restricted to those who suffer persecution *because of righteousness* (cf. 1 Peter 3:13f.; 4:12–16). The believers described in this passage are those determined to live as Jesus lived.

Persecution can take many forms; it need not be limited to the rigorous variety experienced by our fellow-believers in certain repressive countries. A Christian in the West who practices righteousness may be ridiculed by his family, ostracized by his relatives. But even the Christian who comes from a secure and understanding home will face flak somewhere. Perhaps at work, he will discover that some of his colleagues are saying of him, "Well, you know, he's a Christian; but he carries it a bit far. He won't even cheat on his income tax. The other day when I offered to slip him a company binder that I knew he needed for his private papers at home, he turned it down. When I pressed him, he said that taking it would be stealing! And have you ever seen his face cloud over when I tell one of my jokes? What a prig!"

The reward for being persecuted because of righteousness is the kingdom of heaven. In other words, this beatitude serves as a test for all the beatitudes. Just as a person must be poor in spirit to enter the kingdom (5:3), so will he be persecuted because of righteousness if he is to enter the kingdom. This final beatitude becomes one of the most searching of all of them, and binds up the rest; for if the disciple of Jesus never experiences any persecution at all, it may fairly be asked where righteousness is being displayed in his life. If there is no righteousness, no conformity to God's will, how shall he enter the kingdom?

This basic principle reappears again and again in the New Testament. The Christian lives in a sinful world; therefore if he exhibits genuine, transparent righteousness he will be rejected by many. Genuine righteousness condemns people by implication; small wonder that people often lash out in retaliation. Christ's disciples by their righteous living thus divide men: men are either repelled or drawn to our precious Savior. Jesus himself taught:

> If the world hates you, keep in mind that it hated me first. If you belonged to the world, it would love you as its own. As it is, you do not belong to the world, but I have chosen you out of the world. That is why the world hates you. Remember the words I spoke to you: "No servant is greater than his master." If they persecuted me, they will persecute you also. If they obeyed my teaching, they will obey yours also (John 15:18–20).

Paul adds, "For it has been granted to you on behalf of Christ not only to believe on him, but also to suffer for him" (Phil. 1:29). "In fact, everyone who wants to live a godly life in Christ Jesus will be persecuted" (2 Tim. 3:12; cf. 1 Thess. 3:3f.).

This eighth beatitude is so important that Jesus expands it, making it more pointed by changing the third–person form of the beatitudes to the direct address of second person:

Expansion, 5:11f.

> Blessed are you when people insult you, persecute you and falsely say all kinds of evil against you because of me. Rejoice and be glad, because great is your reward in heaven, for in the same way they persecuted the prophets who were before you (5:11f.).

Besides the impact of the direct discourse, this expansion of the eighth beatitude affords three important insights.

First, persecution is explicitly broadened to include insults and spoken malice. It cannot be limited to physical opposition or torture.

Second, the phrase "because of righteousness" (5:10) Jesus now parallels with "because of me" (5:11). This confirms that the righteousness of life that is in view is in imitation of Jesus. Simultaneously, it so identifies the disciple of Jesus with the practice of Jesus' righteousness that there is no place for professed allegiance to Jesus that is not full of righteousness.

Third, there is an open command to rejoice and be glad when suffering under persecution of this type. Elsewhere in the New Testament, many different reasons are advanced for rejoicing under persecution. The apostles rejoiced "because they had been counted worthy of suffering disgrace for the Name" (Acts 5:41). Peter saw trials as a means of grace to prove the genuineness of faith and to increase its purity (1 Peter 1:6ff.). And in the Old Testament the fiery furnace became the place where the divine Presence, even in a visible emissary, was made manifest to three Hebrew young men (Dan. 3:24f.). However, in the passage before us only one reason is given to prompt Jesus' disciples to rejoice under persecution, and that reason is sufficient: their reward is great in heaven. Jesus' disciples, then, must determine their values from the perspective of eternity (a theme Jesus expands in Matt. 6:19–21, 33), convinced that their "light and momentary troubles are achieving for [them] an eternal glory that far outweighs them all" (2 Cor. 4:17). They have aligned themselves with the prophets who were persecuted before them, and thereby testify that in every age God's people are under the gun. Far from being a depressing prospect, their suffering under persecution, which has been prompted by their righteousness, becomes a triumphant sign that the kingdom is theirs.

The Witness of the Kingdom
Matthew 5:13–16

These verses are tied to the preceding ones in two ways. First, Jesus continues to address his hearers in the second person. Second, and more important, a motif implicit in the beatitudes now becomes an explicit theme, that is, the believer as witness.

To see how this works out, we must recognize that it is impossible to follow the norms of the kingdom in a purely private way. The righteousness of the life you live will attract attention, even if that attention regularly takes the form of opposition. In other words, the Christian is not poor in spirit, mournful over sin, meek, hungry and thirsty for righteousness, merciful, pure in heart, a peacemaker—all in splendid isolation. These kingdom norms, diligently practiced in a sinful world, constitute a major aspect of Christian witness; and this witness gives rise to persecution. Nevertheless, the conduct of Jesus' disciples needs to be considered in its effect on the world, just as the opposition of the world has been considered in its effect on the Christian. In verses 13–16, therefore, Jesus develops two telling metaphors to picture how his disciples must by their lives leave their stamp on the world which is so opposed to the norms of the kingdom.

Salt, 5:13

In the ancient world, salt was used primarily as a preservative. Since they did not own deep-freeze refrigerators, the people used salt to preserve many foodstuffs. Incidentally, of course, salt also helps the flavor.

In the first metaphor Jesus likens his disciples to salt. Implicitly he is saying that apart from his disciples the world turns ever more rotten: Christians have the effect of delaying moral and spiritual putrefaction. If their lives conform to the norms of verses 3–12, they cannot help but be an influence for good in society.

But supposing the salt loses its saltiness? What then? It loses its *raison d'être*, and may just as well be thrown out onto the street—the garbage dump of the ancient east—to be trampled by men.

This observation has been interpreted two ways. Because salt by its nature cannot be anything other than salt, it cannot really lose its saltiness; therefore some have taken Jesus to be saying that there is an inner necessity which compels Christians to witness. This interpretation, it seems to me, smacks of the pedantic. Although salt *per*

se cannot lose its saltiness, it can nevertheless be adulterated. If sufficiently adulterated by, say, sand, then salt can no longer be used
as a preservative. It loses its effectiveness in staying corruption, and
so must be jettisoned as a useless commodity. The purpose of salt
is to fight deterioration, and therefore it must not itself deteriorate.

The worse the world becomes and the more its corruption pro-
ceeds apace, the more it stands in need of Jesus' disciples.

Light, 5:14–16

The second metaphor our Lord uses to describe the witness of the
Christian is light. Christians are the light of the world—a world which,
by implication, is shrouded in thick darkness.

Jesus talks about two sources of physical light: the light from a
city set on a hill, and the light from a lamp set on a lampstand. The
first source, the city, is often misunderstood. Some think that
Matthew, in recording Jesus' teaching, became somewhat confused
and put in an irrelevant illustration about a city visible from a great
distance because of its elevation. The illustration is colorful, it is
thought, but out of place in a context concerned with light. Such critics, I think, are only revealing that they live in the industrialized
world where light is so readily available. They do not know how black
nature can be. In Canada it is possible to go camping hundreds of
miles away from any city or town. If it is a cloudy night, and there
is no phosphorus in the area, the blackness is total. A hand held three
inches from your face cannot be seen. But if there is a city nearby,
perhaps a hundred miles away, the darkness is relieved. The light
from the city is reflected off the clouds, and the night, once perfectly
black, is no longer quite so desolate. Likewise Christians who let
their light shine before men cannot be hidden; and the good light
they shed around attenuates the blackness which would otherwise
be absolute.

When once we imagine a world without hundreds of watts of elec-
tric power at our instant personal disposal, we will understand how
darkness can be a terror and a symbol of all that is evil. The light from
the city, even if it is not as powerful as our modern sources of illumi-
nation, makes the darkness a little more bearable than it was before.
Light is so important that it is ludicrous to think that anyone would
want to extinguish the flickering flame from an olive-oil lamp by smoth-
ering it with a peck measure. That burning wick may cast only a little

light by modern standards; but if the alternative is pitch blackness, its light is wonderful, quite sufficient for everyone in the house (5:15).

"In the same way, let your light shine before men, that they may see your good deeds and praise your Father in heaven" (5:16). What is this light by which Jesus' disciples lighten a dark world? In this context, we read of neither personal confrontation nor ecclesiastical pronouncement. Rather, the light is the "good deeds" performed by Jesus' followers—performed in such a way that at least some men recognize these followers of Jesus as sons of God, and come to praise this Father whose sons they are (5:16).

The norms of the kingdom, worked out in the lives of the heirs of the kingdom, constitute the witness of the kingdom. Such Christians refuse to rob their employers by being lazy on the job, or to rob their employees by succumbing to greed and stinginess. They are first to help a colleague in difficulty, last to return a barbed reply. They honestly desire the advancement of the other's interests, and honestly dislike smutty humor. Transparent in their honesty and genuine in their concern, they reject both the easy answer of the doctrinaire politician and the *laissez-fare* stance of the selfish secular man. Meek in personal demeanor, they are bold in righteous pursuits.

For a variety of reasons, Christians have lost this vision of witness, and are slow to return to it. But in better days and other lands, the faithful and divinely empowered proclamation of the gospel of Jesus Christ (who himself is the light of the world *par excellence* [John 8:12]) so transformed men that they in turn became the light of the world (Matt. 5:14). Prison reform, medical care, trade unions, control of a perverted and perverting liquor trade, abolition of slavery, abolition of child labor, establishment of orphanages, reform of the penal code—in all these areas the followers of Jesus spearheaded the drive for righteousness.[3] The darkness was alleviated. And this, I submit, has always been the pattern when professing Christians have been less concerned with personal prestige and more concerned with the norms of the kingdom.

"In the same way, let your light shine before men, that they may see your good deeds and praise your Father in heaven."

---

[1]*Studies in the Sermon on the Mount*, 2 vols. (Grand Rapids: Eerdmans, 1959–60), 1:69–70.

[2]Ibid., 1:74

[3]I recommend the reading of such books as J. W. Bready's *England: Before and after Wesley* (in the abridged American edition, the title is *This Freedom–Whence?*), or D. W. Dayton's more recent *Discovering an Evangelical Heritage*. Although I am not always convinced by their theological analyses, nevertheless such books teach us how almost all valuable social trends were spawned by the Evangelical Awakening under such men of God as George Whitefield, John Wesely, Howell Hariss, Lord Shaftesbury, William Wilberforce, and others.

2

The Kingdom of Heaven

Its Demands in Relation to the Old Testament
(5:17–48)

WE ARE SOMETIMES in danger of treating God's Word as if it were a collection of loose, unclassified gems. The Bible then becomes a mere source book of "precious thoughts." When it is handled in this way, many important things are lost to view: the historical development of God's redemptive purposes; his people's increased theological understanding as he progressively reveals himself and his ways; the literary structure which binds together a book or a discourse into coherent themes and subthemes. On the other hand, when these historical, theological, and literary factors are properly considered, they contribute in important ways to our understanding of each part of the Bible—not least of all the Sermon on the Mount.

Take for example the literary structure. The kingdom of heaven is an important theme in Matthew's Gospel, and we have already noted how, by the literary device of an inclusio (5:3, 10), it becomes central in the beatitudes. Moreover, the first sixteen verses of Matthew 5 introduce or anticipate all the main themes of Matthew 5–7 in such a way as to provoke the reader to self-examination and arouse his interest in what follows. These chapters end with a number of contrasts, demanding that we choose one of two paths, one of two trees, one of two claims, one of two foundations (7:13–27). Between the introduction (5:3–16) of the Sermon on the Mount and its conclusion (7:13–27) is the body of it (5:17–7:12). This body is bracketed by another inclusio, the Law and the Prophets (5:17; 7:12), a common way of referring to the Old Testament Scriptures. So in studying 5:17–48, we recognize two things: first, we are entering the great body of the Sermon; and second, Jesus is taking pains to relate his teaching to the Old Testament.

Of course, we might have expected this emphasis on the Old Testament from our reading of the introduction, the first sixteen verses; for there Jesus says that those who practice the norms of the kingdom and therefore bear witness to the kingdom will not only enjoy great reward in heaven but will find themselves *aligned with the prophets* (5:12).

Thus, from predominantly literary considerations we are plunged into major themes which raise important historical and theological questions. The Sermon on the Mount promises not only to give us some challenging thoughts about poverty of spirit, righteousness, love, forgiveness, and the like, but also promises to reveal something of the way Jesus himself sees his place in history, the relationship between his kingdom-preaching and the Old Testament Scriptures.

Moreover, if we understand that Jesus taught as a first-century Jew to first-century Jews, we shall expect his teaching to be framed in categories comprehensible primarily to his audience, and aimed at least in part at correcting first-century impressions and beliefs which he considered erroneous. This observation grounds the revelation of God through Jesus Christ *in history,* and, as we shall see, enhances our understanding of the Sermon on the Mount.

Jesus as Fulfillment of the Old Testament
Matthew 5:17–20

Matthew 5:17–20 are among the most difficult verses in all the Bible. Superficially it is clear what they are about. Jesus again picks up the theme of the kingdom (mentioned three times in 5:19f.) and now relates it to the Law and the Prophets. These verses then serve as the introduction to the five blocks of material which make up the rest of the chapter.

It is also clear that Matthew 5:17f. portrays Jesus' high view of what we call the Old Testament Scriptures. Jesus did not come to abolish these writings; rather, he acknowledges their immutability right down to the smallest letter, the "jot," or right down to the least stroke of the pen. This least stroke, the "tittle" (KJV), is what we would call a serif, the tiny extension on some letters that distinguishes older type faces from more modern ones. In Hebrew this tiny extension is needed to differentiate between several pairs of letters. Jesus is therefore upholding the reliability and truthfulness of the written text. He is not merely saying that the Old Testament contains some truth, still less that it becomes true when men encounter it meaningfully. Rather, as he says elsewhere, the Scripture cannot be broken (John 10:35).[1]

These observations also bring us into difficulty. If Jesus did not see himself abolishing the Law and the Prophets, but fulfilling them, why, for example, is there good evidence that he abolished the food laws (Mark 7:19)? Why do New Testament writers, after Jesus' death and resurrection, insist that the sacrificial system of the Old Testament is at best no longer necessary, and in principle abolished (see Heb. 8:13; 10:1–18)? Why do not Christians today try to follow the detailed Old Testament law?

Various answers have been put forward. At least as far back as Thomas Aquinas (c. 1225–74), many Christians have divided the law into three categories: moral, civil, and ceremonial. Some say that the civil law of the Old Testament has passed away because God's people today no longer constitute a nation. The ceremonial law has disappeared because it pointed to Jesus, who "fulfilled" it by dying on the cross, thereby rendering the Old Testament ceremonies obsolete. That leaves the moral law; and, it is argued, Jesus in Matthew 5:17–20 is actually referring only to moral law, which never changes.

The first problem with that view is that the expression "not the smallest letter, not the least stroke of a pen" (5:18) sounds much more all-embracing than would be allowed by an exclusive reference to moral law. Moreover, neither the Old nor the New Testaments utilize this threefold distinction. Of course, that fact by itself is not conclusive: many legitimate distinctions may be deduced from Scripture even though they may not be explicitly taught.

The problem with this threefold division is that it's not clear what "moral" then means. If it has to do with what is fundamentally right or wrong, I would want to argue that what God approves is fundamentally right and what he forbids is fundamentally wrong; and in that case, when God approved certain ceremonial sacrifices in the Old Testament, people were *morally* bound to practice them. Again, if God forbade certain *civil* practices in the Old Testament, it would have been *immoral* to proceed with them, just because it was God who prohibited them. So this definition of "moral" runs into problems if the threefold division—moral, ceremonial, civil—is adopted. The three categories are not sufficiently mutually exclusive. If on the other hand moral

law refers to what God *always* approves, then we still face two difficulties: (1) If Jesus in 5:18 is arguing that only moral law never changes,
he is arguing in a circle: "Only law which God always approves (and
which therefore never changes) never changes." (2) Alternatively, if
Jesus means to *establish* this definition of moral law, it is odd that he
should use such inclusive language (5:18). Appeal to the historic threefold division of law undoubtedly has merit in certain contexts; but I
don't think it helps us explain what Jesus means in Matthew 5:17ff.

Another common approach to this passage is the suggestion that
"to fulfill" here means something like "to confirm." Jesus himself fulfilled the law by keeping it perfectly; and now he fulfills it in the lives
of his followers by means of his Spirit: Romans 8:4 says that God sent
his Son "in order that the righteous requirements of the law might
be fully met in us, who do not live according to our sinful nature but
according to the Spirit." In this sense, it is argued, what the law really
means is confirmed by the lives of both Jesus and his disciples. These
points are, no doubt, true; but they do not appear to be taught here.
The language of verse 18 seems tighter than that.

Many commentators argue that Christ fulfills the law and the
prophets in two different ways. The prophets are fulfilled by Jesus in
a predictive fashion: what they predict comes to pass and is thereby
fulfilled. The law, however, is not predictive, and is fulfilled in some
other way. Some say it is fulfilled in the sense argued above—that is,
it is confirmed in its deeper meaning. Others say Jesus fulfilled the
law by dying on the cross, thus satisfying the demands of the law
against all who would believe in him.

I am sure all of these ideas find support elsewhere in the New Testament; but are any of them convincing in this context? Do they conform with the way Matthew uses words, or with the motifs Matthew
emphasizes?

Over the years a somewhat different approach has been suggested
from time to time, and I think it has much to commend it. Elsewhere
Matthew records Jesus as saying, "From the days of John the Baptist
until now, the kingdom of heaven has been forcefully advancing, and
forceful men lay hold of it. For *all the Prophets and the Law prophesied* until John" (Matt. 11:12f.). Not only do the Prophets prophesy,
but the Law prophesies. The entire Old Testament has a prophetic
function; and Jesus came to fulfill the Old Testament.

However, to understand how he fulfills the Old Testament, we must
understand how it prophesies. Some of it is prophecy in the simple
predictive sense; and, from the New Testament perspective, it is clear

that the Old Testament prophecies focused on the Messiah. For example, the place of his birth is foretold (Mic. 5:2; Matt. 2:5f.). But some Old Testament prophecies cited by Matthew are not nearly so clear. For example, Hosea 11:1, "I called my son out of Egypt," is used to point toward Jesus' return from Egypt to Palestine after the death of Herod the Great (Matt. 2:15); but originally it referred to the exodus of the Israelites under Moses. It appears, in this case, that it is the history of the Jews which points forward to Christ, but not in any easy predictive sense.

There are many hints in Matthew's Gospel that this form of "prophecy" is not uncommon. Thus, if in Deuteronomy 8 Moses reminds the people that they wandered for forty years in the desert, where God permitted them to suffer hunger in order that they might learn that man does not live on bread alone, so also Jesus endured hunger for forty days in the desert, and when tempted to doubt God's provision replied that "man does not live on bread alone, but on every word that comes from the mouth of God" (Matt. 4:1–4). This quotation is from the Pentateuch (Deut. 8:2f.), what the Jews called the Law in the narrow sense, and some prophetic function is here presupposed for it.

The New Testament interprets the Old as pointing forward to Christ and the blessings he brings. For example, the sacrificial system pointed toward Jesus' sacrifice (Heb. 9:8f.; 10:1f.). Indeed everything had to be *fulfilled* that was written about Christ in the Law of Moses, the Prophets, and the Psalms (Luke 24:44), and therefore the resurrected Lord could explain to his disciples what was said in all the Scriptures concerning himself—beginning with Moses and all the Prophets (Luke 24:27). The Scriptures testify about him (John 5:39).

In Matthew 5:17f., therefore, we must rid ourselves of conceptions of fulfillment which are too narrow. Jesus fulfills the entire Old Testament—the Law and the Prophets—in many ways. Because they point toward him, he has certainly not come to abolish them. Rather, he has come to fulfill them in a rich diversity of ways, a richness barely hinted at in these paragraphs. Not a single item of the Law or the Prophets shall fail, says Jesus: not ever, until heaven and earth disappear—until everything is accomplished. The clause "until heaven and earth disappear" simply means "never, till the end of time"; but it is qualified by the further clause, "until everything is accomplished."

In other words, Jesus does not conceive of his life and ministry in terms of *opposition* to the Old Testament, but in terms of *bringing to fruition* that toward which it points. Thus, the Law and the Prophets, far from being abolished, find their valid continuity in terms of their outworking in Jesus. The detailed prescriptions of the Old Testament may well be superseded, because whatever is prophetic must be in some sense provisional. But whatever is prophetic likewise discovers its legitimate continuity in the happy arrival of that toward which it has pointed.

All this presupposes that a fresh approach to the Old Testament is being inaugurated by Jesus, concomitant with the transformed perspective brought about by the advance of the kingdom. Indeed, Jesus himself later teaches just that. He says, "Therefore every teacher of the law who has been instructed about the kingdom of heaven is like the owner of a house who brings out of his storeroom new treasures as well as old" (Matt. 13:52).

In the passage previously cited from Matthew 11:12f., we observe further that the Law and the Prophets exercise this prophetic function until John the Baptist. From John the Baptist on, the kingdom of heaven advances (cf. also Luke 16:16f., where the expression is "kingdom of God"). Similarly, in the next two verses of Matthew 5 (19, 20), Jesus moves on from talking about the Law and the Prophets to talking about the kingdom: "Anyone who breaks one of the least of these commandments and teaches others to do the same will be called least in the kingdom of heaven, but whoever practices and teaches these commands will be called great in the kingdom of heaven." The expression "these commands" does not, I think, refer to the commands of the Old Testament law. It refers, rather, to the commands of the kingdom of heaven, the kingdom mentioned three times in verse 19f. They are the commands already given, and the commands still to come, in the Sermon on the Mount.

Some have thought that the Jews expected new law when the Messiah came. I disagree. The flow of the argument in this passage points in a slightly different direction. It runs something like this: Jesus came not to abolish the Old Testament but to fulfill it—fulfill it in the sense that he himself was the object toward which it pointed. Therefore it is the height of folly not to listen to his commands, the commands of the kingdom. (For a similar argument, see Heb. 2:1–3.) What is required is a "righteousness [which] surpasses that of the Pharisees and teachers of the law" (5:20), for otherwise there is no entrance into the kingdom of heaven. Indeed, even ranking within the kingdom is dependent on obedience to Jesus' commands (5:19); but that is not surprising when we remember the tremendous emphasis which the Sermon on the Mount places on obedience to Jesus (cf. Matt. 7:21–23), or Jesus' repeated refrain, "But I tell you" (see Matt. 5:20, 22, 26, 28, 32, 34, 39, 44). The Old Testament pointed to the Messiah and the kingdom he would introduce; Jesus, claiming to fulfill that Old Testament anticipation, introduces the kingdom to his followers. In doing so, he stresses obedience and surpassing righteousness, without which there is no admittance. It is worth noting that Jesus' closing words in Matthew's Gospel again emphasize obedience: the believers are to make disciples of all nations, baptizing them and teaching them *to obey everything Jesus has commanded* (28:18–20). Jesus' commands are highlighted, much as in 5:19.

By now it is clear that the Sermon on the Mount is not soporific sentimentality designed to induce a kind of feeble-minded do-goodism. Nor do these chapters tolerate the opinion that Jesus' views on righteousness have been so tempered with love that righteousness slips to a lower level than when its standard was dictated by law. Instead, we discover that the righteousness demanded by Jesus surpasses anything imagined by the Pharisees, the strict orthodox religious group of Jesus' day. Christ's way is more challenging and more demanding—as well as more rewarding—than any legal system can ever be. Moreover, his way was prophetically indicated before it actually arrived; as Paul says, "But now a righteousness from God, apart from the law, has been made known, to which *the Law and the Prophets testify*" (Rom. 3:21).

Thus, by another route we have returned to the inner purity described in the beatitudes. Just as the beatitudes make poverty of spirit a necessary condition for entrance into the kingdom, so Matthew 5:17–20 ends up demanding a kind of righteousness which must have left Jesus' hearers gasping in dismay and conscious of their own spiritual bankruptcy. By this means the Sermon on the Mount lays the foundation of the New Testament doctrines of justification by grace through faith, and sanctification by the regenerating work of the Holy Spirit. Small wonder Paul, that most faultless of Pharisees (Phil. 3:4–6), when he came to understand the Gospel of Christ, considered his spiritual assets rubbish. His new desire was to gain Christ, not having a righteousness of his own that comes from the law, but one which is from God and by faith in Christ (Phil. 3:8f.).

Application
Matthew 5:21–47

With matchless authority, Jesus has made himself the pivotal point of history. The Old Testament points toward him; and now, having arrived, he introduces the kingdom and shows how the Old Testament finds its ultimate validity and real continuity in himself and his teaching.

At the same time, Jesus must contend with another problem. He cannot assume that everything the people have heard concerning the content of the Old Testament Scriptures was really in the Old Testament. This is because the Pharisees and teachers of the law regarded certain oral traditions as equal in authority with the Scripture itself, thereby contaminating the teaching of Scripture with some fallacious but tenaciously held interpretations. Therefore in each of the five blocks of material which follow, Jesus says something like this: "You have heard that it was said . . . but I tell you. . . ." He does not begin these contrasts by telling them what the Old Testament said, but what they had heard it said. This is an important observation, because Jesus is not negating something from the Old Testament, but something from their understanding of it.

In other words, Jesus appears to be concerned with two things: overthrowing erroneous traditions, and indicating authoritatively the real direction toward which the Old Testament Scriptures point.

Vilifying anger and reconciliation, 5:21–26

The people had heard that it was said to their ancestors, "Do not murder, and anyone who murders will be subject to judgment." The explicit prohibition was the sixth of the ten commandments; the threat of judgment was part of the Mosaic legislation dealing with murder. The person who murdered someone had to appear before a court and be judged.

But is murder merely an action, committed without reference to the character of the murderer? Is not something more fundamental at stake, namely, his view of other people (his victim or victims included)? Does not the murderer's wretched anger and spiteful wrath lurk in the black shadows behind the deed itself? And does not this fact mean that the anger and wrath are themselves blameworthy? Jesus therefore insists that not only the murderer, but anyone who is angry with his brother, will be subject to judgment.

Several observations are in order. First, some early manuscripts of the New Testament add the words "without cause" after "angry with his brother": "But I tell you that anyone who is angry with his brother *without cause* will be subject to judgment." These words are almost certainly a later addition. Some scribe no doubt thought Jesus couldn't possibly have been so rigid as to exclude all anger, and inserted the words to soften the statement.

Second, this categorical and antithetical way of speaking is typical of much of Jesus' preaching, and reflects, I think, a semitic and poetic cast of mind. It is something we shall wrestle with repeatedly in the Sermon on the Mount; but it is also found elsewhere. For example, in Luke 14:26, Jesus says, "If anyone comes to me and does not hate his father and mother, his wife and children, his brothers and sisters—yes, even his own life—he cannot be my disciple." "Hate" is not to be taken absolutely. Jesus is saying rather that love and allegiance must be given in a preeminent way to himself alone; rivals must not be allowed to usurp what is not their due. But Jesus says it in this antithetical fashion (cf. Matt. 10:37), even though elsewhere he upholds the importance, for example, of honoring parents (Mark 7:10ff.). And indeed, it is important to let this antithetical and categorical form of statement speak, in all its stark absoluteness, before we allow it to be tempered by broader considerations. In Matthew 5:21ff., Jesus relates anger to murder: let that relationship stand before going on to observe that some anger, including anger in Jesus' own life, is not only justifiable but good. Of this I shall say more later.

Third, if anger is forbidden, so also is contempt. "Raca" is an Aramaic expression of abuse. It means "empty," and could perhaps be translated "you blockhead!" or the like. Again, no one may say to another, "You fool!"

People who indulge in actions and attitudes of this type are subject to judgment, to the Sanhedrin, to Gehenna. The Sanhedrin was the highest Jewish court in the land. "Gehenna" is a Greek transliteration of two semitic words which mean "Valley of Hinnom," a ravine south of Jerusalem where rubbish was dumped and burned, and which consequently became a euphemism for "the fire of hell."

Some have tried to see in these three steps—anger, "Raca," "You fool!"—a graduation; but it is difficult to believe that Jesus is stooping to such casuistry. Would he resort to hairsplitting distinctions between "Raca" and "You fool"? And could either be meaningfully spit out without anger? Jesus is simply multiplying examples to drive the lesson home. He is a preacher who makes his point and then makes his hearers feel its weight. He confronts his audience: You who think yourselves far removed, morally speaking, from murderers— have you not hated? Have you never wished someone were dead?

Have you not frequently stooped to the use of contempt, even to character assassination? All such vilifying anger lies at the root of murder, and makes a thoughtful man conscious that he differs not a whit, morally speaking, from the actual murderer.

Similarly, it is doubtful that the three punishments—judgment, the Sanhedrin, and the fire of hell—are meant to be taken as a gradation. In the Old Testament theocracy, God himself stood behind the legal system of the state. Judgment, though civil, was also divine. Here, Jesus moves through the accepted system to the ultimate punishment to make it clear that the judgment to be feared is indeed divine, for it is based on God's assessment of the heart and can end in the fire of hell.

These verses make one great point. The Old Testament law forbidding murder must not be thought adequately satisfied when no blood has been shed. Rather, the law points toward a more fundamental problem, man's vilifying anger. Jesus by his own authority insists that the judgment thought to be reserved for the actual murderer in reality hangs over the wrathful, the spiteful, the contemptuous. What man then stands uncondemned?

Someone may well ask, "But didn't Jesus himself get very angry sometimes?" Yes, that is true. He was certainly upset with the merchandising practiced in the temple precincts (Matt. 21:12ff. and parallels). Mark records Jesus' anger with those who for legalistic and hypocritical reasons tried to find something wrong with the healings he performed on the Sabbath (Mark 3:1ff.). And on one occasion Jesus addressed the Pharisees and teachers of the law, "You blind fools!" (Matt. 23:17). Is Jesus guilty of serious inconsistency?

Indeed there is a place for burning with anger at sin and injustice. Our problem is that we burn with indignation and anger, not at sin and injustice, but at offense to ourselves. In none of the cases in which Jesus became angry was his personal ego wrapped up in the issue. More telling yet, when he was unjustly arrested, unfairly tried, illegally beaten, contemptuously spit upon, crucified, mocked, when in fact he had every reason for his ego to be involved, then, as Peter says, "he did not retaliate; when he suffered, he made no threats" (1 Peter 2:23). From his parched lips came forth rather those gracious words, "Father, forgive them, for they do not know what they are doing" (Luke 23:34).

Let us admit it—by and large we are quick to be angry when we are personally affronted and offended, and slow to be angry when sin and injustice multiply in other areas. In these cases we are more prone to philosophize. In fact, the problem is even more complicated than that. Sometimes we get involved in a legitimate issue and discern, perhaps with accuracy, the right and the wrong of the matter. However, in pushing the right side, our own egos get so bound up with the issue that in our view opponents are not only in the wrong but attacking us. When we react with anger, we may deceive ourselves into thinking we are defending the truth and the right, when deep down we are more concerned with defending ourselves.

In the Sermon on the Mount, despite the absolute cast in which anger is forbidden, Jesus forbids not all anger but the anger which arises out of personal relationships. This is obvious not only because of Jesus' teaching and conduct elsewhere, and because the anger in question is that which lies at the heart of murder, but also because of the two examples which Jesus provides to give his point a cutting edge (5:23–26).

The first (5:23f.) concerns the person who comes to perform his religious duty (in this case the offering of a sacrifice at the temple altar) but who has offended his brother. Jesus insists it is far more important that he be reconciled to his brother than that he discharge his religious duty; for the latter becomes pretense and sham if the worshiper has behaved so poorly that his brother has something against him. It is more important to be cleared of offense before all men than to show up for Sunday morning worship at the regular hour. Forget the worship service and be reconciled to your brother; and only then worship God. Men love to substitute ceremony for integrity, purity, and love; but Jesus will have none of it.

The second example (5:25f.) again picks up legal metaphor. In Jesus' day as in recent centuries, a person who defaulted in his debts could be thrown into a debtors' prison until the amount owed was paid. Of course, while he was there he couldn't earn anything, and therefore could scarcely be expected to pay off the debt and effect his own release; but his friends and loved ones who were eager to get him out might well put forth sustained and sacrificial efforts to provide the cash.

It would be making the metaphor run on all fours to deduce that Jesus is teaching that the heavenly court will condemn guilty people to "prison" (hell?) only until they've paid their debts. The debts in question are personal offenses; how then shall they be paid? And shall others pay the debt for the inmate? Rather, what Jesus is stressing is the urgency of personal reconciliation. Judgment is looming, and justice will be done: therefore keep clear of malice and offense toward

others, for even the one "who is angry with his brother will be subject to judgment" (5:22). So we see that in both of these cases, it is
personal animosity which is condemned.

Adultery and purity, 5:27–30

Jesus' contemporaries had also heard that it was said, "Do not commit adultery." This, of course, is a reference to the seventh of the ten
commandments (Exod. 20:14).

Our society has moved a long way from this explicit prohibition.
Many modern thinkers would affirm the legitimacy of adultery—if
there is love. Even Christianity itself is invoked to sanctify this viewpoint. After all, it is argued, isn't love what the gospel is all about? In
fact, as we shall see, such a philosophy distorts the biblical perspective of both love and marriage.

> *In religion*
> *What damned error but some sober brow*
> *Will bless it and approve it with a text,*
> *Hiding the grossness with fair ornament.*

Merchant of Venice

As our society moves away from the seventh commandment in one
direction, Jesus moves in another. He is not content with merely a
formal adherence to it, nor is he simply interpreting it on the side of
stringency. Rather, on his own authority he is underscoring the purity
to which such a law points: "I tell you that anyone who looks at a
woman lustfully has already committed adultery with her in his heart"
(5:28). In effect, by labeling lust adultery, Jesus has deepened the seventh commandment in terms of the tenth, the prohibition of cov-
etousness.

This is not a prohibition of the normal attraction which exists
between men and women, but of the deep-seated lust which consumes
and devours, which in imagination attacks and rapes, which mentally contemplates and commits adultery. If our society is easing off
on the prohibition of adultery, how much more does it cater to our
sexual lust? Our advertisements sell by sexual titillation; our book-
stores fill their racks with both the salacious and the perverted. The
vast majority of pop songs focus on man/woman relations, usually in
terms of satisfying sex, physical desire, infidelity, and the like. Into
this society Jesus speaks his piercing word: "Anyone who looks at a
woman lustfully has already committed adultery with her in his

heart." I write this line with shame. Which one of us is not guilty of adultery? Honesty before God in these matters may bring us the poverty of spirit which our triumphs never will, and prompt us to cry with the hymn writer,

One thing I of the Lord desire—
For all my way has darksome been—
Be it by earthquake, wind or fire,
Lord, make me clean. Lord, make me clean!

Walter Chalmers Smith (1824–1908)

What we require is the attitude described by Jesus in 5:29f.: "If your right eye causes you to sin, gouge it out and throw it away. It is better for you to lose one part of your body than for your whole body to be thrown into hell. And if your right hand causes you to sin, cut it off and throw it away. It is better for you to lose one part of your body than for your whole body to go into hell." The eye is chosen because it has looked and lusted; the hand is chosen, probably because adultery, even mental adultery, is a kind of theft.

Some have taken this language literally. Origen (c. 195–254) castrated himself so that he would not be tempted. But that, I think, quite misses Jesus' point, and the absolute cast of Jesus' preaching noticed earlier; for if I gouged out my right eye because it had looked and lusted, would not my left do as well? And if I blinded myself, might I not lust anyway, and mentally gaze at forbidden things?

What then does Jesus mean? Just this: we are to deal drastically with sin. We must not pamper it, flirt with it, enjoy nibbling a little of it around the edges. We are to hate it, crush it, dig it out. "Put to death, therefore, whatever belongs to your earthly nature: sexually immorality, impurity, lust, evil desires and greed, which is idolatry" (Col. 3:5). Paul adds, "Because of these, the wrath of God is coming" (Col. 3:6)—just as Jesus in Matthew 5:29f. threatens with hell all those who will not deal drastically with sin.

Our generation treats sin lightly. Sin in our society is better thought of as aberration, or as illness. It is to be treated, not condemned and repented of; and it must not be suppressed for fear of psychological damage. I am painfully aware how sin ensnares and entangles and produces pathetic victims; but the victims are not passive victims. In Jesus' teaching, sin leads to hell. And that is the ultimate reason why sin must be taken seriously.

Extrapolation
Divorce and remarriage, 5:31f.

The discussion of adultery and purity leads naturally to the question of divorce. The Jews of Jesus' day had heard it said that the man who wants to divorce his wife must give her a certificate of divorce. Actually, they were hearing something not quite true. The Old Testament passage to which appeal was made was Deuteronomy 24:1–4. The thrust of that passage is this: If a man finds some uncleanness in his wife and divorces her, giving her a certificate of divorce, and she then marries someone else who in time also divorces her, then her first husband cannot remarry her.

By Jesus' day, this main principle was overlooked in favor of concentrating attention on the "uncleanness" which would make legitimate the first divorce. The particular expression for "uncleanness" is used only one other time in the Old Testament, where it refers to human defecation. What the sexual uncleanness is in Deuteronomy 24:1 is not clear; in any case it is, even in the Mosaic perspective, an exceptional thing. By Jesus' day, however, some even taught that it could be some imperfection in the wife as trivial as serving her husband food accidentally burned.

But Jesus will allow no sophistry. Here, as in Matthew 19:3ff., he goes back to first principles. In the beginning God made one man and one woman, and they were joined together. Initially, all divorce was inconceivable; when God made men and women, no allowance was made for it. The Creator said, "For this reason a man will leave his father and mother and be united to his wife, and the two will become one flesh." Jesus adds, "So they are no longer two, but one. Therefore what God has joined together, let man not separate" (Matt. 19:5f.). God in fact hates divorce (Mal. 2:16). Within this framework, therefore, it is obvious that if Moses permitted divorce for some gross uncleanness, it was an exception which found its *raison d'être* in man's hard, sinful heart.

In Matthew 5:31f., Jesus tightens up on the misconceptions, and shows the direction in which the Old Testament points. Anyone who divorces his wife is at fault, because he is causing her to commit adultery if she marries someone else, since the first link is not really broken. It follows therefore that the man who marries a divorcée is likewise committing adultery; before God he is in fact marrying another man's wife (5:32). The only exception which Jesus will allow is "fornication." Different Christians have said this word refers to all sorts of specific sins; but as far as I can see it is an inclusive term which refers to all sexual irregularity. For a married couple, it involves sexual marital unfaithfulness. Even in that case, a man is not commanded to divorce his wife, but permitted to, by way of concession. The same exceptive clause appears also in Matthew 19, and refers both to divorce and remarriage.

This is not all the Bible has to say on the subject, and a great deal of care must be taken in putting it all together. But this is at the heart of it, and our generation needs to be confronted with these demands. It used to be that divorce was a problem rarely found in evangelical circles. To our shame, that is no longer the case. Our society, including many professing Christians, has rejected biblical conceptions of both love and marriage. Love has become a mixture of physical desire and vague sentimentality; marriage has become a provisional sexual union to be terminated when this pathetic, pygmy love dissolves.

How different is the biblical perspective! In God's Word, marriage and love are for the tough-minded. Marriage is commitment; and, far from backing out when the going gets rough, marriage partners are to sort out their difficulties in the light of Scripture. They are to hang in there, improving their relationship, working away at it, precisely because they have vowed before God and man to live together and love each other for better, for worse, for richer, for poorer, in sickness as in health, until death separates them. Love is the determined commitment to seek the other's good, to cherish, shelter, nurture, edify, and show patience with one's partner. And this commitment, worked out because of deep-rooted obedience to God, brings with it the emotional and sentimental aspects of love as well.

Jesus presupposes this high view of marriage when, with one concessive exception, he flatly prohibits divorce. And it is this high view of marriage which likewise underlies Jesus' trenchant remarks on lust (5:27–30), and gives this block of material (5:27–32) its sanity. Marriage is not dirty, sex is not filthy. Both are wonderful gifts from the Creator; but they are prostituted by lust, and demeaned by divorce. The Law and the Prophets, by Jesus' own authority, point to the necessity of absolute purity and must not be trivialized by sophistries which seek to escape that purity.

Oaths and truthfulness, 5:33–37

In the third block of material, Jesus deals with the question of truthfulness. The people had heard that it was said long ago, "Do not break your oath, but keep the oaths you have made to the Lord"

(5:33). This is not a direct quotation from the Old Testament, but an allusion to such passages as Exodus 20:7, Leviticus 19:12, Numbers 30:2, and Deuteronomy 23:21–24. But Jesus now says, "Do not swear at all" (5:34).

Some people think this prohibits them from taking oaths in a courtroom, or from taking an oath of allegiance. Their desire to obey God's Word is admirable; but I submit they have really not understood it. As usual, Jesus is preaching in antithetical fashion; and it is important to discover just what he is saying before we take his statement with such insensitive absoluteness.

It needs to be noticed, first, that the Old Testament does permit men to take oaths, even oaths in God's name. "You shall fear the Lord your God. Him you will serve, to him you will cleave, and you will swear by his name" (Deut. 10:20). Even in the New Testament, Paul, for example, regularly swears by God's name. In particular, he calls God as his witness (Rom. 1:9; 2 Cor. 1:23; 1 Thess. 2:5, 10; cf; Phil. 1:8). Therefore if Paul knew of this teaching of Jesus, he certainly did not take it absolutely. God himself swears: he swears not to send another universal flood (Gen. 9:9–11), he swears to send a redeemer (Luke 1:68, 73), to raise his Son from the dead (Ps. 16:10; Acts 2:27–31), and much more.

Now all of this swearing, these oaths, are designed to encourage truthfulness, or to make truthfulness the more solemn and sure. Sometimes this is even spelled out for us. For example, in one case we read, "Because God wanted to make the unchanging nature of his purpose very clear to the heirs of what was promised, he confirmed it with an oath" (Heb. 6:17). For the same reason, the Mosaic code forbade only false or irreverent oaths, which must be regarded as profaning God's name.

Unfortunately, however, by Jesus' time the Jews had built up an entire legalistic system around the Old Testament teaching. In the Jewish code of law called the *Mishnah,* there is one whole tractate given over to the question of oaths, including detailed consideration of when they're binding and when they're not. For example, one rabbi says that if you swear *by* Jerusalem you are not bound by your vow; but if you swear *toward* Jerusalem, then you are bound by your vow. The swearing of oaths thus degenerates into terrible rules which let you know when you can get away with lying and deception, and when you can't. These oaths no longer foster truthfulness, but weaken the cause of truth and promote deceit. Swearing evasively becomes justification for lying.

Jesus will not allow such casuistry among his followers. If men will play such games with oaths, Jesus will simply abolish oaths. He is interested in truthfulness, its constancy and absoluteness.

Jesus gives examples. Men are not to swear by the heaven or by the earth, for they are God's throne and his footstool respectively. They must not swear toward Jerusalem (if we translate the preposition literally) for it is the city of God, the great King. They must not even swear by their head (compare 1 Sam. 1:26; Ps. 15:4), for they cannot so much as change the color of a single hair: that is, they are swearing by something over which God alone has ultimate sway. In other words, Jesus relates every oath to God; to swear by anything is to swear by God, for God in some way stands behind everything. Therefore no oath is trivial, no oath is justifiable evasion; all oaths are solemn pledges to speak the truth. Jesus enlarges on this point elsewhere:

> Woe to you, blind guides! You say, "If anyone swears by the temple, it means nothing; but if anyone swears by the gold of the temple, he is bound by his oath." You blind fools! Which is greater: the gold, or the temple that makes the gold sacred? You also say, "If anyone swears by the altar, it means nothing; but if anyone swears by the gift on it, he is bound by his oath." You blind men! Which is greater: the gift, or the altar that makes the gift sacred? Therefore, he who swears by the altar swears by it and by everything on it. And he who swears by the temple swears by it and by the one who dwells in it. And he who swears by heaven swears by God's throne and by the one who sits on it (Matt. 23:16–22).

The real question here is truthfulness. For the follower of Jesus, it is best simply to say "Yes" and mean yes, to say "No" and mean no. In the context of Jesus' day, anything beyond this comes from the evil one (5:37), who is well-named the father of lies (John 8:44). Jesus' teaching in this matter of truthfulness left a big impression on the early church, for in what is probably the first epistle in the New Testament to have been written, the epistle of James, the same point is emphasized (James 5:12).

Christians claim to have the truth, and to follow him who is the Truth (John 14:6). In our conversations, therefore, truth must be our watchword. How many of us stoop to telling stories with a reprehensible slant, either to make our point more emphatically or to present ourselves in a more glamorous light than the raw facts will allow? How many of us say we will do things and instead renege on these responsibilities because it is personally inconvenient to go through with them? You who with me are teachers and preachers—how often do we fudge the evidence to make a point, or dogmatize in areas where we know nothing, in the hope that dogma will mask our ignorance? I am not speaking of the honest mistake, but of deceit. Our Lord insists that the Old Testament Scriptures point toward truthfulness; and all who submit to his authority cannot be too careful to speak only truth.

Personal abuse and personal self-sacrifice, 5:38–42

The Jewish people had heard that it was said, "An eye for an eye, and a tooth for a tooth." This famous law is found in Exodus 21, Leviticus 24, and Deuteronomy 19. Two things must be remembered about this law. First, however prescriptive it might have been, it was also restrictive; and therefore it was an excellent tool for eliminating blood feuds and intertribal warfare. Suppose someone cuts off my brother's hand, and I go and knock off the assailant's head. Immediately the initial violence has been escalated, and the assailant's family may feel honor-bound to butcher both me and my family. Where then will it end? But if, instead, the initial act of violence is met with reprisal in precisely the same kind and degree, an eye for an eye and a tooth for a tooth, that is the end of the matter. Second, the law was given to the Jewish people *qua* nation. The law was not designed to be discharged by individuals swept up in personal vendettas, but by the judiciary.

By Jesus' day, however, both of these fundamentals were frequently overlooked. It became all too easy to see the law as prescriptive, and only marginally restrictive. The question then became, How far may my personal retaliation extend, without breaking the law? Worse, the law was thus being dragged into the personal arena, where it could scarcely foster even rough justice, but only bitterness, vengeance, malice, hatred.

Jesus responds with sweeping authority: "But I tell you, Do not resist an evil person" (5:39). How is this statement to be taken? Tolstoy's view that there should be no soldiers, policemen, or magistrates because they resist evil people became famous. But note carefully what Tolstoy is doing: he is extending Jesus' statement to mean that no one may resist an evil person *who is attacking a third party*. For example, twice in my life I have stumbled into a scene in which my physical presence prevented violence. Both occurred late at night in the slums of Toronto. In one, a fellow was attacking a girl; he ran off as I approached. In the other, a drunk was using a bottle to menace a couple as they cowered in a corner. I put myself between the drunk and the couple, whom I urged to leave with appropriate alacrity. Naturally, the drunk turned on me; but as it happened, he never did try to thrust his bottle in my face, and so I was spared the necessity of having to relieve him of it. Nevertheless, it can scarcely be denied that I was guilty of resisting an evil person. Does Jesus' injunction condemn me for my action?

Not many would answer in the affirmative. However, many Christians would be prepared to argue, on the basis of what Jesus here says, that no *Christian* should ever resist evil directed at *him,* and therefore in principle no *Christian* should ever join a police force or an army. They acknowledge that God has given the power of the sword to the *state* (cf. Rom. 13:1–7), but conclude that no Christian should ever be found in any force or position of civil authority which would require him to resist evil people. These committed pacifists feel that any other alternative dilutes what Jesus teaches in the Sermon on the Mount.[2]

This problem is not an easy one, and what I write is not likely to resolve it. However, it is necessary to make due allowance for both the background in which Jesus was preaching, and the antithetical form of his utterances, so typical of him. All interpretations of the text do this at some point or another. For example, Jesus says in 5:42, "Give to the one who asks you." In Cambridge, England, where I first presented this material in lecture form, a large number of beggars prey on the student population, with constant and frequently belligerent demands for handouts. Some of these men are in dire need, and it is a shame there is still no adequate center for them. But many are just using the students. They get to know the softhearted ones, and literally prey on them. Several times when I have been approached for money for food or for shelter, I have offered a meal, offered my time to try to find lodging, and the like; but, when I would not simply give money, my offers were spurned and I was roundly cursed for my pains. The money in question was allegedly to buy food or to provide shelter; but in too many cases it was spent on drink.

Is it the Christian's responsibility to shell out to the professional beggar, or to pay for the drug that is ruining another man? By saying, "Give to the one who asks you," does Jesus mean there are no circumstances where that injunction may not apply? I know a Cambridge research student whose tender conscience led him to an affirmative answer to that question, and who went bankrupt as a result, quite literally doing without food himself while he supplied half a dozen men with the alcohol they would have been better off without. Eventually he was helped to see that his actions, though well motivated, were helping neither the men nor himself, and were honoring neither Jesus nor his teaching.

Thus, no matter how much we wish to follow Jesus seriously, we discover, sooner or later, that seriously following Jesus entails hard thinking about what he said and what he did not say. We may not come to perfect unanimity on all points; but we must agree that absolutizing any text, without due respect for the context and flow of the argument, as well as for other things Jesus says elsewhere, is bound to lead to distortion and misrepresentation of what Jesus means.

As I understand these verses, I do not think that Jesus has policemen and soldiers in view. Explicit New Testament teaching concerning such occupations has more to do with integrity, contentment with wages, and the like.[3]

Instead Jesus is speaking in Matthew 5:38–42 of *personal* abuse and *personal* self-sacrifice, using the misunderstanding of Old Testament law as his starting point. The four examples he gives bear this out.

The first concerns a sharp backhand slap to the cheek, a gross insult. The follower of Jesus is to be prepared to take another one rather than retaliate. There are famous stories of the transformed characters of people like Billy Bray, the pugilist, or of Tom Skinner, leader of the Harlem Lords, when they were converted. Once tough, hostile, and belligerent, they meekly accepted insults and blows (and thereby deeply impressed some of their assailants). This attitude is especially important, of course, when the violence and abuse have come about because of some stand for righteousness (cf. 5:10–12); but the text need not be restricted to that.

The second example concerns a lawsuit in which a man is likely to lose his "tunic," a long garment which corresponds to a modern dress or suit of clothes. The follower of Jesus will throw in the outer coat as well, even though this latter garment was recognized by Jewish law to be an inalienable possession (Exod. 22:26f.). It is unlikely, of course, that a lawsuit would be fought over a suit of clothes. But at stake here is a principle: even those things which we regard as our rights by law we must be prepared to abandon. In another context, Paul enlarges on this principle when he insists that followers of Jesus will prefer to be wronged rather than to enter litigation with another follower of Jesus (1 Cor. 6:7f.).

The third example probably refers to the Roman practice of commandeering civilians. "If someone forces you to go one mile, go with him two miles" (5:41). An ordinary Roman soldier could legally commandeer a civilian to help him, for example, to carry his luggage for a prescribed distance. Jesus' followers are not to feel hard done by and irritable in such cases, as if personally insulted, but are to double the distance and accept the imposition cheerfully.

Jesus' last example demands giving and lending that is cheerful and willing. The issue is not the wisdom or foolishness of lending money to everyone who comes along (for which see Prov. 11:15; 17:18; 22:26), just as Cambridge beggars are not the issue. The burden of the passage is this: Christ will not tolerate a mercenary, tight-fisted, penny-pinching attitude which is the financial counterpart to a legalistic understanding of "An eye for an eye, and a tooth for a tooth." "Give to the one who asks you, and do not turn away from the one who wants to borrow from you" (5:42). Don't be asking yourself all the time, "What's in it for me? What can I get out of it?"

The legalistic mentality which dwells on retaliation and so-called fairness makes much of one's rights. What Jesus is saying in these verses, more than anything else, is that his followers have no rights. They do not have the right to retaliate and wreck their vengeance (5:39), they do not have the right to their possessions (5:40), nor to their time and money (5:41f.). Even their legal rights may sometimes be abandoned (5:40). Hence, it would completely miss the point to interpret 5:41, for example, to mean that the follower of Christ will be prepared to go two miles, but not one inch farther! Personal self-sacrifice displaces personal retaliation; for this is the way the Savior himself went, the way of the cross. And the way of the cross, not notions of "right and wrong," is the Christian's principle of conduct.

Hatred and love, 5:43–47

Consideration of personal abuse and of the response of self-sacrifice leads naturally to the broader question of hatred and love. The people had heard that it was said, "Love your neighbor and hate your enemy" (5:43). Again, they were hearing falsely. The Old Testament Scriptures say, "Love your neighbor" (Lev. 19:18), but nowhere "Hate your enemy." But some Jews took the word "neighbor" to be exclusive: we are to love *only* our neighbors, they thought, and therefore we are to hate our enemies.

This was actually taught in some circles. In the monastic community which lived by the Dead Sea, a common dictum was, "Love the brothers; hate the outsider." The problem of identifying the "neighbor" was a live issue in Jesus' day. It was this very question which prompted Jesus to tell the parable of the Good Samaritan (Luke 10:29ff.), in which Jesus points out that one's neighbor is anyone he is in a position to help. "Love your enemies," Jesus says, "and pray for those who persecute you" (5:44). The particular enemies on whom Jesus focuses attention are the persecutors, presumably those who persecute his followers because of righteousness, because of Jesus himself (5:10–12). To love them and to pray for them is an important part of being a son of the heavenly Father. After all, God "causes his sun to rise on the evil and the good, and sends rain on the righteous and the unrighteous" (5:45). God loved rebellious sinners so much he sent his Son (John 3:16; Rom. 5:8); and, if we are his sons, we will have his character. To be persecuted because of righteousness is to align oneself with the prophets (5:12); but to bless and pray for those who persecute us is to align oneself with the character of God.

Nowhere is this sublime attitude more explicit than in Jesus himself, who, while suffering the unjust agony of the cross, cried, "Father forgive them, for they do not know what they are doing" (Luke 23:34). In the light of such a standard, it will not do merely to love one's friends and let it go at that. "If you love those who love you, what reward will you get? Are not even the tax collectors doing that?"

Tax collectors may have a bad name today; but it is nothing like the reputation they earned in first-century Palestine. The Roman Empire used a tax-farming system. The government would specify the amount to be collected from a certain area, and appoint a man to gather it. This man would in turn appoint men under him, who would appoint others under them. Each appointee had to obtain his quota, and whatever else he got he could keep. The potential for bribery and corruption all the way up the tax-farming ladder was enormous, and every avenue was assiduously exploited. Naturally, the Jewish tax collectors were loathed, and doubly loathed among the Jews because they came into contact with the Gentiles, the Roman overlords, and thus became ceremonially unclean. But even these low, traitorous, disgusting people enjoyed friends—other tax collectors, for a start! So how is a disciple of Jesus in any way superior to the despised tax collector if he only loves his friends?

"And if you greet only your brothers, what are you doing more than others? Do not even pagans do that?" (5:47). A greeting can say a great deal, especially if it brings a wish of welfare and well-being. If certain people are carefully ignored, and only those close to us receive our sincere good wishes, how do we differ from pagans? In other words, the follower of Jesus must not stoop to the low standards of his society. He is, rather, to pattern himself after his heavenly Father. The disciple of Jesus will stand out in the world because of the divine quality of his love. Indeed, elsewhere Jesus even elevates love among Christians to the characteristic or mark that indicates they belong to him (John 13:34f.). Thus it is that Jesus makes clear the real direction toward which the Old Testament law points. It points to a higher standard than legalism and casuistry can ever admit.

Conclusion: The Demand for Perfection
Matthew 5:48

As we have seen, to love one's enemies is characteristic of God (5:45). But love is not the only characteristic of God which Jesus expects his followers to emulate. As the passage continues, it becomes painfully obvious that Jesus is setting out a breathtaking description of morality which makes God himself the standard of all of it. "Be perfect, therefore, as your heavenly Father is perfect" (5:48).

We are to be holy, for the Lord our God is holy (Lev. 19:2); loving, because God is love (1 John 4:7ff.); perfect, as our heavenly Father is perfect (Matt. 5:48).

There are two final points to observe about this section of the Sermon on the Mount. First, Jesus' authority is one of the most dominant features in this chapter. The Law and the Prophets point toward him, but he himself determines their meaning, fulfillment, and continuity, with an authority nothing less than divine. It is important to remember that the Old Testament Scriptures have no intrinsic status apart from God—whatever authority they possess is derived. But because the derivation is *from God*, it takes nothing less than divine authority to interpret it and define it in this way; implicitly, therefore, Jesus is claiming such authority for himself.

Second, that toward which the Law and the Prophets have pointed has come in the person of Jesus and in the kingdom (the saving reign) which he introduces. Jesus authoritatively makes plain the demands of the kingdom and how they stand in relation to the Old Testament Scriptures. The common demand is holiness, perfection; all the Old

Testament laws are rightly understood only when interpreted in the light of this overwhelming concern. The emphasis on transparent purity and unaffected holiness, on imitating the Father's perfection, utterly precludes all religious hypocrisy, all spiritual sham, all paraded righteousness, all ostentatiously performed religious duties. But this deduction Jesus himself makes explicit in Matthew 6.

---

[1]A book which very helpfully sets out Jesus' view of the Old Testament has been written by J. W. Wenham. It is called *Christ and the Bible* (InterVarsity Press).

[2]Perhaps the best recent defense of this position is by J. H. Yoder in his book, *The Politics of Jesus* (Eerdmans).

[3]For those who want to read a Christian perspective on violence and on state authority, written at a popular level and with emphases with which I sympathize, see chapter five of Os Guinness, *The Dust of Death* (InterVarsity Press).

3

Religious Hypocrisy
Its Description and Overthrow *(6:1–18)*

The Principle
Matthew 6:1

WE HUMAN BEINGS are a strange lot. We hear high moral injunctions and glimpse just a little the genuine beauty of perfect holiness, and then prostitute the vision by dreaming about the way others would hold us in high esteem if we were like that. The demand for genuine perfection loses itself in the lesser goal of external piety; the goal of pleasing the Father is traded for its pygmy cousin, the goal of pleasing men. It almost seems as if the greater the demand for holiness, the greater the opportunity for hypocrisy. This is why I suspect that the danger is potentially most serious among religious leaders.

Jesus, having demanded of his followers nothing less than perfection (5:48), is fully aware of the human heart's propensity for self-deception, and issues a strong warning. "Be careful not to do your 'acts of righteousness' before men, to be seen by them. If you do, you will have no reward from your Father in heaven" (6:1). Be perfect (5:48), but be careful (6:1). The question of whose approval we are seeking is thus raised in another form. Just as the beatitudes ask me if it is God's blessing I want, or some other approval, so the demands of righteousness, as presented by Jesus, can never legitimately be confused with forms of external piety: the righteousness in question pleases the Father and is rewarded by him.

The King James Version begins chapter 6 with the words, "Take heed that ye do not your alms before men, to be seen of them. . . ." In other words, it introduces the question of alms in verse 1 instead of verse 2. But the oldest and best manuscripts preserve the reading of the New International Version. Jesus reserves verse 1 for the general principle: All "acts of righteousness" must be preserved from the ostentation of showmanship and from the degradation of the chase for human approval. Then in verses 2–18, he focuses on the three fundamental acts of Jewish piety, almsgiving (6:2–4), prayer (6:5–15), and fasting (6:16–18). He selects these three to represent all other "acts of right-eousness," treating each in the same way. First, he offers a description and a denunciation of that particular form of ostentatious piety typi-cal of the more degenerate forms of Pharisaism, both ancient and mod-ern. Second, he gives an ironic affirmation of the limited results of such pseudo-piety: the actors receive their reward in full. The reward is understood to be the acclaim of the fickle crowd. And that is all the actors get. Third, he presents a contrasting description of true piety and its results. Let us trace this form in the three examples.

The Examples
Matthew 6:2–18

Alms, 6:2–4

The biblical revelation has always held to the importance of alms-giving, of giving to needy people (see Deut. 15:11; Ps. 41:1; Prov. 19:17). But much of our giving is less concerned with meeting needs and pleas-ing God than with earning a reputation for generosity and piety.

"So when you give to the needy, do not announce it with trumpets, as the hypocrites do in the synagogues and on the streets, to be hon-ored by men" (6:2). The trumpets may be metaphorical; philanthropy is not to be accompanied by the repulsive sound of the philanthro-pist blowing his own horn. But the trumpets may be literal, the trum-pets of the Jerusalem temple calling the citizens together to contribute to some particularly urgent need. The opportunity for ostentation under such circumstances is quite unmatched—the trumpets sound, and I quickly close my shop and hasten down the street. Everyone knows where I'm going, and the speed at which I'm moving not only draws attention to my direction but attests to my zeal.

However, Jesus says that people who give in such a fashion, whether in the street or in the synagogue, whether in churches or toward charities, whether as a company public relations gimmick or as a personal effort at self-promotion—these people are hypocrites.

There are several different kinds of hypocrisy. In one kind, the hypocrite feigns goodness but is actually evil, like those who tried to "catch" Jesus in things he said (Matt. 22:15ff.). Such hypocrites know they are being deceptive. In another kind of hypocrisy, the hypocrite is puffed up with his own importance and self-righteousness. Blind to his own faults, he may be genuinely unaware that he is hypocritical—even though he is very harsh toward other people and their sins. Jesus discusses such hypocrites in Matthew 7:1–5, as we shall see. We may at least comfort ourselves that onlookers readily detect this form of hypocrisy, even if the hypocrite himself remains oblivious to his own double standard.

But the kind of hypocrisy involved in Matthew 6:2 is more subtle than either of the other two. In this case, the hypocrite has talked himself into believing that at heart, he is conducting himself with the best interests of the needy in mind. He may thus be unaware of his own hypocrisy. Moreover, the needy themselves are not likely to complain; they will be touchingly grateful, and contribute to the giver's self-delusion. And all but the most discerning of onlookers will speak appreciatively of the philanthropist's deed, for all acknowledge that giving is good.

A hypocrite is basically an actor—consciously or unconsciously. In fact, the classical Greek word, here translated "hypocrite," originally meant actor. Hypocritical piety is not from the heart, it is not genuine; it is play-acting piety. This kind of philanthropy is still motivated by a form of egoism. In the secret recesses of their cherished ambitions, such hypocrites give in order "to be honored by men." And, says Jesus, "I tell you the truth, they have received their reward in full" (6:2b). They get what they're after; but that's all they get. The whole thing turns out to be a successful public relations stunt, and no more. There is no real "act of righteousness," no genuine piety— and no reward from God.

"But when you give to the needy, do not let your left hand know what your right hand is doing, so that your giving may be in secret" (6:3–4a). It is almost as if the Master is using an overwhelming metaphor to express adequately just how quiet and private our giving ought to be. Such privacy is not itself meritorious; but it ensures that our giving is not prompted, even in part, by a love for the praise of peers. No one will know what we have given; and, if there is a danger that secret pride will be nurtured, we ourselves are scarcely to know what we've given: the left hand remains ignorant of what the right hand gives. No one will know about this giving in secret; no one, that is, but God.

Precisely because the Father alone knows, such secret giving is another way of assuring that we are performing a genuine "act of righteousness," one that is pleasing to him. He will detect that we have given because of real compassion for the needy and out of a transparent desire to please him. In this sense, we will be like the Corinthians who first gave *themselves* to the Lord, and then gave their money to the Lord's work (2 Cor. 8:5).

So we are to give "secretly," both to protect ourselves from ostentatious pseudo-piety, and to ensure that we are acting righteously before the Lord. "Then," says Jesus, "your Father, who sees in secret, will reward you" (6:4). It is again made clear that the follower of Jesus is interested in the rewards and blessings of God, and not in the transient approval of men. And, as we understand from the text, Jesus' disciple is not giving secretly *in order* to win some heavenly reward; rather he is giving secretly to avoid the glamour of honor from men, to please his heavenly Father, and to meet real need. The *result* is spiritual reward.

Clearly, Jesus is not opposed to giving; indeed, he presupposes that his followers will give. But his followers, whose goal is perfection, must not delude themselves into thinking that all giving pleases him, or that giving *per se* is an "act of righteousness." The human heart is too crafty to allow so simple a suggestion to stand.

Prayer, 6:5–8

"When you pray, do not be like the hypocrites, for they love to pray in the synagogues and on the street corners to be seen by men. I tell you the truth, they have received their reward in full" (6:5). Play-acting almsgiving now gives way to play-acting praying. As Jesus was not opposed to almsgiving, so is he not opposed to prayer. He presupposes that his followers *will* pray: "*When* you pray. . . ." What he categorically rejects is the attitude found in these who "love to pray . . . to be seen by men."

In synagogue services public prayer was customarily led by a male member of the congregation who stood in front of the ark of the law and discharged this responsibility. A man could easily succumb to the temptation of praying up to the audience/congregation. The acceptable clichés, the appropriate sentiments, the sonorous tones, the well-pitched fervency, all become tools to win approval, and perhaps to compete with the chap who led in prayer last week.

Moreover, at times of public fasts, and perhaps at the time of the daily afternoon temple sacrifice, the trumpets would blow as a sign that prayer should be offered. Right where he was, in the street, a man would turn and face the temple to offer his prayer. This opportunity for a little ostentatious piety was really quite gratifying.

I don't think we should be too hard on the Jews of Jesus' day before examining ourselves thoroughly. I am painfully aware of my own capacity for self-delusion and deceit; and I suspect I am not an isolated case. The believer requested to pray in a Baptist service, the reader asked to participate in an Anglican evensong, the brother asked to preach in a Brethren meeting, the student asked to read the Scripture in Presbyterian worship, and the minister in any of them, have all been sorely tempted in this area. And all receive the same reward, the human praise they desire. But that is their full reward; there is no other, and certainly no answered prayer from the Lord himself.

What, then, is to characterize our prayers? Jesus mentions two things. First: "When you pray, go into your room, close the door and pray to your Father, who is unseen. Then your Father, who sees what is done in secret, will reward you" (6:6). Again, I doubt if Jesus is trying to prohibit all public prayer. If so, the early church didn't understand him, if we may judge by the examples of public praying in the Book of Acts (1:24; 3:1; 4:24ff.; etc.). We will comprehend Jesus' point better if we each ask ourselves these questions: Do I pray more frequently and more fervently when alone with God than I do in public? Do I love the secret place of prayer? Is my public praying simply the overflow of my private praying? If the answers are not enthusiastic affirmatives, we fail the test and fall under Jesus' condemnation. We are hypocrites.

Could it be that the prime reason we do not see more prayers answered is because we are less concerned with bringing our requests to God than with showing off before men? There is a frequently repeated story of a minister in New England who described an elaborate and polished prayer offered in a fashionable Boston church as "the most eloquent prayer ever offered to a Boston audience." Just so. What do I think about when I am praying in public? Am I so busy scrambling to find expressions pleasing to my fellow worshipers that I am not really concentrating my attention on God, and scarcely aware of his presence, even though he is the One to whom my prayers are nominally addressed? Jesus insists that the best way to overcome such evils is to spend time in secret prayer. "Then your Father, who sees what is done in secret, will reward you."

Jesus mentions a second thing which must characterize our praying: "And when you pray, do not keep on babbling like pagans, for they think they will be heard because of their many words. Do not be like them, for your Father knows what you need before you ask him" (6:7f.). Some pagans thought that if they named all their gods, and addressed their petitions to each of them, and then repeated themselves a few times, they would have a better chance of receiving an answer. Jesus tells his contemporary Jewish hearers that much of their praying is akin to this babbling found among pagans; and I am certain that if he were addressing us directly today he would tell us the same thing. Prayer should not consist of heaped-up phrases, idle repetitions, and the ridiculous assumption that the probability of an answer is in proportion to the total number of words in the prayer. "Do not be rash with your mouth or impulsive in thought to bring up anything before God. For God is in heaven and you are on the earth: therefore let your words be few" (Eccles. 5:2). It is shameful to think we can wrest favors from God by the sheer volume of prayer, mechanically intoned.

In one church where I ministered, it was a regular custom in our mid-week prayer meeting for the men and boys to go off and pray in one area of the building and the women and girls in another. Some churches, of course, have much smaller breakdowns. There are advantages to smaller groups—for a start, more people can participate. But there are also disadvantages. There is a genuine need for times when the whole church family prays together, partly to promote unity and partly so that each group within the church learns of the spiritual concerns of the others. In any case, I had inherited this segregated situation and felt it was only one option, not a necessary part of the ecclesiastical tradition. So one night I gently suggested that we all meet to pray together, at least for that week. After the meeting was over, one good man came to me deeply troubled. He felt we had wasted time because "not as much praying could be done." It was true, of course, that not as many individuals led in prayer out loud; but there was no reason why just as many as ever could not have prayed. And in any case, *the sheer volume of words is not the crucial factor*, scarcely even an important factor.

But isn't sustained praying important? What about the parable in Luke 18:1–8, where Jesus tells a story with the explicit purpose of teaching them that men "should always pray and not give up" (Luke 18:1)?

I think we have once more stumbled onto a pattern noticed already in other connections. Jesus has a way of preaching in absolute categories even when he is primarily addressing himself to fairly specific conditions. Unless this is taken into account, we may neglect or distort what he says elsewhere on the same subject but under different conditions.

To put it another way: Jesus offers much of his teaching with certain relationships in view. His teaching never smacks of systematic theology. Such theology is no doubt a legitimate discipline; but if theology systematizes a particular teaching of Jesus too early in its study, it may be guilty of minimizing other relevant teachings of Jesus. It may also negate the implicit limitations imposed on a particular passage by the pattern of relationships Jesus used in that instance.

In the particular example before us, if we absolutize Matthew 6:7f., the logical conclusion is that followers of Jesus must never pray at length, and seldom if ever ask for anything since God knows their needs anyway. If instead we absolutize Luke 18:1–8, we will reason that if we are serious with God we will not only pray at length, but we may expect the blessings we receive to be proportionate to our loquacity. However, if we listen to *both* passages with a little more sensitivity, we discover that Matthew 6:7f. is really not concerned with the length of prayers, but with the attitude of heart which thinks it is heard for its many words. Likewise, we find that Luke 18:1–8 is less concerned with mere length of prayers than with overcoming the quitting tendency among certain of Christ's followers. These Christians, finding themselves under pressure, are often in danger of throwing in the towel. But they must not give up.

The best example in this matter of praying is Jesus himself. Although he prayed much in public, he prayed far more in private; the evangelist Luke takes special pains to demonstrate this (see Luke 5:16; 6:12; 9:18, 28; 11:1; 22:41f.). Although he sometimes prayed with pithy brevity, he also gave himself to long, nighttime vigils. And he taught his followers to address God as their Father, assuring them at the same time that this heavenly Father not only knows the needs of his children before they ask him, yet also encourages those children to ask, in confidence and trust.

In sum: Jesus wants to teach us that praying, to be a genuine act of righteousness, must be without ostentation, directed to the Father and not to men, primarily private, and devoid of the delusion that God can be manipulated by empty garrulity.

How, then, should we pray? Jesus himself gives us a wonderful example, usually referred to as "The Lord's Prayer," but more appropriately designated "The Lord's Model Prayer," since it is less the prayer he prayed than the prayer he gave his disciples as a paradigm for their own praying.

Extrapolation
The Lord's Model Prayer, 6:9–15

It is ironic that the context which forbids meaningless repetition in prayer serves in Matthew's Gospel as the location of the Lord's model prayer; for no prayer has been repeated more than this, very often without understanding. As early as the second century, a document now referred to as the *Didache* prescribes that Christians should repeat this prayer three times a day. That is not necessarily bad, just as it is not necessarily bad to repeat it in unison in our church services. But we must never do so thoughtlessly, and we should remember that Jesus himself conceived of the prayer as a model: "This is how you should pray" (6:9a), he said, not, "This is *what* you should pray."

There are six petitions in this prayer. It is appropriate that the first three concern God directly: his name, his kingdom, his will. The Christian's primary concerns therefore are that God's name be hallowed, that his kingdom come, that his will be done on earth as it is in heaven. Only then are the next three petitions introduced, and they have to do with man directly: our daily food, our sins ("our debts"), and our temptations. It is encouraging that in this model prayer Jesus' thought embraces both our physical and our spiritual needs.

Before looking at these six petitions in a little more detail, we ought to focus attention on the opening invocation: "Our Father in heaven." Jesus did not teach us to pray, "*My* Father in heaven," but "*Our* Father in heaven." Christians are not to pray in splendid isolation, and not to construe spirituality in terms of the rugged individualism which stamps so much Western thought. The apostle John reflects a major New Testament theme when he says, in 1 John 5:1, "Everyone who believes that Jesus is the Christ is born of God, and everyone who loves the father [i.e., God] loves his child as well [i.e., other Christians.]" There is, no doubt, a place for praying as an individual of God; but the general pattern of our praying must be broader than that. Therefore, when I as one follower of Christ among many, address *our*

Father, my concern is to embrace *our* daily bread, *our* sins, and *our* temptations—and not just *mine*.

Concerning the designation "Father," three things need to be said. First, although it is found in Jewish writings about the time of Christ, it is extremely rare. A well-known German scholar, Joachim Jeremias, has shown how exceptional and how stunning Jesus' use of this form of address must have been to his first followers. The Jews of this period preferred exalted titles for God, like "Sovereign Lord," "King of the Universe," and the like. Jesus called him Father (cf. Matt. 11:25; 26:39, 42; Mark 14:36; Luke 23:34; John 11:41; 12:27; 17:1, 5, 11, 21, 24f.). "*Abba*," he said to God; and this is an Aramaic word used by children to address their father. It is not quite as familiar as "My Daddy," but more familiar than "My Father." It reminds me of the way French-speaking Canadian children frequently address their fathers: "Papa."

Of course, Jesus was the Son of God in a unique sense; God was uniquely his Father. Jesus' manner of addressing God forms part of a larger picture in which he claimed, in scores of different ways, to be uniquely one with God. But the remarkable thing about the model prayer before us is that Jesus is here teaching *his disciples* to address God in the same way.

This observation brings us to another major New Testament theme. It is common for New Testament writers to describe the process of becoming a disciple of Jesus in terms of becoming a child of God, a son of God. Those who repent of their sins and trust Jesus as the one who paid for their sins by dying in their behalf, those who vow allegiance and obedience to Jesus, those who confess, "Jesus is Lord!"— these are the same ones who are said to be born of God (John 3), sons of God by adoption (Rom. 8). Once headed for wrath (Eph. 2:3), now these people have been made alive before God. They relish the new relationship with God himself. Although their sonship is in some respects qualitatively different from Jesus' sonship, nevertheless they along with Christ will inherit the splendors of a new heaven and earth (Rom. 8:15ff.). Even now, God has sent the Spirit of his Son into their hearts, the Spirit who calls out, "*Abba, Father*" (Gal. 4:6). Small wonder that Jesus, after his death and resurrection, could triumphantly instruct Mary, "Go to my brothers and tell them, 'I am returning to *my* Father and *your* Father, to *my* God and *your* God'" (John 20:17). By his ministry, death, and resurrection, Jesus brought about the means whereby men could come to God Almighty and say, meaningfully, "Our Father."

This, then, is the second thing that needs to be said about such a designation: The way in which God is seen as a Father in the Scripture is usually related, not to the general "Fatherhood of God" ("God is the Father, and all men are brothers"), but to the special relationship between God and followers of Jesus. It is true, of course, that all men everywhere are "God's children" (Acts 17:29) in the sense that God made them all and stands over them as Creator and Sustainer, and yet that is not the way New Testament writers most commonly use the "father-son" imagery with respect to God and men. For example, in 1 John 3:1 John distinguishes between "children of God" and "the world." Writing to believers, he says, "How great is the love the Father has lavished on us, that *we* should be called *children of God!* And that is what we are! The reason the *world* does not know *us* is that it did not know him."

There is, therefore, an abundant relationship between God the heavenly father, and those who have become his children by faith in and obedience toward his Son. There is life, forgiveness, acceptance, inheritance, family, and discipline in this relationship. Yes, discipline; but our perfect and loving Father bestows even that discipline in order "that we may share in his holiness" (Heb. 12:10; cf. 12:4–11).

We must, moreover, observe that God is our Father "in heaven." That is the third observation about this designation. The Jews of Jesus' day were inclined, on the whole, to conceive of God as so exalted that personal relationships with him could scarcely be imagined. He was so transcendent that the richness of personality was frequently lost to view. By contrast, much modern evangelicalism tends to portray him as exclusively personal and warm. Somehow his sovereignty and exalted transcendence disappear. If you enter certain American churches you will hear the enthusiastic singing of some such ditty (I can scarcely grace it with "chorus") as "He's a great big wonderful God." Regrettably, I never fail to think of a great big wonderful teddy bear. Such "choruses" are not quite heretical, not quite blasphemous. I sometimes wish they were, for then they could be readily condemned for specific evil. They are something much worse than isolated blasphemy and heresy. They constitute part of a pattern of irreverence, shallow theology, and experience-dominated religious criteria, which has eviscerated a terribly high proportion of evangelical strength in the Western world.

This does not contradict my earlier comments concerning the personal nature of God as portrayed by the designation "our Father." When Jesus taught his disciples to pray in this fashion, he was addressing men who were already convinced of the awesomeness of God's transcendence, the grandeur of God's ineffable exaltation. When they first timidly prayed, "Our Father in heaven," no doubt they deeply felt the tremendous privilege of approaching this marvelous God in so personal and intimate a fashion. But today, those who have lost sight of God's transcendence can no longer cherish the sheer privilege of addressing him as Father.

Fortunately, there are still believers who, with solemnity, meaning, and dignity, join together to sing some such praise as this:

> Immortal, invisible, God only wise,
> In light inaccessible hid from our eyes,
> Most blessed, most glorious, the Ancient of Days,
> Almighty, victorious, thy great name we praise.
>
> Great Father of glory, pure Father of light,
> Thine angels adore Thee, all veiling their sight;
> All laud we would render: O help us to see
> 'Tis only the splendour of light hideth Thee.
>
> Walter Chalmers Smith (1824–1908)

When such believers then pray, "Our Father in heaven," they cannot but be hushed and humbled.

With such a balanced opening, it is significant that the first petition concerns this exalted Father: "Hallowed be your name." In the semitic perspective, a person's name is closely related to what he is. Therefore, when God in the Old Testament reveals that he has this name or that, he is using his name to reveal himself as he is. The names are explanatory, they are revelatory. God's names include *God the Most High, Almighty, I am*; and compounds of the last one, which might be translated *I Am Who Is Our Help, I Am Who Is Our Righteousness*. And as we think of the character of God hidden behind these names, we are to pray, "Hallowed be your name."

"To hallow" means "to sanctify," to make holy, or to consider holy. The same verb is used in 1 Peter 3:15, where it would not be incorrect to translate, "But in your hearts hallow (or sanctify) Christ as the holy Lord." We are to reverence, honor, consider holy, and acknowledge Christ as the holy Lord. Similarly we are to reverence, honor, consider holy, and acknowledge the name of God, and therefore God himself.

One intriguing aspect of this petition, I think, is that although it is a prayer that God's name be hallowed, and therefore presumably a request that God will hallow his own name, it is nevertheless a prayer which, when answered, means that *we* will hallow God's name. In other words, Christ's followers are asking their heavenly Father to act in such a way that they and an increasing number of others will reverence God, glorify him, consider him holy, and acknowledge him. Many men use "God" and "Jesus" as oaths, or as expressions of disgust or of anger, or in connection with jokes. But to the degree that this prayer is answered, not only will they put aside such habits, but they will regard God's name as so holy that the thought of it will be sufficient to incite a spirit of reverence and holy fear.

In a way, to pray, "Hallowed be your name" is to pray, "Make me holy. Grant that I may reverence you. Work in me and in other men so that we will acknowledge your unsurpassed and glorious holiness always." But the petition as Jesus teaches it is framed not so much in terms of what must happen to us for the prayer to be fulfilled, as in terms of the goal itself. The highest goal is not that we be made holy; the highest goal is rather that God's name be hallowed. This removes man from the center of the picture, and gives that place to God alone. Man—even transformed man—is not the chief goal of this universe. Man's chief *raison-d'être* is indeed, as the theologians have told us, to glorify God and to enjoy him forever. This one brief petition has so much meat in it for profitable meditation, so many implications about how we are to think about God, that it is sufficient in itself to drive us to our knees.

The second petition is no less brief: "Your kingdom come" (6:10). This cannot be a request that God's universal sovereignty will be exercised, for that is always in force. The reference is to God's saving reign, which, as we have seen, is in one sense already present, but which awaits the future for its consummation. To pray, "Your kingdom come," is to pray that God's saving reign will be expanded even now, and, much more, that God will usher in the consummated kingdom. When God's kingdom fully comes, it will do so because it is inaugurated by Jesus' return. If early Christians were eager for Jesus' power and authority to be manifested through them in their ongoing witness (see Acts 4:28f.), they were even more eager for Jesus' return, and prayed *"Maranatha!"*—"Come, O Lord!" (1 Cor. 16:22). They were "looking forward to a new heaven and a new earth, the home of righteousness" (2 Peter 3:13). The last book of the Bible concludes with the prayer, "Come, Lord Jesus" (Rev. 22:20).

"Your kingdom come." Christians ought not utter this petition lightly or thoughtlessly. Throughout the centuries, followers of Jesus suffering savage persecution have prayed this prayer with meaning and fervor. But I suspect that our comfortable pews often mock our sincerity when we repeat the phrase today. We would have no objection to the Lord's return, we think, provided he holds off a bit and lets us finish a degree first, or lets us taste marriage, or gives us time to succeed in a business or profession, or grants us the joy of seeing grandchildren. Do we really hunger for the kingdom to come in all its surpassing righteousness? Or would we rather waddle through a swamp of insincerity and unrighteousness?

The third petition broadens and somewhat specifies the boundaries of the second. "Your kingdom come" is followed by "Your will be done on earth as it is in heaven." This may well be a prayer that the kingdom of God might come in its fullness; for the most wonderful feature of that arrival will be the perfect accomplishment of the Father's will, without rebellion, prevarication, delay, evil agencies, and those mysterious twists by which God now works even through men's evil (see Gen. 50:20; Isa. 10:5–19).

The ambiguity of the language permits a broader application of this petition. God's ethical will (if I may use such an expression to speak of his desire to see righteousness practiced) will be completely fulfilled only in the consummated kingdom. But those who now belong to that kingdom, as that kingdom is at present manifest among us, are already under special obligation to fulfill that will. Much of Matthew 5 is saying just this: Surpassing righteousness is required to enter the kingdom (5:20). In the consummated kingdom, it will of course not be necessary to lay down guidelines about divorce, face-slapping, hate, lust, hypocrisy, and other foul things; but at present, an essential part of the pursuit of kingdom ethics is that such ethics must be worked out in a context in which evil still abounds. In the consummation, I shall not be tempted to retaliate against someone who slaps my face, because there will be no face-slapping; I shall not be tempted to hate my enemies, because I will have no enemies. Thus, although the absolute demands for righteousness are not diminished or diluted by appeal to the pressure of the present evil age, nevertheless they are framed in terms of opposition to the evil of the age. It is in this way that they point forward to the perfection of the consummated kingdom, when God's will shall be done openly, plainly, freely, without exceptions or caveats, *and without the painful necessity of framing it in terms of opposition to evil.*

Perhaps I can sum this up another way. When Jesus uses the phrase, "Your will be done *on earth as* it is *in heaven*," I think he chooses language which allows for several contrasts. He may be teaching us to pray (1) that God's desires for righteousness will be as fully accomplished *now* on the earth as they are *now* accomplished in heaven; (2) that God's desires for righteousness may *ultimately* be as fully accomplished on the earth as they are *now* accomplished in heaven—that is, this phrase is analogous to "Your kingdom come"; (3) that God's desires for righteousness may ultimately be accomplished on the earth *in the same way* that they are accomplished in heaven—that is, without reference to contrasting evil, but purely.

We need to realize that if we are praying that God's will be done on earth, we are committing ourselves to two important responsibilities. First of all, we are committing ourselves to learning all we can about his will. That means sustained and humble study of the Scriptures. It pains me to hear Christians insist on the authority and infallibility of the Scriptures, if those same Christians do not diligently work at learning the Scriptures. What are the themes of Zechariah and Galatians? What do we learn of God's will from Exodus and Ephesians? How do the portraits of Jesus painted by Matthew and John differ from and complement each other? In studying God's will, what have we learned this week that has prompted improvements in our lives?

That brings us to the second responsibility. If my heart hunger is that God's will be done, then praying this payer is also my pledge that, so help me God, by his grace *I will do his will*, as much as I know it!

These are the three first petitions of the Lord's model prayer. The primary concerns and delights of Jesus' follower will be God's glory, God's reign, and God's will. After that, the Christian will take thought for the needs of himself and others.

The first petition in this connection is, "Give us today our daily bread" (6:11). The word translated "daily" occurs very rarely in Greek. In fact, it is found with one hundred percent certainty only in this prayer; but most likely it appears also in one of the papyri, which breaks off halfway through the word. It seems to be an adjective meaning "of the day that is coming." If in the morning we ask for our food for the day that is coming, we mean today's food; if we ask at night, we mean tomorrow's.

The point is the same in any case; and unfortunately, that point is lost in the complicated structures of contemporary Western society. In Jesus' day, laborers were commonly paid each day for the work they had achieved that day; and the pay was frequently so abysmally low that it was almost impossible to save any of it. Therefore the day's pay purchased the day's food. Moreover, the society was largely agrarian: one crop failure could spell a major disaster. In such a society, to pray "Give us today our daily bread" was no empty rhetoric. Living a relatively precarious existence, Jesus' followers were to learn to trust their heavenly Father to meet their physical needs.

But an even larger principle is at stake here. James, the half-brother of Jesus, reminds us, "Every good and perfect gift is from above, coming down from the Father of the heavenly lights, who does not change like shifting shadows" (James 1:17). Paul is more pungent: "For who makes you different from anyone else? What do you have that you did not receive? And if you did receive it, why do you boast as though you did not?" (1 Cor. 4:7)—that is, as if you earned it, or grew it yourself. In other words, the Scriptures teach that God himself is the ultimate source of every good, whether food, clothing, work, leisure, strength, intelligence, friendship, or whatever. Moreover, he does not owe us these things. Since all of us have at some time or other gone our own tawdry way, effectively shaking our puny fists in his face and affirming our own independence, he would not be at all unjust were he to withhold his blessings. Our very ingratitude is an insult to Deity; the present thankless generation is an affront to him. We have taken his gifts for granted; and then when they begin to dry up we complain and, call into question the very existence of this beneficent God.

Life in Western society is not quite as precarious as it was in the first century. We have received so much more. But sadly, our very wealth has contributed to our thanklessness, to our spiritual bankruptcy. As I pen these lines, news is pouring in of drought in Europe, Australia, and elsewhere. I would not want to argue that Europe is more evil than the rest of the world; rather, I wonder if God is beginning to call to the Western world in the terrible language of judgment, until we learn some lessons of repentance, gratitude, poverty of spirit, and, perhaps more than anything else, conscious dependence on him.

If difficult times do descend on us, it is the follower of Jesus who will find refuge in this petition, "Give us today our daily bread" (Matt. 6:11). Nor is it simply a question of praying such a prayer in order to teach us dependence on God, although it is partly that. Rather, the annals of Christian experience overflow with the witness that God is able to answer such a petition in the most faithful way.[1]

The second petition is found in verse 12: "Forgive us our debts, as we also have forgiven our debtors." Jesus goes on to enlarge the point after he has finished his model prayer, for in verses 14f. he adds, "For if you forgive men when they sin against you, your heavenly Father will also forgive you. But if you do not forgive men their sins, your Father will not forgive your sins." Sin is pictured in the prayer as a debt. Sin incurs a debt which must be discharged. If then someone owes us such a debt, and we fail to release him by forgiving him, our own debts before the Father will not be forgiven by him, and we will not be released. Actually, in Aramaic, which is the language Jesus probably used in preaching this sermon, it is not uncommon to refer to sin as a debt.

Is Jesus giving us some tit-for-tat arrangement here? Do I forgive Johnny and then the Lord forgives me—indeed, *so that* the Lord will forgive me? The New International Version (hereafter called NIV) of verse 12 strengthens such an interpretation, although the Greek behind it may simply mean "as we herewith forgive our debtors," and not necessarily "as we also have forgiven our debtors." But what then do the very explicit conditions of verses 14 and 15 mean?

Some light is shed on the passage by a parable Jesus tells in Matthew 18:23–35:

> [23] "Therefore, the kingdom of heaven is like a king who wanted to settle accounts with his servants. [24] As he began the settlement, a man who owed him ten thousand talents was brought to him. [25] Since he was not able to pay, the master ordered that he and his wife and children and all that he had be sold to repay the debt.
>
> [26] "The servant fell on his knees before him. 'Be patient with me,' he begged, 'and I will pay back everything.' [27] The servant's master took pity on him, cancelled the debt and let him go.
>
> [28] "But when that servant went out, he found one of his fellow servants who owed him a hundred denarii. He grabbed him and began to choke him. 'Pay back what you owe me!' he demanded.
>
> [29] "His fellow servant fell to his knees and begged him, 'Be patient with me, and I will pay you back.'
>
> [30] "But he refused. Instead, he went off and had the man thrown in prison until he could pay the debt. [31] When the other servants saw what had happened, they were greatly distressed and went and told their master everything that had happened.
>
> [32] "Then the master called the servant in. 'You wicked servant,' he said, 'I cancelled all that debt of yours because you begged me to. [33] Shouldn't you have had mercy on your fellow servant just as I had on you?' [34] In anger his master turned him over to the jailers until he paid back all he owed.
>
> [35] "This is how my heavenly Father will treat each of you unless you forgive your brother from your heart."

The point of the parable it seems does not so much turn on temporal sequence (X must forgive Y before Z can forgive X) as on attitude. There is no forgiveness for the one who does not forgive. How could it be otherwise? His unforgiving spirit bears strong witness to the fact that he has never repented.

It is of the essence of the Christian way to walk in self-denial. Whoever sees himself and his own life as central to meaningful existence loses everything; whoever takes up his cross, follows Christ, and loses his life, actually finds it. In this sense, the famous prayer attributed to St. Francis of Assisi explores the categories by which this petition in the Lord's model prayer is to be understood:

> Lord, make me an instrument of your peace.
> Where there is hatred, let me sow love;
> where there is injury, pardon;
> where there is doubt, faith;
> where there is despair, hope;
> where there is darkness, light;
> and where there is sadness, joy.
>
> O Divine Master, grant that I may not so much seek
> to be consoled as to console,
> to be understood as to understand,
> to be loved as to love.
>
> For it is in giving that we receive,
> it is in pardoning that we are pardoned,
> and it is in dying that we are born to eternal life.

The final petition of the prayer is this: "And lead us not into temptation, but deliver us from the evil one" (6:13). At first sight this is a very strange request. Why should we have to ask God *not* to lead us into temptation? Couldn't we take that for granted? To ask God to keep us out of temptation would be more understandable; but to ask that he not lead us into it is difficult.

Many pages have been written on this petition, but I suspect the real explanation of this puzzling phrase is simpler than most of the proposed solutions. I think this is a *litotes*, a figure of speech which expresses something by negating the contrary. For example, "not a few" means "many"; by negating "a few" we have produced this litotes. In John 6:37, Jesus says, "All that the Father gives me will come to me, *and whoever comes to me I will never drive away*." Many people think the latter clause is a litotes meaning, "I will certainly receive all who come to me." In fact, it is an even stronger litotes than that. As the succeeding verses clearly show, it means "I will certainly keep in all who come to me." Thus, by negating "drive away," a forceful and somewhat ironic expression for "keep in" is generated.

It appears to me that "Lead us not into temptation" is a litotes akin to these examples. "Into temptation" is negated: Lead us, *not* into temptation, but away from it, into righteousness, into situations where, far from being tempted, we will be protected and therefore kept righteous. As the second clause of this petition expresses it, we will then be delivered from the evil one.

This petition is a hefty reminder that, just as we ought consciously to depend on God for physical sustenance, so also ought we to sense our dependence on him for moral triumph and spiritual victory. Indeed, to fail in this regard is already to have fallen, for it is part of that ugly effort at independence which refuses to recognize our position as creatures before God. As Christians grow in holy living, they sense their own inherent moral weakness and rejoice that whatever virtue they possess flourishes as the fruit of the Spirit. More and more they recognize the deceptive subtleties of their own hearts and the malicious cunning of the evil one, and fervently request of their heavenly Father, "Lead us not into temptation, but deliver us from evil."

When did you last pray such a prayer? Is it not a mark of spiritual carelessness, and insensitivity to the spiritual dimensions of human existence, when such prayers are neglected?

The fact that the plea to avoid temptation is placed between the petition concerning forgiveness (6:12) and its further elucidation (6:14f.) may possibly suggest that the temptation primarily in view is the temptation to be bitter, the temptation to maintain a veneer of true religion even while one's secret attitudes are bursting with the corruption of grapes gone sour. This also suits the dominant theme of this passage (6:1–18), the description and overthrow of religious hypocrisy.

The doxology printed in some English versions ("for yours is the kingdom and the power and the glory forever. Amen.") appears not to have been added before the late second century, at the earliest. This observation does not call into question the fact that the kingdom and the power and the glory really do belong to God forever; many other passages say similar things. However, it remains doubtful that Jesus taught such a clause as part of his model prayer.

There is so much to be learned about praying; most of us are little more than novices. One of the most profitable studies of the Scripture is the examination of the prayers recorded in its pages. Then, of course, the student needs to practice what he has discovered. But, regardless how many riches he finds, he will not come across a prayer more all-encompassing, more pointed, more *exemplary*, than the Lord's model prayer.

Blessed is the follower of Jesus who can sing, without embarrassment, insincerity, or a trace of a blush (despite the quaintness of some of the wording):

> Sweet hour of prayer! Sweet hour of prayer!
> That calls me from a world of care,
> And bids me at my Father's throne
> Make all my wants and wishes known.
> In seasons of distress and grief
> My soul has often found relief,
> And oft escaped the tempter's snare
> By thy return, sweet hour of prayer.
>
> Sweet hour of prayer! Sweet hour of prayer!
> Thy wings shall my petition bear
> To him whose truth and faithfulness
> Engage my waiting soul to bless.
> And since he bids me seek his face,
> Believe his word and trust his grace,
> I'll cast on him my every care,
> And wait for thee, sweet hour of prayer.
>
> William W. Walford (1772–1850)

Fasting, 6:16–18

Jesus' third example of ostentatious piety is fasting. "When you fast," he says, "do not look sombre as the hypocrites do, for they disfigure their faces to show men they are fasting. I tell you the truth, they have received their reward in full" (6:16). Just as Jesus did not demean almsgiving and prayer, so likewise does he refrain from speaking against fasting *per se*: he assumes his disciples will fast. On the other hand, in another context he is found defending his disciples for *not* fasting (Matthew 9:14–17). In any case, here in the Sermon on the Mount Jesus is interested in condemning the abuses of the practice and in exposing its dangers.

In the Jewish calendar there were certain special fasts in which everybody participated. These took place in connection with the high feast days, such as the Day of Atonement or the Jewish New Year. Fasts might also be called when, for example, the autumn rains failed to appear; these fasts, too, would be national in scope. In addition, many individuals would fast at other times, allegedly for reasons of moral and religious self-discipline, and especially as a sign of deep repentance and brokenness before the Lord, and perhaps as part of some important request offered up to the Lord.

But what began as spiritual self-discipline was prostituted into an occasion for pompous self-righteousness. Some would wear glum and pained expressions on their faces, go about their business unwashed and unkempt, and sprinkle ashes on their head, all to inform peers that they were fasting. What was once a sign of humiliation became a sign of self-righteous self-display.

Tragically, we do similar things today. At one time people wore nice clothes on Sunday as a sign of respect and reverence before the Lord. It was not long before the quality of the clothes became more important than the reverence; and pretty soon people were competing to look better than their neighbors. Small wonder many youths finally rejected every trace of this clothes contest and started wearing blue jeans to church. Many of them may have done so for unworthy motives, but their parents' motives for dressing up were equally unworthy.

In one campus outreach group, Christian students were strongly urged to carry their Bibles to school and college as a sign of their faith and a witness to others. After all, if they were not embarrassed to carry Freud or a chemistry text or a novel, why should they balk at carrying their Bibles? But pretty soon I noticed some Christians were carrying exceptionally *big* Bibles. . . . Like hypocrites in Jesus' day, they were trying to establish a reputation for piety.

Almost anything that is supposed to serve as an outward sign of an inward attitude can be cheapened by this hypocritical piety. Jesus told those who wanted to fast, "But when you fast, put oil on your head and wash your face, so that it will not be obvious to men that you are fasting, but only to your Father, who is unseen; and your Father, who sees what is done in secret, will reward you" (6:17f.). Jesus is telling his followers that when they fast they are to act normally so that no one but God will know it. They are to take off the ashes, wash their faces, use their deodorant or talc or oil or whatever, and act normally. No voluntary act of spiritual discipline is ever to become an occasion for self-promotion. Otherwise, any value to the act is utterly vitiated.

The thrust of Matthew 6:1–18 is humbling. The Matthew 5 demand for righteousness is now complemented by the insistence that such righteousness must never become confused with pious ostentation, with play-acting piety. The question is raised in its most practical form: Whom am I trying to please by my religious practices? Honest reflection on that question can produce most disquieting results. If it does, then a large part of the solution is to start practicing piety in the secret intimacy of the Lord's presence. If our "acts of righteousness" are not primarily done secretly before him, then secretly they may be done to please men.

The negatives of these verses are actually an important way of getting to the supreme positive, namely, transparent righteousness. Genuine godliness, unaffected holiness, unfeigned piety—these are superlatively clean, superlatively attractive. The real beauty of righteousness must not be tarnished by sham.

God help us.

---

[1]Perhaps the most remarkable narrative in this connection is the biography *George Müller of Bristol,* by A.T. Pierson.

4

Kingdom Perspectives

(6:19–34)

THE FIRST PART of Matthew 6, as we saw in the last chapter, confounds hypocrisy. As such, it is largely negative in tone; yet by that negative tone the positive lesson is driven home. In the pursuit of the righteousness of the kingdom, a man must make sure that his specifically religious "acts of righteousness" are preserved from hypocrisy. He can best avoid hypocrisy by guaranteeing that his ultimate objective is to please God and be rewarded by him. In practical terms, he must eschew all showiness in acts of piety.

At stake are the perspectives of the kingdom. Life in the kingdom is not simply a question of crossing one hurdle or passing one test, followed by relative indifference to kingdom norms. Involved, rather, is that deep repentance which willingly orients all of life around these norms. The second half of Matthew 6, therefore, builds on what has come before. Followers of Jesus not only shun hypocrisy in religious duty, but, more positively, they comprehend that all of life is to be lived and all its attitudes are to be formed according to the perspectives of the kingdom.

Jesus enunciates two general but all-embracing kingdom perspectives. The first is unswerving loyalty to kingdom values, and the second is uncompromised trust in God.

Unswerving Loyalty to Kingdom Values
Three Metaphors, Matthew 6:19–24

Treasure, 6:19–21

"Do not store up for yourselves treasures on earth, where moth and rust destroy, and where thieves break in and steal. But store up for yourselves treasures in heaven, where moth and rust do not destroy, and where thieves do not break in and steal. For where your treasure is, there your heart will be also." The treasures on earth here envisaged clearly include rich oriental garments, the sort of clothing any self-respecting moth would dearly love to find. The word translated "rust" may mean just that, and therefore be connected with the corrosion of metals; but it can refer to other kinds of decay and destruction as well. For example, it can refer to something which eats away at a supply of grain. Older commentators, rightly I think, picture a farm along with its products and supplies being eroded, corroded, fouled, destroyed.

Even valuables which cannot be corroded or eaten can be stolen. Many "treasures of earth" are the delight of thieves, who break in and steal. Actually, they "dig through" and steal; for most homes in ancient Palestine were made of mud brick which easily succumbed to any thief with a sharp tool.

In principle, by "treasures of earth" Jesus refers to any valuable which is perishable or which can be lost in one way or another. The means by which the treasure is lost is unimportant (but in our day certainly includes galloping inflation).

By contrast, followers of Jesus must store up for themselves treasures in heaven, where moth and rust do not destroy, where thieves do not break in and steal—and where inflation cannot possibly operate. The treasures in question are things which are the result of the divine approval and which will be lavished upon the disciples in the consummated kingdom. The treasures of the new heaven and the new earth are wonderful beyond our wildest expectation. Sometimes the pages of Scripture give us glimpses couched in glittering metaphor as the resources of language are called up to tell us of things still barely conceivable. At other times Scripture extrapolates the advance tastes we enjoy here, and pictures love undiluted, a way of life utterly sinless, integrity untarnished, work and responsibility without fatigue, deep emotions without tears, worship without restraint or disharmony or sham, and best of all the presence of God in an unqualified and unrestricted and personal way. Such treasures cannot be assailed by corrosion or theft.

I do not think that Jesus is condemning all wealth, any more than he is condemning all clothes. He is not prohibiting things, but the love of things. Not money, but the love of money, is a root of all kinds of evil (1 Tim. 6:10). Jesus forbids us from making mere things our treasure, storing things up as if they had ultimate importance.

The preacher, Ecclesiastes, can help us here. Ecclesiastes pictures the construction of buildings, the work ethic, sex, reputation, power, various philosophies, and then dismisses each of them as vanity and a striving after wind. My friend and colleague Dr. Harold Dressler has convinced me that the word translated "vanity" is not to be taken to mean that all these things are equally useless, stupid, "vain," but that all these things are transient. They are "vanity" in the sense that they are nonenduring. Such things, if you will, are cursed with temporality, with transience. When I die, I will take out with me exactly what I brought in—nothing. Therefore even if thieves and rust spare my goods for the span of my life, it is vain to store up treasures which have such time-limited value.

Of course, to argue as Jesus here argues presupposes belief in rewards and punishments from heaven. Therefore only the man of faith will acknowledge that the argument is valid; for as the writer of the Epistle to the Hebrews puts it, "Without faith it is impossible to please God, because anyone who comes to him must believe that he exists and that he rewards those who earnestly seek him" (Heb. 11:6). But if I am genuinely committed to the kingdom of God, my most cherished values will be established by God.

Just as the kingdom is already present, at least incipiently, so even now the disciple of Jesus is accumulating, and enjoying, treasure in heaven. And just as the kingdom is still to come in the fullness of its splendor, so also the disciple of Jesus awaits that consummation in order to enter the fullness of the blessings the Father has prepared for him. He lives by faith; but granted the reality of the objects of that faith, the restraints here expounded are reasonable. We must ask ourselves (if once again I may refer to eternity in the categories of time) how important contemporary transient values will appear to us in fifty billion trillion millennia. It is a poor bargain which exchanges the eternal for the temporal, regardless of how much tinsel is used to make the temporal more attractive. And it is tragic if we have to follow the examples of Achan, Solomon, the rich young ruler, and Demas, in order to discover this basic truth for ourselves.

It is not merely a question of ultimate rewards. It is much more than that, for the things we treasure actually govern our lives. What we value tugs at our minds and emotions; it consumes our time with planning, day-dreaming, and effort to achieve. As Jesus puts it, "For where your treasure is, there your heart will be also." If a man wants *above all else* to make a lot of money, buy an extravagant house, ski in the Alps or sail in the Mediterranean, head up his company or buy out his competitor, build his reputation or achieve that next promotion, advance a political opinion or seek public office, he will be devoured by these goals, and the values of the kingdom will get squeezed out. Notice that none of the goals I mentioned is intrinsically bad; but none is of ultimate value, either. Therefore any of them can *become* evil if it is valued as ultimate treasure and thereby usurps the place of the kingdom. And how much uglier is the situation when the goals *are* positively evil! But the principle remains the same: We think about our treasures, we are drawn toward our treasures, we fret about our treasures, we measure other things (and other people) by our treasures. This is so painfully true that a person who honestly examines himself can pretty well discover what his real treasures are, simply by studying his deepest desires.

In Canada, freshly fallen snow is usually dry and powdery, not wet and sticky. A large field of new snow is so inviting as it glistens in the winter sun. No mark is on it, no footprint; yours is the privilege of tramping across it and establishing any pattern you like. If you look fixedly at your feet and try to cross the field in a straight line, you will make a most erratic pattern. If instead, you fix your eye on a tree or boulder on the other side and walk straight toward it, the path you leave will be quite remarkably straight.

While we were engaged to be married, Joy and I lived in Cambridge, England. Sometimes we enjoyed long bicycle rides together along the tow path beside the river Cam. Pedaling along, I was never more than two or three feet from the sharp bank: an accidental swerve would mean a tumble into the river. Where the path is wide enough to ride two abreast, Joy would be on the inside. If in conversing back and forth she then started to look at me, I would have to slam on my brakes to avoid either tangling with her bicycle or being forced into the river.

Such illustrations teach us that we tend to move toward the object on which we fix our gaze. In the same way, our whole lives drift relentlessly toward the spot where our treasures are stored, because our hearts will take us there. To follow Jesus faithfully entails therefore a consistent development of our deepest loves, to train ourselves to adopt an unswerving loyalty to kingdom values and to delight in all that God approves. Small wonder that Paul writes in these terms: "Since, then, you have been raised with Christ, set your hearts on things above, where Christ is seated at the right hand of God. Set your minds on things above, not on earthly things" (Col. 3:1f.). Or again: "Command those who are rich in this present world not to be arrogant nor to put their hope in wealth, which is so uncertain, but to put their hope in God, who richly provides us with everything for our enjoyment. Command them to do good, to be rich in good deeds, and to be generous and willing to share. *In this way they will lay up treasure for themselves as a firm foundation for the coming age,* so that they may take hold of the life that is truly life" (1 Tim. 6:17–19).

Light, 6:22f.

The next metaphor is a little more difficult to understand. Jesus says, "The eye is the lamp of the body. If your eyes are good, your whole body will be full of light. But if your eyes are bad, your whole body will be full of darkness. If then the light within you is darkness, how great is that darkness!"

It is possible that this thought has its roots in the preceding paragraph. If so, the eye is the lamp of the body in the sense that it enables the body to find its way. Your eye must be "good," in order for it to direct "your whole body" (a semitic expression meaning "you yourself") toward what is good.

Alternatively, it is possible (and in my judgment, preferable) to interpret verses 22f. in a somewhat simpler fashion. The whole body— that is, the whole person—is pictured as a room or a house. The purpose of the eye is to illuminate this room, to ensure that it is "full of light." The eye thus serves as the source of light; we might think of a window in an otherwise windowless room, although in fact Jesus uses the figure of a lamp, not a window.

For the individual to be full of light, then, the eyes must be "good." If they are bad, if their flame is smoky or their glass caked with soot, if their wick is untrimmed or their fuel depleted, the person remains in utter darkness. Clearly, it is important to discover just what Jesus means, in nonmetaphorical terms, by demanding that the eye be "good."

But this adjective "good" is a little perplexing. The word in the original was used in the Septuagint to mean "singleness of purpose, undivided loyalty": hence "single" in the King James Version. However, among the rabbis, the "evil eye" indicated selfishness; and in that case the good eye might well indicate committed generosity. Being full of light is equivalent to being generous; and that seems to fit in well enough as an elaboration of the preceding paragraph's warnings about foolishly selected treasure.

I suggest that the Septuagint meaning of the word is best, if we may judge by the context. Although at first glance the alternative idea concerning generosity seems to mesh well with the preceding paragraph's interest in treasure and the next paragraph's warning against money, closer inspection reveals that the fit is not so good. Verses 19–20 are less concerned with financial wealth and giving it away than with a man's scale of values whereby he establishes what is his ultimate treasure. Similarly, verse 24 is not so much focused on money as it is on servitude and commitment.

In other words, verses 19–21 and verse 24 all demand unswerving loyalty to kingdom values; the particulars used are treasure and money. The accent remains on singleness of purpose—heart fidelity—toward God. Therefore the word translated "good" by the NIV most probably means "singleness of purpose, undivided loyalty"—which, context apart, is the most natural interpretation. The good eye is the one fixed on God, unwavering in its gaze, constant in its fixation.

The result is that the entire person is "full of light." I think this expression is lovely. If light is taken in its usual connotations of revelation and purity, then the individual with a single eye toward kingdom values is the person characterized by maximum understanding of divinely revealed truth and by unabashedly pure behavior. Moreover, the expression "full of light" is probably not limited to what the person is in himself, isolated; but that person will also be so full of light that he will *give off* light. It is by this unreserved commitment to kingdom values that Christians become "the light of the world" (Matt. 5:14).

The alternative is to be "full of darkness," devoid of revelation and purity. That darkness is especially appalling if the person deceives himself. If he thinks his eye is good when it is bad, he talks himself into believing that his nominal loyalty to kingdom values is deep and genuine, when in fact it is shallow and contrived. That person's darkness is greatest who thinks his darkness is light: "If then the light within you is darkness, how great is that darkness!"

Slavery, 6:24

"No one can serve two masters. Either he will hate the one and love the other, or he will be devoted to the one and despise the other. You cannot serve both God and Money" (6:24).

Superficially, the text appears somewhat extreme in its polarization. But two things must be kept in mind if we are to understand it correctly. First, by "masters" Jesus does not have twentieth-century employers in mind (most of whom are limited in authority by trade unions), but something closer to slave owners (although perhaps not quite that stereotyped). It is possible to work for two employers; it is not so easy to serve two masters.

Second, the contrast between love and hate is a common semitic idiom, neither part of which may legitimately be taken absolutely. To hate one of two alternatives and to love the other simply means the latter is strongly preferred, especially if there is any contest between the two. This idiom sheds light on other words of Jesus: "If anyone comes to me and does not hate his father and mother, his wife and children, his brothers and sisters—yes, even his own life—he cannot be my disciple" (Luke 14:26). This same Jesus elsewhere insists that people should honor their parents with integrity (Mark 7:9–13); so clearly, he is not advocating hatred. He means that any man's best love and first allegiance must be directed toward the Father and toward the Son whom he sent, and that even family ties must be considered secondary.

In the same way, Matthew 6:24 warns us that during crises our allegiances get sorted out, and only one can come out on top. One "master" will be preferred: what or whom we want to serve most will be revealed. And then Jesus gives us one pithy example: "You cannot serve both God and Money."

The word translated "Money" in the NIV is transliterated in most other versions as "Mammon." Originally the word meant "something in which one puts confidence," or the like. Eventually, no doubt because man's confidence is so often deposited in riches, the word came to refer to all material possessions: profit, wealth, money. No one can be simultaneously devoted to both God and money.

Let us admit it. Many, many of us try very hard to compromise in this area. Two jobs become available, and for most of us the weightiest factor prompting us to select the one or the other will be the salary, not the opportunity presented by each option to serve the Lord. Or we make a needless move to a bigger and better car or a bigger and better home, for no other reason than to keep up with (or surpass) peers.

Contrast the attitude of the commentator Matthew Henry (1662–1714) who, when he was robbed, returned home and wrote in his diary words to this effect:

> *Lord, I thank you*
> *that I have never been robbed before;*
> *that although they took my money, they spared my life;*
> *that although they took everything, it wasn't very much;*
> *that it was I who was robbed, not I who robbed.*

Matthew Henry was a man who served God.

These three metaphors—treasure, light, and slavery—join forces to demand unswerving loyalty to kingdom values.

Uncompromised Trust
Matthew 6:25–34

"Therefore I tell you, do not worry about your life, what you will eat or drink; or about your body, what you will wear. Is not life more important than food, and the body more important than clothes?" What is the "Therefore" there for? It is a logical connective directing attention to what has preceded: *Because* transient earthly treasures do not satisfy and do not last (6:19–21), *because* moral and spiritual vision is easily distorted and darkened (6:22f.), *because* a choice must be made between God and Money (6:24), *because* the kingdom of God demands unswerving allegiance to its values (6:19–24), *therefore* do not worry, and in particular do not worry about mere things.

But let us consider a more subtle connection. Jesus has been minimizing the ultimate significance of material possessions; and no doubt not a few among his hearers find themselves wondering, "But what about necessities? It's all very well to turn your back on wealth when you're rich; but I've got a wife and children, and I can barely provide them with food, clothing, and shelter. What are you saying to me?" In effect, Jesus answers that just as earthly possessions can become an idol which deposes God by becoming disproportionately important, so also can earthly needs become a source of worry which deposes God by fostering distrust. Loyalty to kingdom values rejects all subservience to temporal things, whether that subservience be the type which accumulates endlessly, or the type stamped by a frenetic, faithless, and worried scurry for essentials.

Before examining what Matthew 6:25–34 says about worry, I think it wise to make some general observations about worry and the response of the New Testament to it. This is because anxiety and tension have become a major point of discussion in our society, and attitudes toward it have degenerated into several polarized positions. It is necessary to make an appeal for balance and caution.

Picture three people. The first is a happy-go-lucky, cheerful, almost irresponsible person. He rarely gets anything done, and never gets anything done on time. He doesn't worry about the next five minutes, let alone tomorrow. Responsibility he wears too lightly; life is a lark. If he is a Christian, it is very difficult to get him to work faithfully at any task. He probably won't cause any tension by stooping to bitterness or vindictiveness: everyone knows him as a "nice guy." On the other hand, he remains insensitive to the needs and feelings of others, and is consistently carefree about the spiritual lostness of millions of men.

The second person is almost hyper-responsible. He takes every grief and burden seriously. If there is any trouble, he frets so much over it that he produces outsize ulcers. The state of the economy is a constant weight on his mind: not only does he worry about tomorrow, he wonders how he'll make out when he retires in forty-two years. He may spread the objects of his worry around, so that every bit of bad news, or even a whiff of potentially bad news, prompts a new outbreak of anxiety; or he may focus his worry and inflated sense of responsibility on a few restricted areas, with the result that he utterly excludes other people and topics.

The third person is a balanced and sane young Christian, noteworthy for his integrity and disciplined hard work. Married with two children, he is supporting them faithfully while he tries to finish his doctorate. With about one year to go, he wakes one night to discover that his wife can't speak and can't move her right side. A brain tumor is discovered; but major surgery proves useless. The doctor tells the young man that the recovery period will be lengthy, and will not return his wife to normal strength and mental clarity in any case. In fact, the prognosis is three years, during which time she will become more and more like a vegetable; and then she will die.

These three people hear some preacher use Matthew 6:25–34 as the basis for a long sermon on the wickedness of worry. The preacher says that worry involves distrust in God, and this is shameful.

How will each react?

The first will be quite happy. He always knew that other people were too uptight all the time. Why bother studying so hard for an "A"? Just passing the course is good enough. Why get so hung up with binding commitments? He's happy and free, and cheerfully obeying the Lord's injunction not to worry.

The second may feel quite rebuked by the sermon. He knows it is for him. He worries that he has been denying the Lord, and despairs of himself and his sins. Quite without any sense of irony, he begins to worry about worry.

The third person listens to the sermon, and, unless he is remarkably mature and full of grace, bitterly sneers under his breath something to the effect that the preacher should watch his own wife die before venturing on so difficult a subject. And if this third man is tired and feeling a trifle vindictive, he may start to tick off on his mental fingers a few of the things that somebody jolly well *ought* to start worrying about: ecological problems, threat of nuclear holocaust, runaway inflation, widely scattered wars, racial prejudice, totalitarian cruelty, economic oppression, rampaging alcoholism in France, and rampaging venereal disease in America. He may also list other more personal problems: divorce, competition for promotion at work, deadlines, family feuding, rebellious teenagers, and so on. These personal frustrations and enmities somehow coalesce with national and international concerns because they are all deposited in our minds by newspapers, radio, and television. Not worry? Man number three hears such an injunction and weighs it against the gnawing anxieties which plague the spirit and endanger health, and he mutters, "You don't understand. It can't be done."

These three represent only a small number of possible reactions, but they illustrate the kind of problem this exposition of the text has confronted again and again. Interpreting the Scriptures demands both balance and precision: balance to weld together diverse teachings, and precision so that no one teaching is thoughtlessly extrapolated out of proportion.

Moreover, the application of these diverse emphases requires a certain pastoral awareness of the needs of each individual. This first man needs to hear something about discipline, self-sacrifice, and hard work, and he needs to have illegitimate worry differentiated from these. The second man ought to hear of God's providence, of the means and results of prayer, and of the self-centeredness which is frequently a large constituent of nagging worry. The third man needs to have a close and loving brother weep with him, pledge support, and perhaps point afresh to the final proof of divine benevolence, the cross of Christ.

I shall offer two propositions:

(1) There is a sense in which worry is not only good, but its absence
    is, biblically speaking, irresponsible.
(2) There is a sense in which worry is not only evil, but its presence
    signifies unbelief and disobedience.

The first sort of "worry" is simply the concern of the follower of
Jesus to be faithful and useful in his master's service. Even a casual
reading of the Pauline corpus makes it clear that Paul lived and ministered with a certain intensity, a throbbing commitment not only
to become more Christ-like himself, but also to fight spiritual bat-
tles on behalf of an exponentially increasing number of other believers. His commitment cost him the hardship and sufferings detailed
in 2 Corinthians 11:23ff. "Besides everything else," Paul adds, "I face
the daily pressure of my concern for all the churches. Who is weak,
and I do not feel weak? Who is led into sin, and I do not inwardly
burn?" (2 Cor. 11:28f.).

In addition to these concerns the Christian can be greatly exercised
concerning sin, as the beatitudes themselves testify (cf. also Pss. 38
and 51). Small wonder the Christian way can be described in terms
of wrestling, boxing; or as a fight, a struggle, a race that demands
every effort if the goal is to be reached and the prize won. There is
little justification in Scripture for picturing the Christian life in terms
of constantly effervescent joy, unbounded peace, unbroken serenity;
and still less is there warrant for irresponsibility toward the Lord in
the use of his gifts. Joy and peace and freedom there are, but only
within the matrix of unadulterated commitment to Jesus, along with
all the pressures such commitment must inevitably bring.

None of these "worries" is purely selfish. Moreover, such concerns
(a less emotive term than "worries") are essentially God-directed. That
is, they are a result of looking at things from God's perspective, and
seeking to ensure that his will be done on earth as it is in heaven. The
absence of such "worries" is irresponsible.

On the other hand, many worries are both illicit and harmful.
There is nothing wrong with puttering about the kitchen; but if commitment to the kitchen prompts impatience and distorted values, it
deserves rebuke (Luke 10:38–42). Some seed gets planted and grows
in a most promising way at first, before thorn bushes choke the life
out of it; and those thorn bushes are "the worries of this life and the
deceitfulness of wealth" (Matt. 13:22). We sense Paul's desire to
eliminate corrupting worry in Philippians 4:6f.: "Do not be anxious
about anything, but in everything, by prayer and petition, with

thanksgiving, present your requests to God. And the peace of God, which transcends all understanding, will guard your hearts and your minds in Christ Jesus." Too many Christians overlook the fact that the apostle here gives us the *means* of overcoming worry, as well as his prohibition.

I dare not neglect prayer and thanksgiving if I am to enjoy God's transcendent peace and overcome my worries. I must abhor thankless bitterness and eschew sulkiness. My worries must be enumerated before the Father, along with thoughtful requests framed in accordance with his will. These requests must be offered to the accompaniment of sincere gratitude for the many undeserved blessings already received, and for the privilege of stretching my faith by exposure to this new and improved hardship. Thus the follower of Jesus learns really to trust the all-wise and all-gracious sovereignty of God (Rom. 8:28), as he begins to experience the profundity of Peter's injunction: "Humble yourselves, therefore, under God's mighty hand, that he may lift you up in due time. Cast all your anxiety on him because he cares for you" (1 Peter 5:6f.).

Most—if not all—illicit worries indicate an acute shortage of confidence in God; and therefore to some extent they are self-centered. Most are bound to temporal categories; and where they are not, as in the fearful brother who fears God's grace is insufficient to pardon him, all the rich promises of the gospel are available to quell them.

Perhaps the trickiest forms of worry are those which marry legitimate concern with self-centered worry. For example, the preacher may be honestly exercised about an impending address he is to give, that it be true, helpful, anointed by the Spirit of God, and spoken in love. But he may also be worried about his reputation. We humans are very skilled at developing mixed motives and mixed worries. God help us to reinforce the good and hold the evil in abomination.

With what sort of worry is our Lord concerned in Matthew 6:25–34? Quite clearly, he is not advocating carefree irresponsibility. What he teaches is that even material necessities are not valid causes of worry among the heirs of the kingdom. Therefore our physical needs, however legitimate they may be, must never supplant our prior commitment to the kingdom of God and his righteousness. Furthermore, he teaches that these same needs become opportunities for living a life distinctive from the surrounding pagans who never learn to trust God for even the basic necessities.

The general principle, 6:25

"Therefore I tell you, do not worry about your life, what you will eat or drink; or about your body, what you will wear. Is not life more important than food, and the body more important than clothes?" The New International Version's "Do not worry" is superior to the King James Version's "Take no thought," since the injunction is not designed to promote thoughtlessness, but freedom from care.

There is an implicit *a fortiori* argument here. An *a fortiori* argument is one with the form, "If this, then how much more that?" There are some famous examples of such reasoning in the New Testament. Perhaps the best known is Romans 8:32: "He who did not spare his own Son, but gave him up for us all—how will he not also, along with him, graciously give us all things?" God has already given us his best gift; how much more will he give us lesser gifts! Another excellent example of an *a fortiori* argument lies in the chapter under study: "If that is how God clothes the grass of the field, which is here today and tomorrow is thrown into the fire, will he not much more clothe you, O you of little faith?" (Matt. 6:30). Again, in Matthew 7:11 we find: "If you, then, though you are evil, know how to give good gifts to your children, how much more will your Father in heaven give good gifts to those who ask him!"

In Matthew 6:25, the *a fortiori* argument is only implicit, because the form isn't present; but the thought seems to be something like this: he who provides us with life, with bodies (which from our perspective are most important), how much more will he also provide things of lesser importance like food and clothes! Therefore, the follower of Jesus is not to worry about such needs, as basic as they are.

This point is driven home by two examples.

Two examples, 6:26–30

Life and food, 6:26f.

"Look at the birds of the air; they do not sow or reap or store away in barns, and yet your heavenly Father feeds them. Are you not much more valuable than they? Who of you by worrying can add a single hour to his life?"

During three enjoyable years in Cambridge, England, I spent most of my time working in the excellent facilities of the Tyndale Library. Outside the window by my desk stretched a pleasant, well-kept garden. Every morning, and often throughout the day, scores of birds would come to scratch and peck and pull up worms. But for all their constant activity, they seemed carefree and alert; they chirped and sang, the high note of the robin mingling with the more mellow warble of the thrush and the common note of the sparrow.

These creatures live from day to day, "they do not sow or reap or store away in barns." Jesus, however, is not arguing that they should be our paradigm, and that we should therefore abolish farming. Rather, he goes on to tell us that despite the day-to-day kind of existence among birds, "yet your heavenly Father feeds them." The conclusion is inevitable: "Are you not much more valuable than they?" If your heavenly Father feeds them, will he not undertake to feed you, especially in the light of the fact that he considers you more valuable than they? And therefore is not constant worry about how future meals will be provided an affront to God, a charge that we cannot trust his providence? Has not Jesus already taught the heirs of the kingdom to pray, "Give us today our daily bread"? And will this prayer, taught by Jesus himself, be mocked by the Almighty?

Jesus' argument, both in this example and the next, depends for its validity on a biblical cosmology. Consider four models. The first might be called the *open universe*.

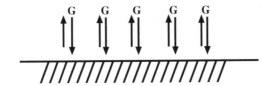

In this model, the Gs represent gods; the bottom of the diagram is the physical universe as it may be perceived by primitive peoples. My sister lived for years among the people of a certain New Guinea highland tribe. This tribe was pre–Stone Age in its technology—that is to say, however sophisticated they were in other areas, their arrowheads were made of teak or bamboo, not stone (much less metal!). Their cosmology was much like the above model. They thought their activity affected the gods in some way; and these gods or, better, spirits (a more appropriate term, since the people were animists) in turn affected things, people, and events in the perceived world. Such spir-

its are somewhat whimsical and capricious; and so a great deal of
time and care go into placating them and winning their favor. Right
religious practice, avoidance of taboos, and the appropriate propiti-
ating sacrifices, all help to ensure good crops, victory in the impending skirmish with the next tribe, the survival of the newborn baby,
and the like. In this open universe, of course, science (as we think of
it) is inconceivable. The gods (spirits) are too unpredictable; "laws"
of cause and effect could not be discovered because they are unexpected, and, if they were somehow unearthed, they would be otherwise interpreted.

The second cosmology is the *closed universe*. It might be schema-
tized like this:

Everything that is, lies within the circle. And everything that takes
place is to be explained by what is already in the circle. The best modern representative of this model of cosmology is science of a purely
mechanistic and atheistic variety. There is nothing other than matter, energy, and space. Even time and chance are secondary. And every
thing, every person, every event, every emotion, is to be explained by
mechanistic principles of cause and effect. Science is not only possible; it is the only perspective considered legitimate.

Some might make an alteration to this model:

At first sight, this is quite an improvement: God is at the center of
things. In fact, however, it differs little from the second model, because

God is merely part of the mechanism. The best contemporary examples of this sort of cosmology are found among certain philosophers and theologians. These men are not atheists in the sense that they deny the existence of a god; but they are atheists in the sense that they deny that there is a personal and transcendent God. God becomes to them the ground of being, the impersonal force which directs man to authentic existence, and the like. God-words are common; but they refer to some "Being" far removed from the God portrayed in the Bible. And in terms of the way men see reality, science (and its laws of cause and effect) is the dominant force. Men may be called upon to make decisions, but sober reflection reveals that even such decisions are determined by the facts of science (either absolutely or according to the vagaries of statistical accident). I think this cosmology might be labeled the *quasi-theistic existentialist universe.*

A fourth model may be used to picture biblical cosmology. It is *the controlled universe.*

G

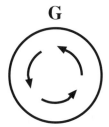

In this diagram, everything in the phenomenal universe is found, without exception, within the circle, along with every other created thing or being. Within this universe there are scientific laws to be discovered, and a patterned order which supports principles of cause and effect. Above this universe stands God. Actually, because of God's omnipresence, he stands both above this universe and in it (to use spatial categories). However, the infinite-personal God cannot be identified with his creation. In this sense, God stands ontologically over against his creation as its Creator and Sustainer. Designed by him, the universe hums along according to regular and predictable laws; but it does so only because he constantly exercises his sovereignty over the whole. No part of the system ever operates completely independently.

Moreover, at any instant he chooses, he is free to suspend or abolish scientific "laws"; that alone will account for such a miracle as the resurrection of Jesus from the dead. Man can discover scientific "laws"; indeed, he must, he is commissioned to do so as the steward of the creation. But the scientist who has adopted this biblical cosmology will not only recognize such laws and allow for divinely initiated exceptions, he will realize that those laws continue faithfully because of God's sustaining power. More specifically, since divine sovereignty is mediated through the Son, the Christian will hold that it is the Son who is, even now, "sustaining all things by his powerful word" (Heb. 1:3).

This biblical cosmology must be carefully distinguished from two counterfeits. The first is offered by Deism: God has started the whole machine running, like a giant watch; but he has now more or less left it to its own devices. The Bible pictures God, rather, as Sustainer. The second counterfeit recognizes God's sovereignty and transcendence, but pictures divine control as so immediate that science is excluded. The model becomes akin to the open universe I mentioned first, with all the Gs coalescing into one God. But this ill accounts for the orderliness and structure God has built into the system, and for the mandate he has given man concerning it.

Old Testament believers were quite aware that water evaporates, forms clouds which drop their rain, which provides rivulets, streams, and rivers which run to the sea; but more customarily they preferred to speak of God sending the rain. Such is the biblical cosmology.

This cosmology stands behind Matthew 6:26. Only those who have adopted such a cosmology will sense the thrust of the passage. The Christian looks at a beautifully plumed bird, or an eagle in flight, or a robin straining valiantly in a tug-of-war against a fat worm, and sees his Father's design and his Father's care. A bat swoops low at dusk; and the Christian does not say, "Ha! Marvelous aerodynamics, there! Evolution is quite remarkable." Rather, ornithologist or no, he testifies to God's activity behind the flight. And the wren who works all day to feed her chicks is evidence of God's provision for tiny baby birds. The believer who has understood and adopted this biblical cosmology has a constant, abundant array of evidence around him concerning divine providence and beneficence.

Jesus adds one more emphasis to this example. He asks, "Who of you by worrying can add a single hour to his life?" (6:27). This verse has been translated in many different ways. For example, in addition to the rendition of the NIV just given, we find:

Which of you by taking thought can add one cubit unto his stature? (KJV).

Can any of you, however much he worries, make himself an inch taller? (Phillips).

And which of you by being anxious can add one cubit to his span of life? (RSV).

Is there a man of you who by anxious thought can add a foot to his height? (NEB).

The problem is that the word translated "life" by the NIV can either mean stature or age. Zacchaeus was little in *stature* (Luke 19:3); Abraham was past the *age* to father children (Heb. 11:11). In the Greek New Testament, the same word is used in both verses. So in Matthew 6:27, we are asked which of us can add a single cubit (a linear measure of perhaps eighteen inches) to his stature or to his age. The latter seems inappropriate: linear measure can scarcely be added to age. But stature seems no more appropriate, because the force of the question in this case would depend on a very short linear measure, certainly not a cubit. All of the above efforts at translation have been generated by these difficulties.

I am inclined to follow those who see an idiom here, something like this: "Who of you by worrying can add to the pathway of his life a single cubit?" In America a person might say on his birthday, "Well, I've reached another milestone." Of course, he hasn't; what he has done is used linear measure as a metaphor for age. As a person walks the pathway of life, the time comes when God determines it will end. Worrying will not change that decree; he cannot travel a single cubit farther. So why worry about it?

Body and clothes, 6:28–30

Clothes are scarcely less important than food; and Jesus treats both in the same way. "And why do you worry about clothes? See how the lilies of the field grow. They do not labor or spin. Yet I tell you that not even Solomon in all his splendor was dressed like one of these. If that is how God clothes the grass of the field, which is here today and tomorrow is thrown into the fire, will he not much more clothe you, O you of little faith?" (6:28–30). The word rendered lilies is, in the original, an obscure word which probably means "wild flowers," flowers of the field, complementing the "birds of the air" in verse 26.

Watch those flowers grow: they do not work to earn or buy their beauty. They grow. Each flower individually, and all of them in a field as they collectively decorate the green grass, make the opulent splendor of Solomon's clothing pale by comparison. This is God's work; the biblical cosmology is again presupposed. The Christian sees the fresh greenness of well-watered grass, and, whether or not he acknowledges the effect of chlorophyll, he certainly acknowledges the God behind the chlorophyll. God clothes the grass with spectacular arrays of flowers, even though the grass is destined to be mowed down and burned up. Shall he not be even more concerned to clothe us, his children?

In other words, biblical cosmology plus observant eyes engender real trust in God. Small wonder Jesus calls those who do not perceive these lessons, "men of little faith" (6:30).

Distinctive living, 6:31f.

At the end of Matthew 5, Jesus insists that his followers must love their enemies, for even pagans and public sinners love their friends. The norms of the kingdom require that our lifestyle be distinctive. Now in chapter 6 we discover—as in love, so also in freedom from worry: "So do not worry, saying, 'What shall we eat?' or 'What shall we drink?' or 'What shall we wear?' For the pagans run after all these things, and your heavenly Father knows that you need them" (6:31f.).

Lack of uncompromising trust in God is not only an affront to him, but also essentially pagan. In other words, verse 32 provides two important reasons why we are not to sound worried and frustrated like secular men. The first is that if we worry as pagans do, it is transparent that we are pursuing the same things they are; but if we are, then because the kingdom values are so different, the kingdom is necessarily being denied. Second, such worry on the part of those who profess faith in God constitutes some sort of denial of that profession, since the heavenly Father is well aware of our needs (cf. also 6:8), and our conduct is advertising loudly that we don't believe it.

Our worries must not sound like the worries of the world. When the Christian faces the pressure of examinations, does he sound like the pagan in the next room? When he is short of money, even for the essentials, does he complain with the same tone, the same words, the same attitude, as those around him? Away with secular thinking. The follower of Jesus will be concerned to have a distinctive lifestyle, one that is characterized by values and perspectives so un-pagan that his life and conduct are, as it were, stamped all over with the words, "Made in the kingdom of God."

What does this principle imply for Christians in the professions, in trade unions, in big business? Suppose even one-tenth of contemporary nominal evangelicals pored over the pages of Scripture to establish what their lifestyles should be like, and, with balance, determination, meekness, and courage, found grace to live accordingly. What transformation would be effected in our world! How the light would alleviate the darkness; how the salt would preserve society!

In the fourth century, the Roman Emperor Julian the Apostate failed in his efforts to suppress Christianity, largely because of the distinctive living he found among believers. He told his officials, "We ought to be ashamed. Not a beggar is to be found among the Jews, and those godless Galileans [he meant the Christians] feed not only their own people but ours as well, whereas our people receive no assistance whatever from us." We have some things to learn from the early Christians (not to mention many later ones, such as the Anabaptists) about the sharing of material things; but, more broadly, we have even more things to learn about the importance of the kind of living which is eager to pursue kingdom perspectives.

The question immediately at hand is worry. Would it not be wonderful if some world leader were forced to say today, "We ought to be ashamed. Not a worrier is to be found among those fanatics who call themselves Christians. They cope not only with the pressures faced by other men, but the pressures we put on them as well. And then they go and give comfort to some of us when we worry, whereas our people are constantly gulping down tranquilizers, visiting assorted counselors, and mass-producing overweight ulcers."

The heart of the matter, 6:33

Because our heavenly Father knows what we need and has committed himself to be gracious to his children, Jesus gives this pledge: "But seek first his kingdom and his righteousness, and all these things will be given to you as well" (6:33). Our part is to avoid consuming worry, even over essentials, and to pursue the kingdom of God. The word "seek" here is present imperative, suggesting unceasing quest. God's part is then to provide his children with what they need.

Three limitations must be observed. (1) This promise is to the children of God, not to all men indiscriminately. This is made clear by the contrast between Jesus' disciples and pagans in 6:31f., as well as by the condition in 6:33a itself: Seek first his kingdom and his righteousness. (2) Jesus promises that necessities will be provided (in context, food, drink, and clothes are specified), not luxuries. Many Christians in the West would think it very hard indeed if they had to live at subsistence level, for they have long since come to take as necessities things which others would assess as luxuries. God in his lavish mercy often gives much more than the essentials; but he here pledges himself only to the latter. (3) I think the major exception to this pledge occurs when Christians are suffering for righteousness' sake. Some are martyred by starvation and by exposure. The overwhelming importance of the kingdom may require self-sacrifice even to this ultimate degree.

God does keep this promise. In the affluent West, too few of us, especially if we are young, have experienced his faithfulness in this regard. But some have been privileged to experience pressure to the point where they have had absolutely no recourse but God. I know a couple who, some years ago, were serving a small, lower class church in Montreal. On Christmas Day, the man distributed food packages, gathered by the church, to the destitute in the vicinity. He returned home to his wife, and both of them thanked the Lord for the food with which he had provided them—one can of beans. One half hour later they were invited out to a Christmas dinner.

Such stories could be multiplied endlessly. God answers prayer and supplies the needs of his own. To this I testify from many experiences of his grace, especially during the long years while I was a student, frequently without any money at all.

But at least I *was* a student. What shall we say of the desperate hunger that stalks so much of the globe today? I have seen little of it; but what I have seen of it in a Christian context confirms the promise of Matthew 6:33. God provides for his own. This *in no way* reduces our responsibility to share what we have; rather, it enhances it, for God's most common way of meeting the material needs of his poor children is by laying such needs on the hearts and consciences of others among his children.

This prompts two other reflections which, even if they are not explicitly stated in the text itself, are quite important. They speak to questions lurking in the back of our minds in these days when evangelicals are reassessing their social responsibility, and at the same time the so-called "Protestant work ethic" has come under attack.

On the first point, we Christians desperately need to assess our goals and commitments in the light of what the Scriptures teach about caring for the hungry (see Prov. 22:9; 25:21f.; Isa. 32:6; 58:6ff.; Ezek. 16:49; 18:7; Matt. 25:42; Luke 3:11; 12:48; Acts 4:32ff.). Christians first of all ought to support their own, but they must reach out to others as well. Sooner or later the mad race toward more and more possessions must cease: let Christians choose to get out of the race now, before there is no choice.

On the second point, work and profit are not to be despised. The Puritans receive much bad popular press; but they have a great deal to teach us about working with integrity. They saw their work as a form of service to the Lord, and, believing that they should be faithful in small things as in great, worked with zealous industry. Moreover, their desire for education brought them advancement, and their simple lifestyle multiplied their savings. (How much does an "average" family of four spend *per annum* on cigarettes, junk and excess food, alcohol, and questionable entertainment? This arithmetical exercise produces staggering results.) The tragedy of the Puritans was that later generations came to believe, though few would be so crass as to express it, that righteousness and industry were worthwhile virtues *because* they led to thrift and wealth. They disciplined themselves *so that* they might accumulate things. Gradually a biblical perspective was subverted into an abhorrent materialism.

Disciples of Jesus must think clearly about these things. They will seek first their Father's kingdom and righteousness, assured that he will provide enough to cover their needs. And, industrious and honest as they may be, they will refuse to tie their lives and happiness to treasures which can be corrupted and stolen. And rich or poor, they will struggle to understand how best to please their Father by using the wealth he has entrusted to them.

The goal, then, is always the kingdom of God. For the Christian, the disciple of Jesus, there is no other. The logic entailed by this simple fact orients his thinking to kingdom values and concomitantly abolishes worry over merely temporal things, a worry which compromises his trust in his heavenly Father.

Final reason for reducing worry, 6:34

I think Jesus must have said the words in Matthew 6:34 with a wry smile. So far his reasons for sending worry to oblivion have been essentially theological. They have turned on the compassion and providence of God, and on the superlative value of the kingdom. But this last reason is purely pragmatic: "Therefore do not worry about tomorrow, for tomorrow will worry about itself. Each day has enough trouble of its own" (6:34).

It is as if Jesus recognizes that there will be some unavoidable worry today after all. But let's limit it to the concerns of today! Our gracious God intends us to take one step at a time, no more; to be responsible today and not fret about tomorrow. "Each day has enough trouble of its own." And if there will be new troubles tomorrow, so also will there be fresh grace.

The person who enters the kingdom adopts the perspectives of the kingdom. In broadest terms, this entails unswerving loyalty to the values dictated by God, and uncompromised trust in God. In the light of so high a calling, our self-examination will produce some bleak results; and we shall want to pray the words of T. B. Pollock (1836–1896):

> We have not known Thee as we ought,
> Nor learned Thy wisdom, grace, and power;
> The things of earth have filled our thought,
> And trifles of the passing hour.
> Lord, give us light Thy truth to see,
> And make us wise in knowing Thee.
>
> We have not feared Thee as we ought,
> Nor bowed beneath Thine awful eye,
> Nor guarded deed, and word, and thought,
> Rememb'ring that our God was nigh.
> Lord, give us faith to know Thee near,
> And grant the grace of holy fear.
>
> We have not loved Thee as we ought,
> Nor cared that we are loved by Thee;
> Thy presence have coldly sought,
> And feebly longed Thy face to see.
> Lord, give a pure and loving heart
> To feel and own the love Thou art.
>
> We have not served Thee as we ought;
> Alas, the duties left undone,
> The work with little fervor wrought,
> The battles lost or scarcely won!
> Lord, give the zeal, and give the might,
> For Thee to toil, for Thee to fight.

When shall we know Thee as we ought,
And fear, and love, and serve aright?
When shall we, out of trial brought,
Be perfect in the land of light?
Lord, may we day by day prepare
To see Thy face, and serve Thee there.

5

Balance and Perfection

(7:1–12)

WE HUMAN BEINGS display a vast capacity for self-deception. For example, we prostitute righteousness into self-righteousness, and perfection into a perfect reputation; but we accomplish this prostitution so cleverly that we are at best only vaguely aware of the monstrosity we have wrought. Against all such aped religion Jesus has already spoken trenchantly (Matt. 6:1–18), filling out the warning with searching counter-demands which require heart-adherence to kingdom perspectives (Matt. 6:19–34).

Before Jesus winds up the Sermon on the Mount and drives home the alternatives which men must face (Matt. 7:13–27), he warns against three other dangers. The first two are cast in negative terms— we are not to be judgmental (7:1–5) and yet we are not to be undiscriminating (7:6). The third is formulated positively: We must persist in our pursuit of God, exercising childlike trust as we do so (7:7–11). By looking closely at these three warnings, we shall discover how they build toward the golden rule (7:12).

The Danger of being Judgmental
Matthew 7:1–5

The principle, 7:1

It is easy to see how powerful and dangerous the temptation to be judgmental can be. The challenge to be holy has been taken seriously, and a fair degree of discipline, service, and formal obedience have been painstakingly won. Now, I tell myself, I can afford to look down my long nose at my less disciplined peers and colleagues. Or perhaps I have actually experienced a generous measure of God's grace, but somehow I have misconstrued it and come to think that I have earned it. As a result I may look askance at those whose vision, in my view, is not as large as my own; whose faith is not as stable; whose grasp of the deep truths of God not as masterful; whose service record is not as impressive (in men's eyes, at least); whose efforts have not been as substantial. These people are diminished in my eyes; I consider their value as people inferior to my own value.

The harping, critical attitude may become so poisonous that men whose spiritual stature, personal integrity, and useful service are all vastly superior to my own, somehow emerge as spiritual pygmies and intellectual paupers by the time I have finished my assessment. Perhaps some small deficiency or inconsistency in their lives has, in my view, utterly vitiated their stature. If in Matthew 6 love of money and distrustful anxiety ruin Christian character, in Matthew 7 the same result is achieved by this scurrilous sort of zeal.

All this, of course, is a form of raw hypocrisy (see 7:5), the second of the three forms of hypocrisy I mentioned earlier. Lest the challenges and impeccable standards of the Sermon on the Mount evoke such ugly sin, Jesus warns, "Do not judge, or you too will be judged" (7:1).

We will be wise to consider first what this text does *not* say. It certainly does not command the sons of God, the disciples of Jesus, to be amorphous, undiscerning blobs who never under any circumstance whatsoever hold any opinions about right and wrong. Are we to say nothing about the rights and wrongs of a Hitler, a Stalin, a Nixon? of adultery, economic exploitation, laziness, deceit? The New Testament itself excludes such a fatuous interpretation. A few verses on, the Lord Jesus himself alludes to certain people as pigs and dogs (7:6)—some sort of negative judgment has certainly taken place! A little further on, Jesus warns, "Watch out for false prophets. They came to you in sheep's clothing, but inwardly they are ferocious wolves" (7:15). By these words Jesus not only labels certain teachers with the most damning epithets, but demands that his followers recognize such teachers for what they are; and that is certainly an exercise which requires the use of discriminating faculties.

Elsewhere, the apostle Paul is prepared to hand over a certain promiscuous man to Satan (1 Cor. 5:5), demanding that his local church discipline him; such discipline requires judgment. In Galatians 1:8f. Paul calls down an anathema on all who preach some version of the gospel other than the true gospel which Paul himself preaches. In Philippians 3:2 he uses strong language to warn his readers against certain false teachers: "Watch out for those dogs, those men who do evil, those mutilators of the flesh." And this language is mild compared with that in Galatians 5:12. John likewise demands some kind of judgment when he writes, "Dear friends, do not believe every spirit, but test the spirits to see whether they are from God, because many false prophets have gone out into the world" (1 John 4:1). Moreover, when a crowd misjudges Jesus because his healing ministry extends to the Sabbath, he does not forbid all judgment, but replies rather, "Stop judging by mere appearances, and make a right judgment" (John 7:24).

What then does Jesus mean by his imperative in Matthew 7:1, "Do not judge, or you too will be judged"? Much of the confusion here is resolved when the semantic range of the Greek word translated "judge" is understood. "To judge" can mean to discern, to judge judicially, to be judgmental, to condemn (judicially or otherwise). The context must determine the precise shade of meaning. The context here argues that the verse means, "Do not be judgmental." Do not adopt a critical spirit, a condemning attitude. The same verb is found twice, with identical meaning, in Romans 14:10ff.: "You, then, why do you *judge* your brother? Or why do you look down on your brother? For we will all stand before God's judgment seat. It is written: 'As I live,' says the Lord, 'every knee will bow before me; every tongue will confess to God.' So then, each of us will give an account of himself to God. Therefore, let us stop *passing judgment* on one another. Instead, make up your mind not to put any stumbling block or obstacle in your brother's way." Jesus himself commands, "Do not be judgmental."

This is not an easy area of one's life to sort out. On the one hand, some people are so critical that they feast on roast preacher every Sunday lunch; and some preachers are so critical they level verbal barrages at most of their colleagues, especially those more fruitful than they. On the other hand, Jesus' disciples ought to recognize some preachers as false because of their fruit (7:16), and dismiss them accordingly; the preacher who credits all his peers with precisely the same grace and insight falls far below Paul's discriminating attitudes. The problem is that the Christian's responsibility to discern, once granted, is readily warped into justification for harping criticism. The arch-critic is thoroughly at home with all the passages which encourage us to spot false prophets by their fruit. "I'm not being judgmental," he protests, "I'm just a fruit inspector." But by his own mouth, he stands condemned; he has become a fruit *inspector*, he has taken on himself some special role.

What is fundamentally at stake, I think, is attitude. This is clearly seen in that particular kind of critical spirit found in the gossip. It is not always the case that what the gossip says is malicious; what he says might, in fact, be strictly true. But it is always the case that he says it maliciously; that is, he speaks without any desire to build up, or any real concern to instill discernment. He wants only to puff himself up, or to be heard, or to enhance his own reputation, or to demean the person about whom he is speaking.

If a Christian's *attitude* is right, provision is made for him to face another brother with his fault (see Matt. 18:15ff.). Indeed, spiritual leaders will not ignore open sin in one of their Christian brothers, but will try and restore him—gently, and aware of their own weakness (Gal. 6:1).

"Do not be judgmental," Jesus says, and then adds, "or you too will be judged" (7:1). The latter clause may perhaps be taken like the first: if you are judgmental, others will be judgmental toward you. Alternatively, depending on the ambiguity of the Greek verb, the sentence may mean: do not be judgmental, or you will be condemned (whether by God or others). Either way, the clause adds stinging pungency to the injunction, and introduces the theological justification for abolishing all judgmental attitudes.

The theological justification, 7:2

"For in the same way you judge others, you will be judged, and with the measure you use, it will be measured to you" (7:2). It is theoretically possible to understand these words, like the words of 7:1b, in more than one way. They may mean that the measure we use on others will be the measure others use on us; the person with a critical spirit is inviting a lot of criticism. Alternatively, verse 2 may mean that the measure we use on others will be the measure God himself will use on us.

I think it is the latter meaning that is in view; and if so, the ambiguity in 7:1b must be interpreted in a similar way. The point of these two verses is not that we should be moderate in our judging in order that others will be moderate toward us, but rather that we should abolish judgmental attitudes lest we ourselves stand utterly condemned before God. A judgmental attitude excludes us from God's pardon, for it betrays an unbroken spirit. The thought is akin to 5:7

and 6:14f.: "Blessed are the merciful, for they will be shown mercy.
. . . For if you forgive men when they sin against you, your heavenly
Father will also forgive you. But if you do not forgive men their sins,
your Father will not forgive your sins. For in the same way you judge
others, you will be judged. . . ."

Some rabbis said that God had two measures by which he assessed
men, the measure of justice and the measure of mercy. It may be
that Jesus in 7:2 is using this belief to drive home his point—the
measure we use, of these two, will be applied to us. For example,
suppose we come across a wretched liar. How do we look upon him?
If we measure him by justice alone, we will be very critical and condemning. But that measure will then be turned on us: How truthful
are we? How often do we slant reports and stories to make a point
or earn favor? Or perhaps we apply the standard of justice to the
adulterer or prostitute. How will we fare when the same standard is
applied to us, especially in the light of Matthew 5:27–30? Or again,
perhaps we apply God's standard of justice to wealthy men who
exploit the poor by unfair practices and greed. But how often have
we been greedy? How often have we robbed others of value for money
(even, for example, in our work)? Do we really want the standard of
God's justice to be applied to ourselves in the way we are prone to
apply it to others?

As we have seen, this does not mean that the disciple of Jesus must
never speak against any sin, exercising a sort of insipid, overlooking
mercy. God's standard of justice will not go away. These verses attack
judgmental attitudes, but they do not deny that real sins may well be
present. In the example which follows (7:3–5), the speck of sawdust
in the patient's eye does in fact require removal, even if the operation
should not be performed by a surgeon with a plank in his own eye.

Moreover, this passage does not suggest that we can earn God's
mercy by exercising a little mercy ourselves. Mercy by definition cannot be earned. But we may exclude ourselves from mercy by sustained haughtiness and arrogance, by an attitude which reflects the
antithesis of true poverty of spirit. God, in fact, exercises both justice and mercy, even toward his own people (of this I shall say more
at the beginning of the next chapter). Therefore his people must
reflect God's character by living justly and showing mercy. And
because they are conscious of their own shortcomings and rebellion,
they cannot but be profoundly grateful for mercy they have experienced even while they strive for perfection and magnify holiness.

This balanced perspective keeps them both from a judgmental spirit and from moral apathy.

Perhaps I should say in passing that some people relate 7:1f. to the "Golden Rule" in 7:12. They feel this is strong evidence that 7:2 has to do with the way men will judge us, not at all with the way God will judge us. They understand 7:1f. to mean that one important reason we should not be judgmental to others is so that as a result others will not be judgmental toward us; this, they say, is one aspect of the "Golden Rule." For reasons I have already given, I think such an interpretation fails to comprehend 7:1f.; but I hasten to add that it equally fails to understand the "Golden Rule" (7:12). This rule tells us to do to others what we would have them do to us; it does not tell us to do nice things to others *in order that* they might do nice things to us. Doing to others what we would have them do to us establishes a code for our own behavior; it does not establish a *reason* for that behavior. The reason is given in the next clause: such behavior sums up the Law and the Prophets.

An example, 7:3–5

"Why do you look at the speck of sawdust in your brother's eye and pay no attention to the plank in your own eye? How can you say to your brother, 'Let me take the speck out of your eye,' when all the time there is a plank in your own eye? You hypocrite, first take the plank out of your own eye, and then you will see clearly to remove the speck from your brother's eye" (7:3–5).

This colorful illustration must not be permitted to lose its power because of its familiarity, still less because it is set in the categories of ophthalmology. The situation depicted by this brief scenario occurs so frequently and so pathetically in professing Christian circles that the contrast between a speck of sawdust and a plank or log is not at all exaggerated.

The most obvious example in the Bible, I suppose, is found in 2 Samuel 12:1–7. King David steals another man's wife. Despite his large harem, he lusts after this particular woman, seduces her, and later discovers that she has become pregnant by him. Her husband is absent at the military front (fighting the king's wars) and so David arranges to have him killed. The king is now guilty of both adultery and murder. The prophet Nathan enters the royal court; but instead of confronting his monarch outright, he tells a parable, a short story about a poor farmer whose one little lamb has been stolen by a rich, powerful neighbor with a large flock of his own. David is incensed; perhaps some of the force of his wrath arises from his own suppressed guilt. In seething indignation, and quite unconscious of any irony, he asks who this wicked farmer is. Nathan replies, "You are the man."

Somehow, King David, incredibly blind, had been unconscious of the plank in his own eye as he fumed over the speck of sawdust in the rich farmer's eye.

It is terribly easy to imitate David's conduct, in one way or another. Sometimes we accomplish this by focusing on certain public sins which others are prone to commit, and denouncing those sins with gusto, while remaining disturbingly oblivious to the sins to which we ourselves are especially attracted. Doctrinal critics can be among the most offensive in this regard. The doctrinal critic may agree that another person is a brother in Christ, has been significantly used of the Lord, is thoughtful and sincere in his submission to Scripture; but because the critic focuses on the one area of doctrine in which the two disagree, this other brother may be painted publicly in hues of gray and black. That Christians are to demonstrate observable love (John 13:34f.; 17:20–23) is lost to view while the critic "defends the truth."

I am not minimizing the significance of truth, nor denying that there are limits to fellowship. I am saying two things. First, genuine believers have more in common than they recognize when, with a sectarian mentality, they focus attention and energy on points of difference, largely to reinforce what they construe as their own *raison d'être*. If I wholeheartedly embrace only those fellow Christians who see things exactly the way I do, I will never embrace anyone, except, perhaps, a handful of weak-minded followers. Second, we must never lose sight of the stress in Matthew 7:1–5 on attitudes. Christians will honestly disagree on doctrinal points, but to become very heated helps no one. There ought to be clear-headed discussion of the differences, with honest submission to the Word of God and a repudiation of arguments which consistently and without cause ascribe unworthy motives to the opposing brothers. Who knows? Perhaps frank discussion and humble examination both of the Scriptures and of the way the other man understands them will bring about consensus of opinion. At the very least it will produce an awareness of the dimensions of the debate, and establish the points where there is, at present, irreconcilable difference of opinion, some of which may be removed by further reflection and research.

Ironically, the worst fault-finder, whether in doctrinal or other realms, cannot be convinced of his fault. If the speck he has discovered in another person's eye is shown to be an illusion, or if the large log in his own eye is gently pointed out, he hunts and pecks until he finds another speck in his target's eye. This critic always looks for something else to criticize; he cannot feel he is sound unless he is constantly denouncing and condemning. I am not sure how he envisages his responsibility to love his neighbor as himself, nor what he thinks of the words, "Love is patient, love is kind. It does not envy, it is not proud. It is not rude, it is not self-seeking, it is not easily angered, it keeps no record of wrongs. Love does not delight in evil, but rejoices in the truth. It always protects, always trusts, always hopes, always perseveres. . . . The end of all things is near. Therefore be clear-minded and self-controlled so that you can pray. Above all, love each other deeply, because love covers over a multitude of sins" (1 Cor. 13:4–7; 1 Peter 4:7f.).

The more I reflect on this passage, the more I find I am self-condemned. God grant me grace to practice what I preach.

I used to think that those who most needed Matthew 7:1–5 were young people, especially students. They are struggling to establish their own identities, trying to come to terms with new ideas. These new ideas are quickly espoused and stoutly defended or as quickly rejected and unthinkingly mocked. But young people and students are far from being the only ones who go through periods of identity crisis and of critical exposure to new thinking. Older people, fearful of their positions, concerned with their prestige, and often disturbed by what they take to be the lack of productivity in their lives, often become singularly defensive, rigid, judgmental, intolerant, even nasty and petty. The young, at least, may grow out of it; but for the old to reject such a long-established pattern of behavior may take a dramatic display of divine intervention, perhaps in the form of a crushing, devastating experience that engenders humility.

The person who is scrupulously careful about removing the planks from his own eyes is not thereby absolved from all further responsibility. Having gained the ability to see clearly, he can help remove the speck from his brother's eye (7:5). Indeed, only then will his brother welcome his assistance.

The Danger of being Undiscriminating
Matthew 7:6

We come now to what is essentially the converse danger to the one treated by our Lord in Matthew 7:1–5: the danger of being undiscriminating. It is easy to see how this new danger arises. The disciple of Jesus has been told to love his neighbor as himself, and to love his enemies. He is to mirror God's graciousness, the God who evenhandedly sends his rain upon both the just and the unjust. He has just been told never to adopt a judgmental mentality. As a result, he is in chronic danger of becoming wishy-washy, of refusing legitimate distinctions between truth and error, good and evil. He may even try to treat all men in *exactly* the same way, succumbing to a remarkable lack of discrimination.

And so, after warning us against judgmentalism, Jesus warns us against being undiscriminating, especially in our choice of people to whom we present the wonderful riches of the gospel. However, in seeking to do full justice to this warning in 7:6, we ought not fail to note that five verses are reserved for judgmental people, and only one for undiscerning people. That ratio reflects an accurate assessment of where the greater danger lies.

The Lord Jesus says, "Do not give dogs what is sacred; do not throw your pearls to pigs. If you do, they may trample them under their feet, and then turn and tear you to pieces." The dogs in view are not cuddly pets with wagging tails and affectionate natures, friendly creatures that love to have their ears scratched. They are semi-wild hounds that roam the streets and hills, tongues hanging from their mouths and burrs clinging to their filthy coats as they forage for food in savage packs. And the Palestinian domestic pig was not only an abomination to the Jew, but, most probably derived from the European wild boar, it was capable of certain violence. The two animals together serve as a model of people who are savage, vicious, held in abomination. These two are brought together again in 2 Peter 2:22, in an equally negative context: "Of them [certain people] the proverbs are true: 'A dog returns to its vomit,' and, 'A sow that is washed goes back to her wallowing in the mud.'"

Jesus sketches a picture of a man holding a bag of precious pearls, confronting a pack of hulking hounds and some wild pigs. As the animals glare hungrily, he takes out his pearls and sprinkles them on the street. Thinking they are about to gulp some bits of food, the animals pounce on the pearls. Swift disillusionment sets in—the pearls are too hard to chew, quite tasteless, and utterly unappetizing. Enraged, the wild animals spit out the pearls, turn on the man, and tear him to pieces.

Camping can be enjoyed in vast wilderness areas of North America. But one of the rules to be observed unfailingly is, Don't feed the bears! Feed the ground squirrels, feed the deer, feed the raccoons, even feed the coyotes; but don't feed the bears. If they aren't satisfied, they will turn and tear you to pieces.

In metaphorical language (which makes his warning even more shocking than if he had spoken without metaphor), Jesus is commanding his disciples not to share the richest parts of spiritual truth with persons who are persistently vicious, irresponsible, and unappreciative. Just as the pearls were unappreciated by the savage animals, but only enraged them and made them dangerous, so also many of the riches of God's revelation are unappreciated by many people. And, painful as it is to see it, these rich truths may only serve to enrage them.

In the New Testament, there are several examples of this principle in action. In Matthew 15:14, Jesus, speaking of certain Pharisees, tells his disciples, "Leave them; they are blind guides. If a blind man leads a blind man, both will fall into a pit." According to Acts 18:5f., Paul abandons his ministry to the Jews in Corinth because they oppose him and become abusive. Instead he turns to the Gentiles to minister to them. Paul recommends a similar course of action to Titus concerning divisive people within the professing Christian community: "Warn a divisive person once, and then warn him a second time. After that have nothing to do with him. You may be sure that such a man is warped and sinful; he is self-condemned" (Titus 3:10f.).

I would like to draw attention to five implications or allusions embedded in this pithy injunction. First, it is no accident that Jesus speaks of pearls, and not gravel. The man in the scenario is in possession of great wealth. Interpreting the metaphor, we learn that the good news of Jesus Christ, with all of history and revelation pointing toward it, really is a priceless treasure. It is wonderful beyond words. All physical wealth pales to insignificance beside it. Because this is God's world, nothing is more important to me than to have my sins forgiven and to be accepted by him; and nothing is more wonderful than the way God has accomplished this by sending his own Son to die in my behalf. God has graciously given to men, both in human language (the Bible) and in a human person (Jesus), true and sure revelation of himself; and nothing, absolutely nothing, is richer or more important or of more consequence than that.

Second, however, is the somber recognition that not all men will receive this revelation. Some, like dogs and pigs confronting pearls, remain utterly insensitive to this revelation. It does not gratify their immediate appetites, and they have no other criteria by which to assess it. Thus, by these verses we are being prepared for the division of the human race into two groups, portrayed by the Lord Jesus in Matthew 7:13ff.

Third, it is not simply that some do not receive this revelation. For the chief thrust of 7:6 is that Jesus' disciples are not even to present the riches of that revelation to certain people of vicious and unappreciative disposition. Their cynical mockery, their intellectual arrogance, their love of moral decay, and their vaunted self-sufficiency make them utterly impervious to the person and words of Christ. Over the years I have gradually come to the place where I refuse to attempt to explain Christianity and introduce Christ to the person who just wants to mock and argue and ridicule. It accomplishes nothing good, and there are so many other opportunities where time and energy can be invested more profitably.

This unavoidable conclusion must be balanced with a fourth observation, that this injunction from the Lord Jesus himself is set in a broader context, which demands love for enemies and a quality of life characterized by perfect righteousness. In other words, the fact that Christians ought not throw their pearls to dogs and pigs does not give them a license to be nasty and vindictive, still less to ignore all else that Jesus has taught. Moreover, there is no justification in this verse for neglecting all verbal witness on the grounds that there are only dogs and pigs out there who are, without exception, vicious. Many—if not most—thinking adults who have become sincere disciples of the Lord Jesus Christ begin this pilgrimage by balking, and not a few begin by mocking.

There are many situations in which Christians need to persist in their witness and be patient with their sowing of God's truth. The harvest will come in due time if we do not faint from cowardice or laziness first. What Jesus is calling for is discernment; and the essence of discernment is knowing that simple rules cannot be expected to crank out an infallible answer. Here, again, we do well to try to follow the example of the Teacher himself. It is eminently profitable to examine his approach to different individuals and groups. He can dismiss a group (as we have seen him do, in Matt. 15:14), write off a Herod (Luke 13:31–33), promise judgment to whole cities (Matt. 11:20–24); but he can be patient with a group (see Luke 9:51–55; Mark

6:31–34), offer indisputable evidence to a doubting Thomas (John 20:24ff.), and weep over a city (Luke 19:41ff.). Christians dare not decide which side of Jesus' reactions they will follow most closely; they must follow both. And I suspect that the stronger the inclination to follow one side at the expense of the other, the greater the danger of imbalance, and the stronger the need to grow in discernment and conformity to Christ.

Moreover, although Christians must learn discretion and spiritual discernment, and therefore refrain from throwing around their pearls with reckless abandon, nevertheless the bearing and quality of their life may conceivably be used of God to prompt the dogs and pigs to reflect. If there is hope for lost and hardened people, it lies, as James Montgomery Boice has said, "in the sovereignty of God and in the demonstrable reality of true Christian living." While writing these lines I was called aside to explain the fundamentals of biblical Christianity to a medical student from one of the universities nearby. It is worth noting that, according to him, his first attraction to the Bible and to Christ was prompted in part by intellectual curiosity, but more particularly by the quality of life of some Christian students he has known. The salt had not lost its savor; the light was still shining.

In sum, we are to be careful in our handling of the truths of biblical revelation, for they are holy things, and must not be thrown around indiscriminately, but thoughtfully, carefully, responsibly, strategically. And, it is probably valid to deduce that the discrimination explicitly required by this text constitutes only a part of the larger responsibility to be discriminating.

The Danger of Lacking a Trusting Persistence
Matthew 7:7–11

It is painfully easy to understand how those who lack persistence in the Christian faith develop. Someone gets all excited about the teaching of Jesus. So many things attract him: the noble sentiments, the call to self-sacrifice, the sublime moral tone, the uncompromised purity, the emphasis on untarnished truth, the farsighted faith, the winsome freedom from a judgmental mentality—splendid stuff! And in committing himself to this fine teaching he experiences a sort of catharsis which he takes to be a sign of spiritual life. Thus encouraged, he spurts ahead, his behavior promising a rich harvest of spiritual graces. No one is more eager to volunteer for spiritual work, no one more faithful in attendance at Bible studies and prayer meetings, no one more concerned to follow Christ's teachings in all spheres of human existence.

And then he fizzles, ignominiously flickers once or twice, and sputters out. It is as if he bloomed in some rocky place without much depth of earth. The seed of truth falls into this soil, and grows up quickly for no other reason than that the soil is so shallow. But when the full heat of the summer sun pelts down its searing rays, the plant's young roots have nowhere to go for moisture. The plant is scorched, and it withers and dies. In Jesus' words, "What was sown on rocky places is the man who hears the word and at once receives it with joy. But since he has no root, he lasts only a short time. When trouble or persecution comes because of the word, he quickly falls away" (Matt. 13:20f.; cf. 13:1–9).

What has gone wrong with this person? First, he lacks persistence, he is short on sticking power. True Christian commitment perseveres. "No one who puts his hand to the plow and looks back is fit for service in the kingdom of God" (Luke 9:62), Jesus insists—an attitude reflected equally in John, who says that those who draw back have never really belonged to Christ's people (1 John 2:19). But second, and more important, this flash-in-the-pan disciple has been motivated by high sentiment and noble thought, and has somehow entirely missed the significance of the first beatitude: "Blessed are the poor in spirit, for theirs is the kingdom of heaven" (5:3). He is riding on his determination, his own recently stimulated lofty ideals. Incredibly, the Sermon on the Mount makes him think he can live by its precepts all by himself. Instead of seeing his own spiritual bankruptcy by the light of the Sermon on the Mount, he sees only the beauty of the light itself; and therefore instead of turning to God and asking for the grace, mercy, forgiveness, acceptance, and help which his spiritually bankrupt state requires, he merely turns over a new leaf. Small wonder he is soon discouraged and defeated.

That is why Jesus says, "Ask and it shall be given you; seek and you will find; knock and the door will be opened to you. For everyone who asks receives; he who seeks finds; and to him who knocks, the door will be opened" (7:7f.). In the perfect threefold symmetry of these two verses, the imperatives are emphatic and in the present tense. Keep on asking, keep on seeking, keep on knocking; ask, seek, knock, and keep on doing it; for "everyone who asks receives; he who seeks finds; and to him who knocks the door will be opened."

Persistence is required. But persistence in what? The answer is persistence in prayer—not prayer envisaged as an occasional pious request for some isolated blessing, but, in the context of the Sermon on the Mount, prayer that is a burning pursuit of God. This asking is an asking for the virtues Jesus has just expounded; this seeking is a seeking for God; this knocking is a knocking at heaven's throne room. It is a divinely empowered response to God's open invitation: "You will seek me and you will find me when you search for me with all your heart" (Jer. 29:13).

The kingdom of heaven requires poverty of spirit, purity of heart, truth, compassion, a nonretaliatory spirit, a life of integrity; and we lack all of these things. Then let us ask for them! Are you as holy, as meek, as truthful, as loving, as pure, as obedient to God as you would like to be? Then ask him for grace that these virtues may multiply in your life! Such asking, when sincere and humble, is already a step of repentance and faith, for it is an acknowledgment that the virtues the kingdom requires you do not possess, and that these same virtues only God can give. Moreover, I suspect that this asking, seeking, and knocking has a total package as its proper object. It does not seek holiness but spurn obedience; it does not seek obedience but hedge when it comes to purity. It is a wholehearted pursuit of the kingdom of God and his righteousness. And this pursuit is stamped by stamina: it is a *persistent* asking, seeking, knocking (cf. also Luke 11:5–10; 18:1–8; 1 Thess. 5:17).

The Western world is not characterized by prayer. By and large, to our unspeakable shame, even genuine Christians in the West are not characterized by prayer. Our environment loves hustle and bustle, smooth organization and powerful institutions, human self-confidence and human achievement, new opinions and novel schemes; and the church of Jesus Christ has conformed so thoroughly to this environment that it is often difficult to see how it differs in these matters from contemporary paganism. There are, of course, exceptions; but I am referring to what is characteristic. Our low spiritual ebb is directly traceable to the flickering feebleness of our prayers: "You do not have, because you do not ask God. When you ask, you do not receive, because you ask with wrong motives, that you may spend what you get on your pleasures" (James 4:2b–3).

There is an unavoidable correlative to this asking. It follows inescapably that if we must ask, we cannot receive the virtues characteristic of those in the kingdom unless they are given by God. This observation is of extreme importance because it forms part of a motif which flows through the entire New Testament. To put it another way, no one earns his place in the kingdom of God. No one chalks up merit points until he has accumulated enough to inherit eternal life. No one is capable, by himself, of even approaching the quality of life characterized by the Sermon on the Mount. And certainly no one will ever enter the consummated kingdom simply because he has determined to improve himself and make himself presentable before God.

The first beatitude has already set the tone: God's approval rests on the person who is poor in spirit. Such a person, recognizing his personal spiritual bankruptcy and his personal inability to conform to kingdom perspectives, will be eager to ask God for grace and help, impatient to seek the blessings only God can give, delighted to knock at the portals of heaven. He also recognizes that salvation now—and the full richness of that salvation in the consummated kingdom—depends on God's grace, God's free unmerited favor. This man rejoices to read Jesus' invitation to ask, seek, and knock. He comes as a humble petitioner, seeking pardon and grace.

It becomes clear, then, how Jesus' words serve as an antidote to the danger of withering in rocky soil. The person who becomes all excited about the lofty ideals of the Sermon on the Mount must learn that no spiritual progress is made apart from God's grace; then he will understand that there is nothing more crucial than to ask God for that grace. Moreover, he will begin to grasp the solemn fact that biblical Christianity is not some temporary high to be assumed or discarded at will according to the present level of excitement or discouragement. Rather, it is an orientation of the whole life, an eternal commitment that depends for its success on the trustworthiness of God. Failures and setbacks there may be; but God remains utterly faithful and free from partiality and the vagaries of human whims, and still gives to the one who asks, presents spiritual treasure to the one who seeks, and opens to the one who knocks.

Does God do this begrudgingly? This is a question of considerable importance, for we frame our requests in accordance with what we know of the character of the one whom we are addressing. The child with the kind, gentle, and firm father does not fear to ask him for things, but deep down he enjoys the assurance that his father will not give him something which greater wisdom and experience assess as not in the child's best interests. The child with the extravagant but thoughtless father approaches him with arrogance and lays down his next demand, knowing he will not be refused. The child with the stingy, ill-tempered, and abusive father will seldom ask for anything, fearing another meaningless beating.

How then shall we approach God? Jesus gives a brief but telling illustration to reinforce the main point: as sons of the kingdom we are to approach God with trust in his goodness, and persistence as we ask for the day's supply. "Which of you," Jesus asks, "if his son asks for bread, will give him a stone? Or if he asks for a fish, will give him a snake?" This scenario is desperately silly. What father would think it a fine joke to replace a bun with a stone that looked like a bun? Jesus' conclusion to his rhetorical question is inevitable: "If you, then, though you are evil, know how to give good gifts to your children, how much more will your Father in heaven give good gifts to those who ask him!" (7:9–11).

Sadly, many of God's children labor under the delusion that their heavenly Father extracts some malicious glee out of watching his children squirm now and then. Of course, they are not quite blasphemous enough to put it in such terms; but their prayer life reveals they are not thoroughly convinced of God's goodness and the love he has for them. Jesus' argument is *a fortiori:* If human fathers, who by God's standards of perfect righteousness can only be described as evil, know how to give good gifts to their children, *how much more* will God give good gifts to them who ask him? We are dealing with the God who once said to his people, "Can a mother forget the baby at her breast and have no compassion on the child she has borne? Though she may forget, I will not forget you!" (Isa. 49:15).

The Christian is to remind himself often of the sheer goodness of God, and therefore of the resources available to him from his heavenly Father:

> *Come, my soul, thy suit prepare;*
> *Jesus loves to answer prayer;*
> *He himself has bid thee pray,*
> *Therefore will not say thee nay.*
>
> *Thou art coming to a King;*
> *Large petitions with thee bring;*
> *For his grace and power are such,*
> *None can ever ask too much.*

John Newton (1725–1807)

Balance and Perfection
Matthew 7:12

I have titled this chapter, which deals with Matthew 7:1–12, "Balance and Perfection"; and those themes reach their apex in verse 12: "In everything do to others what you would have them do to you, for this sums up the Law and the Prophets."

I explained in the second chapter that 5:17–20 and 7:12 form an inclusio—that is, they bracket the main body of the Sermon on the Mount as it is recorded in Matthew, and indicate that the sermon is concerned with the way the kingdom of God fulfills the Law and the Prophets. Much of this is expounded in Matthew 5. The Old Testament, as we saw, points forward to Jesus and the kingdom he announces and finds its real continuity in them. But the righteousness demanded by the kingdom might be prostituted by some into hypocritical "acts of righteousness," and so Jesus goes on to warn against such hypocrisy in Matthew 6, insisting on sincere adherence to the perspectives of the kingdom.

At the beginning of Matthew 7, then, Jesus deals with final possible misconceptions. Precisely because he is given to preaching in absolute categories, he takes special pains to bring the parts together in balance and proportion. Of course, we do not know all Jesus said that day on the hillside in Galilee; but there is good reason to believe that Matthew has captured its thrust and balance. The first danger Jesus deals with is the danger of being judgmental (7:1–5); but he balances that against the danger of being undiscriminating (7:6). And the whole discourse is tempered by his warning against lacking a trusting persistence (7:7–11); for by this means it becomes clear that Jesus is not advocating a mere determination to improve. Rather, he is insisting that both entrance into the kingdom and progress in the kingdom require God's saving hand. Thus the whole body of the Sermon on the Mount has been rounded out and knit together with exceptional balance.

Then, Jesus caps it off with the so-called "Golden Rule." The *negative* form of this rule is known to many religions—that is, it often appears elsewhere in the form, "Do not do anything to anyone that you would not want him to do to you." For example, Rabbi Hillel taught, "What is hateful to you, do not do to your fellow creatures. That is the whole law. All else is explanation." But Jesus gives the *positive* form of this rule, and the difference between the two forms is profound. For example, the negative form would teach behavior like this: If you do not enjoy being robbed, don't rob others. If you do not like being cursed, don't curse others. If you do not enjoy being hated, don't hate others. If you do not care to be clubbed over the head, don't club others over the head. However, the positive form teaches behavior like this: If you enjoy being loved, love others. If you like to receive things, give to others. If you like being appreciated, appreciate others. The positive form is thus far more searching than its negative counterpart. Here there is no permission to withdraw into a world where I offend no one, but accomplish no positive good, either. What would you like done to you? What would you really like? Then, do that to others. Duplicate both the quality of these things, and their quantity—"in everything."

Why are we to act in this way? Jesus does *not* say that we are to do to others what we would like them to do to us *in order that* they will do it to us. At stake is no such utilitarian value as "honesty pays" or the like. Rather, the reason we are to do to others what we would like others to do to us is that such behavior sums up the Law and the Prophets. In other words, such behavior conforms to the requirements of the kingdom of God, the kingdom which is the fulfillment of the Law and the Prophets. It constitutes a quick test of the perfection demanded in 5:48; of the love described in 5:43ff.; of the truth portrayed in 5:33ff.; and so forth.

That the "Golden Rule" does not lay great stress on our relationship to God is not really surprising. The preceding verses have already insisted on our conscious and continually formulated dependence upon him if we are to grow to meet the norms of the kingdom. Elsewhere Jesus teaches that the greatest commandment is, "Love the Lord your God with all your heart, with all your soul, and with all your mind," and that the second greatest is, "Love your neighbor as yourself" (Matt. 22:37, 39). But in Jesus' teaching it is axiomatic that the second will never be obeyed without the first: we will never love our neighbors in the way we would like to be loved until we love God with heart and soul and mind.

As the overwhelming distance between these demands and our own conduct drives home our spiritual bankruptcy, God give us a burning desire to turn to him with humble, persistent asking, seeking, knocking. Out of this we shall become "doers" of the Word, and not just "hearers."

6

Conclusion to the Sermon on the Mount

(7:13–28)

BEFORE STUDYING MATTHEW 7:13–27, the conclusion of the Sermon on the Mount as it is recorded by Matthew, it may be wise to step back a pace and consider how the teaching of these chapters relates to one or two other important emphases in the New Testament. In particular, I would like to raise the question of how Matthew 5–7 meshes with major Pauline emphases, especially his stress on justification by grace through faith, preeminently expounded in his epistles to the Romans and the Galatians. I am persuaded that this pause will bring the final verses of the Sermon on the Mount into sharper focus.

Excursus
The Sermon on the Mount and Pauline Emphases

Balance
Joyful Christian submission to the authority of the Scriptures brings with it commitment to a certain balance in the way we approach these Scriptures. For the Christian, the Bible is to be believed as a whole, the later revelation complementing and sometimes modifying the earlier. Within the New Testament itself, different writers stress themes which interest them or which are of particular concern to the believers among whom they minister. In giving us this sacred book, God did not choose to provide us with a textbook of systematic theology,

nor a dictated letter. Rather, he sovereignly moved and inspired men to write various accounts, descriptions, letters, experiences, visions, and injunctions so that what was put down was a true reflection of the human author's impressions, assessments, research, convictions, experiences—and yet at the same time the very words of God. To put it more concretely, John does not write like Paul; their vocabularies are different, their historical and theological interests differ, their styles are their own. God, however, uses both men. Because of this fact, it is not legitimate to pit one against the other, or to accept one as a normative expression of Christianity at the expense of the other.

So then, biblical revelation is not monochromatic; therefore it must not be interpreted monochromatically. Granted that this is so, we must nevertheless learn how to blend the different light rays into one unbroken spectrum.

The Sermon on the Mount contains a great deal of ethical instruction—so much so that some people have concluded that it lays out a series of conditions which must be met if a person is to enter the kingdom of God. In this view, an individual enters the kingdom because his obedience merits entrance. Such a deduction is, of course, false; we observed in the last chapter how Jesus' insistence on poverty of spirit (in 5:3), coupled with the accent on humbly petitioning God (in 7:7–11), combine to vitiate such a conclusion. However, it is understandable, to say the least, how a superficial reading of the Sermon on the Mount might lead the inattentive reader to this false conclusion.

Paul

Let us contrast Paul's teaching on salvation. In particular, let us examine three elements of that teaching. First, Paul insists that men are saved by God's free grace, and by nothing else. Certainly they cannot be saved by their works, by the merits they accumulate. He takes the first two and one half chapters of Romans to prove that all men, without exception, stand guilty before God. God is just and holy; he cannot overlook sin and pretend it doesn't matter. However, he is gracious and loving, and therefore takes no pleasure in condemning guilty people. Acting therefore in perfect conformity with both his justice and his grace, he sends his Son to become a man, Jesus of Nazareth. Jesus, God's "Anointed One" (that is, God's chosen one, his "Christ"), voluntarily, as a man, obeys his Father in all things, and dies as a representative and a substitute for men who could not save themselves. God did this "to demonstrate his justice at the present time, so as to be just and the one who justifies the man who has faith in Jesus" (Rom. 3:26). "Where, then, is boasting?" Paul asks; and he replies, "It is excluded. . . . For we maintain that a man is justified by faith apart from observing the law" (Rom. 3:27f.).

Second, this salvation which comes by God's grace, through faith, does not, according to Paul, condone irresponsibility. If someone argues that God pours out his grace in proportion to the sin ("But where sin increased, grace increased all the more. . . ," Rom. 5:20) and therefore it is best to go on sinning so that grace may go on increasing, Paul will have none of it (Rom. 6:1ff.). Moreover, Paul argues further that because Jesus' death met the law's righteous demands forensically, Jesus' disciples, pardoned by their Lord's supreme act of self-sacrifice, will themselves be controlled by the Spirit of God (Rom. 8:1ff.). Indeed, *only* those who possess this Spirit, and whose lives demonstrate it, have truly been pardoned; and *all* those who possess this Spirit, and whose lives demonstrate it, have truly been pardoned.

To put it another way, the salvation which God gives by grace is not static; it inevitably results in good works. Good works may not earn salvation, but they will certainly result from it. In this connection, Ephesians 2:10 needs to be weighed alongside the more commonlycited pair of verses preceding it: "For it is by grace you have been saved, through faith—and this not from yourselves, it is the gift of God—not by works, so that no one can boast. *For we are God's workmanship, created in Christ Jesus to do good works, which God prepared in advance for us to do*" (Eph. 2:8–10). According to this passage, good works can be construed as both the goal of salvation and the test of salvation.

Third, from the perspective of the Christian who looks back on a longer period of God's revelation than his Old Testament counterpart could, it becomes clear that the Old Testament law was never by itself designed to save anyone. It pointed forward to the salvation that was coming, and it did this in a number of ways. For example, it taught the Jews the real extent of their guilt (Rom. 2:17ff.), just as natural revelation and commonly recognized morality taught the Gentiles the extent of theirs (Rom. 1:18–2:16). As far as the Jews are concerned, the law was introduced as a stop-gap measure until the promise of redemption was fulfilled in Jesus (Gal. 3:19). Its entire sacrificial system pointed to the supreme sacrifice of the Savior himself. Thus the law, by pointing to Christ and by compounding human guilt and human awareness of that guilt, was designed to lead men to Christ, in order that they might be justified by grace, through faith (Gal. 3:24).

In fact, Paul can argue that no one was ever saved by law (Gal. 3:11)—that is, by simply doing enough of what the law says.

To construct a model in which a man's good points are totted up and measured against his bad points is ridiculous from the Pauline point of view. After all, the good ought to be done without exception. Therefore there is nothing meritorious in doing good and obeying God's law; and failure to do good (that is, breaking God's law) is such unequivocal evil that we have no means of making it up. That by which we would like to think we can make it up—namely, doing good—we are supposed to do anyway; and so it can scarcely atone for the evil. Paul argues that even before Christ came, and the real object of faith was fully unveiled to our view, Old Testament believers were acceptable to God only on the basis of his grace. The law looked forward to Christ's cross and resurrection, somewhat the way the gospel now looks back on those climactic events. Old Testament believers, even while seeking to obey the formal law, had to approach God by faith—in poverty of spirit, desiring divine grace—or not at all.

Current Christianity
Of course, Paul is referring primarily to the function of law within the history of the Jewish race. However, this account of things also holds up at the personal level. It is usually true that a man won't cry to be found until he knows or suspects he's lost. He won't beg for pardon until he thinks he's condemned. He will not ask for forgiveness until he is conscious of his guilt. I am aware, of course, that some people become Christians without passing through deep traumas in these areas; but I suspect some of the same features apply anyway. For example, some are converted because they are drawn by the humbling magnificence of Jesus' love, as expressed in his self-sacrifice. But that means they recognize some need in their own lives, or some claim he has on them, or an essential superiority in him which they admit they do not possess and would like to establish as their goal. And these people, I suspect, do not make up the majority of genuine conversions. To go farther, I would argue that the reason we are currently seeing such an embarrassingly high percentage of spurious conversions to Christ is precisely because we have not first taught people their need of Christ.

In one of his letters to a young man who wanted to know how to preach the gospel, John Wesley offers a quite different approach. He says that whenever he arrived at any new place to preach the gospel, he began with a general declaration of the love of God. Then he preached "the law" (by which he meant all of God's righteous standards and the penalty of disobedience) as searchingly as he could. This he kept up until a large proportion of his hearers found themselves under deep conviction of sin, beginning even to despair of the possibility of forgiveness from this holy God. Then, and only then, did he introduce the good news of Jesus Christ. Wesley explained the saving significance of Christ's person, ministry, death, and resurrection, and the wonderful truth that salvation is solely by God's grace, through faith. Unless his audiences sensed that they were guilty, and quite helpless to save themselves, the wonder and availability of God's grace would leave them unmoved. Wesley adds that after quite a number had been converted, he would mix in more themes connected with "law." He did this to underline the truth that genuine believers hunger for experiential righteousness, and continue to acknowledge poverty of spirit, recognizing constantly that their acceptance with God depends always and only on Christ's sacrifice.

In much contemporary evangelism, there is little concern for whether or not God will accept us, and much concern for whether or not we will accept him. Little attention is paid to whether or not we please him, and much to whether or not he pleases us. Many popular evangelistic methods are molded by these considerations. As a result, there is far too little stress on God's character and the requirements of the kingdom, and far too much stress on our needs. Worse, our needs are cast in preeminently psychological categories, not moral ones (alienation and loneliness, not bitterness and self-seeking and hatred; frustration and fear, not prayerlessness and unbelief). To top it off, peace, joy, and love are preached as desirable goals. These *are* desirable, but they suffer from two defects. First, virtues such as peace, joy, and love can easily be interpreted in merely personal, almost mystical terms. As a result, the biblical emphases on peace *with God* and with men, joy *in the Lord,* and tough-minded love which gives sacrificially to both God and men, are reduced to a warm, pleasant glow. Second, these virtues need to be set alongside complementary virtues such as justice, integrity, righteousness, truth, humility, and faith.

Imagine a large cone:

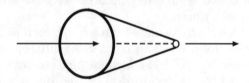

If the entrance to the kingdom is presented as large and wide, many people will take the first steps. However, they soon discover that the cone narrows down inside. To continue would mean lightening the load they are carrying; the final terms for entrance are very restrictive. They have been induced to enter the cone by much talk of life, forgiveness, peace, and joy; and suddenly they discover more confining notions. They learn of sin and repentance, obedience and discipleship. Not surprisingly, there is often an eruption and they blow back out.

But the cone might face the other way:

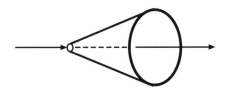

Now, the entrance seems very narrow. There is no admittance until a person comes without any baggage. He enters solely on the conditions laid down. But once inside, to his delight he discovers expanding horizons and growing freedom.

Paul, we have seen, understands that in general the cone lies in the second position. He explains that one of the major functions of the law is to condemn men. That is, far from providing a convenient code by which men may earn merits before God, the law functions to expose sin and condemn it. Paul writes, "Now we know that whatever the law says, it says to those who are under the law, so that every mouth may be silenced and the whole world held accountable to God. Therefore no one will be declared righteous in his sight by observing the law; rather, through the law we become conscious of sin" (Rom. 3:19f.). As a result, when a person comes to Christ, he comes stripped of all pretense of self-righteousness, all claims to personal moral merit. I am not saying that a person is worthless. Far from it—each person is made in the image of God and therefore possesses immense significance, not the least of which is his eternal destiny. But before God no one possesses any *meritorious moral worth* that would earn him forgiveness, salvation, and entrance to the kingdom of God.

In other words, it is typical of Paul to stress, on the one hand, salvation by grace through faith; and, on the other, the unequivocal surrender by which men must approach God.

Christ

How often does Jesus' own ministry reflect the same perspectives! He
has an uncanny knack of putting his finger on the sorest spot or the
biggest hindrance in the life of the person with whom he is dealing.
The rich ruler, in love with his wealth, needs to get rid of it (Luke
18:18ff.). The Samaritan woman is prepared to talk about religion,
but Jesus brings up her adulterous relationships (John 4:7ff.). He
warns prospective disciples to count the cost (Luke 14:25ff.), con-
cluding his illustrations of this point with the penetrating statement,
"In the same way, any of you who does not give up everything he has
cannot be my disciple" (Luke 14:33). There it is—the narrow end of
the cone. This idea emerges again when he actually rebuffs half-
hearted or premature volunteers (Luke 9:57–62).

Of course, this is only one side of the picture. Jesus can also be
found giving broad invitations (see Matt. 11:28–30; John 7:37f.); and
he is known as the one who will not break bruised reeds nor quench
smoldering wicks (Matt. 12:20). But this only means that to the
crushed, bruised, downtrodden, and weary he shows himself to be
gracious. Jesus is called as a doctor to the sick, not the well; as a Savior for sinners, not for the righteous (Matt. 9:12f.). The broken people do not need large lessons on poverty of spirit: they've already
learned them, and now need words of grace and hope.

I am coming now to the nub of the issue, as far as the Sermon on
the Mount is concerned. Paul makes it clear that the law makes men
conscious of sin, that men are saved by grace through faith, and that
no one is acceptable to God if he brings along conditions and caveats.
Paul *explains* the function of law; and *what Paul is explaining in
Romans and Galatians, Jesus is doing in the Sermon on the Mount.*

It is not for nothing that the Sermon on the Mount begins with the
demand for poverty of spirit. It begins by demanding that kingdom
hopefuls acknowledge their spiritual bankruptcy, their need. Moreover, just as Paul is explaining some of the relationships between law
and the gospel, so also is Jesus (cf. Matt. 5:17–20); but he does so in
such a way as to underscore the demand for righteousness in the kingdom. Whatever binding authority Old Testament law still possesses,
it possesses in that which has fulfilled it, that is, in the kingdom. Therefore in one sense Jesus is preaching the law: he is preaching that toward
which the law and the prophets pointed. In thus proclaiming the norms
and requirements of the kingdom, he is simultaneously providing genuine disciples with the kingdom's perspectives, and making all others
painfully aware of their insurmountable shortcomings.

Of course, Jesus is preaching to people who still have not wrestled with the significance of his death, nor rejoiced at the historical fact and eschatological dimensions of his resurrection. This pre-Passion setting undoubtedly influences how much Jesus tells them, and in what terms. Nevertheless, I insist that if the Sermon on the Mount be construed merely as legal requirement to kingdom entrance, no one shall ever enter: can anyone meditate long on Matthew 5–7 and remain unashamed? The Sermon on the Mount provides us with a crushing blow to self-righteousness and follows it up with an invitation to petition God for favor (7:7–11), without which there can be no admittance to the kingdom. At the same time it sketches in the quality of life of those who do enter, those who petition God (7:7–11), ask for forgiveness (6:12), and who by God's grace discover not only forgiveness but a growing personal conformity to kingdom norms. It is not long before their own lives begin to sum up the law and the prophets.

Nothing could be more calamitous than to meditate long and hard on Matthew 5:1–7:12 and then to resolve to improve a little. The discipleship which Jesus requires is absolute, radical in the (etymological) sense that it gets to the root of human conduct and to the root of relationships between God and men. A person either enters the kingdom or he does not. He walks the road that leads to life, or he walks the road that leads to destruction. There is no third alternative. Nothing, nothing at all, could have more crucial significance than following Jesus. Even if today this is far from being a universally admitted truth, yet one day all men without exception shall confess it, some to their everlasting grief.

Jesus therefore concludes the Sermon on the Mount with a number of paired alternatives. He speaks of two paths (7:13f.), two trees (7:15–20), two claims (7:21–23), two houses (7:24–27). By these pairs he insists that there are two ways, and only two. These final verses of the Sermon on the Mount demand decision and commitment of the type that beseeches God for mercy and pardon. Such discipleship is characterized by that deep repentance which hungers for nothing more than conformity to God's will. But because there are only two ways, simple failure to make such deep commitment is already a commitment not to do so. Jesus' way demands repentance, trust, and obedience. Therefore refusal, stemming as it must from an unrepentant arrogance, unbelief, and/or disobedience—in short, self-centeredness instead of God-centeredness—can only be construed as rebellion.

Two ways, and only two. The Sermon on the Mount does not end with lofty thoughts of human goodness, sprinkled liberally with naive hope about the inevitability of human progress. It offers two ways, and only two. The one ends in life (7:14), good fruit (7:17), entrance into the kingdom of heaven (7:21), stability (7:25); the other ends in destruction (7:13), bad fruit and fire (7:19), exclusion from the kingdom along with other evildoers (7:23), ruination (7:27). Solemn thoughts, these; a man will ignore the weight of these blessings and curses only at his own eternal peril.

TWO PATHS
Matthew 7:13f.

Jesus says, first of all, "Enter through the narrow gate. For wide is the gate and broad is the road that leads to destruction, and many enter through it. But small is the gate and narrow the road that leads to life, and only a few find it" (7:13f.).

The metaphor is straightforward enough. We are to picture two paths, two roadways. The first is broad (not "easy," RSV) and its gate is wide. It accommodates many people, all enjoying its spacious contours. But although it is so well-traveled, it ends in destruction. The other path is narrow, and the way into it is small. It is confined, and relatively few travelers are to be found on it. But it leads to "life"—a synonym for the kingdom.

What legitimate deductions can be drawn from these two verses? I shall mention five things. First, God's way is not spacious, but confining. Poverty of spirit is not easy; prayer is not easy; righteousness is not easy; transformed God-centered attitudes are not easily achieved. In fact, these things are impossible for us, apart from God's grace. They are alien to much of what is in us and which cries out to be heard; and therefore the re-alignment that is part and parcel of genuine conversion is a confining thing. There is no room for me to set my opinion against the Lord's, no room to set goals in any way at cross-purposes to his, no room to form attachments which vie for the central place the Lord Jesus must have.

There is considerable danger that the picture I am painting will be thought dull gray, not to say morbid; and so I hasten to add certain caveats to what I have just said. There is a whole spectrum of joys and freedoms for the Christian. The deepest joy is joy in personally knowing God through Christ, just as the deepest human joys have always been close, personal friendships. There is the liberty of sins forgiven and of progressive triumph over temptation. New loves and friendships mushroom with other disciples of Christ, so much so that Jesus can say, "I tell you the truth, no one who has left home or brothers or sisters or mother or father or children or fields for me and the gospel will fail to receive a hundred times as much in this present age (homes, brothers, sisters, mothers, children and fields—and with them, persecutions) and in the age to come, eternal life" (Mark 10:29f.). As the Godhead becomes the center of the Christian's thinking, all of life takes on a new and fascinating attraction as he glimpses the wholeness of things under God.

> Heaven above is softer blue,
> Earth around is sweeter green;
> Something lives in every hue
> Christless eyes have never seen:
> Birds with gladder songs o'erflow,
> Flowers with deeper beauties shine,
> Since I know, as now I know,
> I am His, and He is mine.
>
> George W. Robinson (1838–1877)

Yet the way is confining nevertheless. Indeed, the more hesitation there is about going Christ's way wholeheartedly, without reserve, the more confining his way seems. However, the more enthusiasm there is for following him regardless of personal opinion or peer pressure, regardless of cost, the more liberating his way appears.

Second, we may deduce from Matthew 7:13f. that God's way cannot be discovered by appeal to majority opinion, for the majority is on the road that leads to destruction. Christians will apply Paul's words to many perspectives: "Let God be true, and every man a liar" (Rom. 3:4). If someone asks directly, "Does this mean that only relatively few will be saved, and that the rest are lost?" then the safest answer is that of Jesus himself (Luke 13:22–30):

> [22]Then Jesus went through the cities and villages, teaching as he made his way to Jerusalem. [23]Someone asked him, "Lord, are only a few people going to be saved?"
> He said to them, [24]"Make every effort to enter through the narrow door, because many, I tell you, will try to enter and will not

be able to. [25]Once the owner of the house gets up and closes the door, you will stand outside knocking and pleading, 'Sir, open the door for us.'

"But he will answer, 'I don't know you or where you come from.'

[26]"Then you will say, 'We ate and drank with you, and you taught in our streets.'

[27]"But he will reply, 'I don't know you or where you come from. Away from me, all you evildoers!'

[28]"There will be weeping and grinding of teeth when you see Abraham, Isaac and Jacob and all the prophets in the kingdom of God, but you yourselves thrown out. 29People will come from east and west and north and south, and will take their places at the feast in the kingdom of God. 30Indeed there are those who are last who will be first, and the first who will be last."

Strong words! They were spoken first of all to the Jews of Jesus' own day who were rejecting their own Messiah; but the thrust of Jesus' response will not change. He demands of his questioners less speculation on the precise number of those who are "going to be saved," and more personal concern about their own salvation.

In the third place, it follows that the narrow way to life cannot be pursued as long as we are motivated by a desire to please the mass of men. Most men travel the broad road; the narrow road is a little lonelier. This is another way of expressing a truth which emerges repeatedly in the Sermon on the Mount, that true disciples of Jesus will not play to the galleries, nor form their values according to the passing approval of faddish whim. The beatitudes tell us that it is God's approval alone which is of ultimate importance. In Matthew 6 Jesus excoriates that form of hypocrisy which practices piety to win the approval of men. And here in Matthew 7 he tells us that the way to life is narrow and not as popular as the way to destruction.

"Choose for yourselves today whom you will serve . . . ; but as for me and my household, we will serve the Lord" (Josh. 24:15). Joshua's challenge to Israel comes to us today with the same vigor, a vigor born of clear-headed analysis. It reminds me of the spirit of Athanasius, the fourth-century theologian who for a while stood virtually alone in his defense of the deity of Christ. His work has largely stood the test of time; and in his own time he eventually won the day. But during the darker periods when he was being sucked into the maelstrom of theological controversy and seemed to be isolated from his friends and colleagues, he was advised to give up his opinions because the whole world was against him. His reply was devastatingly simple: "Then is Athanasius against the whole world."

Of course, it is possible to take such a position out of sheer arrogance and stubborn independence. Anyone who stoops to such obnoxious egotism has not learned even the first lessons of the Sermon on the Mount. The distinctions by which such a person seeks to preserve his isolation are more traditional and personal than biblical. Nevertheless, when all allowances have been made, it remains a fact that the narrow way wins few popularity contests. This is so partly because the full-blooded righteousness of the Sermon on the Mount is too comprehensive and demanding to be universally attractive to a race that prefers compromise and assorted personal corruptions. Also, the Sermon's concern for truth is so great that personal intolerance of false teaching is necessarily entailed (as we shall see in Matt. 7:15–20).

In the fourth place, the two paths are not ends in themselves, but have eternal significance beyond themselves. The one ends in destruction, the other in life. Ironically, it is the spacious and popular path which leads to destruction, and the confined and relatively unpopular one which leads to life. The point remains the same in each case; not the path but the path's destination is of ultimate significance. The tragedy is that otherwise reasonable men become so enamored with the spaciousness and the popularity of their path that they take little thought as to its destination. Should they hear that it leads to destruction, they will deny it, arguing that they are no worse than most others on the same road, and that in any case God would not permit the destruction of so many. Let me state emphatically that the Scriptures do not encourage such optimism. Jesus himself insists that only the narrow way leads to life. Only the path that seems confining explodes in the end into vitality, the consummation of the kingdom of God.

Lastly, let it be noted once more that there are only two ways. To put this point in other terms, we might say that there is no other way to life, no other way to avoid destruction, than the narrow way. Men will not gain the kingdom by worshiping nature, nor by pious sentiment, nor by drifting into salvation without decision and commitment, still less by hedonism and self-expression. They will enter life by coming under the kingdom's norms, and be saved by God's grace through faith in Christ, or they will head for destruction. On this point Jesus insists.

TWO TREES
Matthew 7:15–20

Disciples of Jesus Christ are not very susceptible to open invitations to sin. They are not likely to be taken in by the teacher/preacher who advocates raw hedonism, anarchy, or various forms of unbelief. The problem will lie with the preacher who seems pious, who prays, who at first glance seems to have all the marks of the Christian. He uses all the right religious clichés, and the very dogmatism he exudes seems to testify to his orthodoxy. He appears as one of the sheep in Christ's flock, and most of the genuine sheep fail to notice he is really a savage wolf. "Watch out for false prophets," Jesus warns. "They come to you in sheep's clothing, but inwardly they are ferocious wolves" (7:15).

The problem of false prophets has always been with us. A prophet is fundamentally a messenger for someone else, and these false prophets claim to be speaking for God. The acuteness of the danger they present is that they are accepted at face value—they appear within the church and gather a following within the church. Elsewhere Jesus warns that "many false prophets will appear and deceive many people" (Matt. 24:11). Toward the end of his ministry, the apostle Paul warned the elders of the church in Ephesus, "I know that after I leave, savage wolves will come in among you and will not spare the flock. *Even from your own number* men will arise and distort the truth in order to draw away disciples after them. So be on your guard! Remember that for three years I never stopped warning each of you night and day with tears" (Acts 20:29–31). Or consider the solemn words in 2 Peter 2:1–3, 17–22:

> [1]But there were also false prophets among the people, just as there will be false teachers among you. They will secretly introduce destructive heresies, even denying the sovereign Lord who bought them—bringing swift destruction on themselves. [2]Many will follow their shameful ways and will bring the way of truth into disrepute. [3]In their greed these teachers will exploit you with stories they have made up. Their condemnation has long been hanging over them, and their destruction has not been sleeping.

> [17]These men are springs without water and mists driven by a storm. Blackest darkness is reserved for them. [18]For they mouth

empty, boastful words and, by appealing to the lustful desires of sinful human nature, they entice people who are just escaping from those who live in error. [19]They promise them freedom, while they themselves are slaves of depravity—for a man is a slave to whatever has mastered him. [20]If they have escaped the corruption of the world by knowing our Lord and Savior Jesus Christ and are again entangled in it and overcome, they are worse off at the end than they were at the beginning. [21]It would have been better for them not to have known the way of righteousness, than to have known it and then to turn their backs on the sacred commandment that was passed on to them. [22]Of them the proverbs are true: "A dog returns to its vomit," and, "A sow that is washed goes back to her wallowing in the mud."

Perhaps we should not be surprised, if we remember the archetype behind these false prophets. Paul, writing of certain men with whom he had to deal, unveils their real model: "For such men are false prophets, deceitful workmen, masquerading as apostles of Christ. And no wonder, for Satan himself masquerades as an angel of light. It is not surprising, then, if his servants masquerade as servants of righteousness. Their end will be what their actions deserve" (2 Cor. 2:13–15).

How, then, are we to recognize these wolves in sheep's clothing? Many suggestions for unmasking them are scattered throughout the Scriptures, but only two are in view here.

The first is based on a contextual observation. Within the context of the Sermon on the Mount, the false prophet can only be someone who does not advocate the narrow way presented by Jesus. He may not be wildly heretical in other areas; indeed, he may set himself up as a staunch defender of orthodoxy. But the way which he commends is not narrow or disturbing, and therefore he can gain quite a hearing. These people remind me of certain religio-political prophets in the time of Jeremiah, concerning whom God says, "For from the least of them even to the greatest of them, every one is covetous, and from the prophet even to the priest, every one deals falsely. And they have healed the wound of my people slightly, saying 'Peace, peace,' but there is no peace. Were they ashamed because of the abomination they have done? They were not even ashamed at all; they did not even know how to blush" (Jer. 6:13–15; cf. Jer. 8:8–12). There is nothing in their preaching which fosters poverty of spirit, nothing which searches the conscience and makes men cry to God for mercy, nothing which excoriates all forms of religious hypocrisy, nothing which prompts such righteousness of conduct and attitude that some persecution is inevitable. It is even possible in some instances that everything these false prophets say is true; but because they leave out the difficult bits, they do not tell the whole truth, and their total message is false.

The second test is not based on contextual observations, but on the explicit argument of the text. Jesus says, "By their fruit you will recognize them. Do people pick grapes from thornbushes, or figs from thistles? Likewise every good tree bears good fruit, but a bad tree bears bad fruit. A good tree cannot bear bad fruit, and a bad tree cannot bear good fruit. Every tree that does not bear good fruit is cut down and thrown into the fire. Thus, by their fruit you will recognize them" (7:16–20).

This semitic way of putting things (that is, both positively and negatively: every good tree bears good fruit, no good tree bears bad fruit, and so forth) makes the test very sure. In Jesus' day, everyone knew that the buckthorn had little black berries which could be mistaken for grapes, and that there was a thistle whose flower, from a distance, might be mistaken for a fig. But no one would confuse the buckthorn and the grape once he started to use the fruit to make some wine. No one would be taken in by thistle flowers when it came to eating figs for supper.

In other words, from a certain perspective, false prophets can look like real prophets, and even their fruit may appear to be genuine. But the nature of the false prophet cannot be hidden forever: sooner or later he will be seen for what he is. Just as he does not advocate Jesus' narrow way, so also does he fail to live it; this fact must one day be exposed to all who cherish the narrow way. In this manner, Matthew 7:15–20 serves as a bridge between 7:13f. and 7:21–23. Matthew 7:13f. deals with the two ways; 7:21–23 (as we shall see) pictures a man who has all the trappings of discipleship to Jesus but is not characterized by obedience to Jesus. The bridge (7:15–20) presents false prophets who do not teach the narrow way, nor practice it. The falseness of their teaching erupts in the disobedience of their lives.

I must emphasize that Jesus is not encouraging a heresy-hunting mentality here. After all, the same Jesus has only recently condemned judgmental attitudes. Yet false teachers must be identified. If they are not recognized immediately by their doctrine, then sooner or later they may be recognized by their lives; for what a man believes must sooner or later manifest itself in what he does. Jesus affirms an indissoluble link between belief and conduct. Moreover, these verses are not as much given to threaten the false prophets themselves (even though the bad trees are cast into the fire), as to encourage ordinary disciples to spot them: "By their fruit you will recognize them."

This test must not be superficially applied. It will not do to use only this text, find some socially useful pagan, and regard him as a true prophet. Still less will it suffice to adopt secular criteria by which to assess a man's fruit: success, style, aplomb, popularity. Nor will patterns of speech and conduct acceptable to contemporary evangelicalism suffice. The fruit the Lord Jesus looks for is a life in growing conformity to the norms of the kingdom: righteousness, transparent humility, purity, trusting and persistent prayerfulness, obedience to Jesus' words, truthfulness, love, generosity, rejection of all that is hypocritical. It may take time for the test to prove very helpful; but where doctrinal aberration cannot be detected immediately and unequivocally, the "fruit test" is eventually a safe guide.

This is a day when pluralism is popular. However, although everyone may have the right to his own opinion, it does not follow that every opinion is right. To some it will appear terribly intolerant even to speak of "false" prophets; yet that is Jesus' designation of would-be spokesmen for God who do not teach what Jesus himself teaches. "Watch out for false prophets," he says; "by their fruit you will recognize them." The kingdom of God is the issue. Failure to heed Jesus' warning means that the threat of judgment looming over the heads of the false teachers becomes a threat to others as well. Not only their destiny, but ours, yours and mine, are at risk, if we fail to identify and avoid the false prophets.

TWO CLAIMS
Matthew 7:21–23

"Not everyone who says to me, 'Lord, Lord,' will enter the kingdom of heaven, but only the one who does the will of my Father who is in heaven. Many will say to me on that day, 'Lord, Lord, did we not prophesy in your name, and in your name drive out demons and perform many miracles?' Then I will tell them plainly, 'I never knew you. Away from me, you evildoers!'" (7:21–23).

Two claims are made, and two kinds of claimants are portrayed. The first group approaches Jesus reverently on that day, the day of judgment; and they address him as "Lord." Probably their belief is perfectly orthodox. Moreover, they have an impressive record of spiritual experience. They have prophesied in Jesus' name, they have exorcised demons in Jesus' name, and in Jesus' name performed many miracles. The Lord does not deny any of their claims, and neither should we. We may therefore expect that even in our own day there are *many* (7:22) people who use the right language and who have performed spiritual wonders in Jesus' name, but who are not genuine disciples. One of the most tragic ingredients to this scenario is the way these people take themselves to be genuine believers. They clearly expect admission to the consummated kingdom.

Sometimes, of course, people who attempt using Jesus' name to do various things get caught long before the last judgment. In Acts 19, for example, the seven silly sons of Sceva are exposed for the charlatans they are. For their pains they get beaten up and chased down the street by one particularly aggressive demon. Whether now or on the day of judgment, the false claimants will be exposed. Eventually Jesus will disown them: "I never knew you." He will banish them from his presence: "Away from me." And he will dismiss them as "evildoers," literally as those who practice lawlessness.

What, then, is the *essential* characteristic of the true believer, the genuine disciple of Jesus Christ? It is not loud profession, nor spectacular spiritual triumphs, nor protestations of great spiritual experience. Rather, his chief characteristic is obedience. True believers perform the will of their Father, consistent with their prayer, "Your will be done on earth as in heaven." They cannot forget that at the beginning of the Sermon on the Mount, Jesus said, "Anyone who breaks one of the least of these commandments and teaches others to do the same will be called least in the kingdom of heaven, but whoever practices and teaches these commands will be called great in the kingdom of heaven. For I tell you that unless your righteousness surpasses that of the Pharisees and the teachers of the law, you will certainly not enter the kingdom of heaven" (5:19f.). And so they practice obedience. The Father's will is not simply admired, discussed, praised, debated; it is done. It is not theologically analyzed, nor congratulated for its high ethical tones; it is done. The test is rephrased by a famous second-century document, the *Didache*, which says, "But not everyone who speaks in the Spirit is a prophet, except he have the behavior of the Lord."

There are several different ways to become self-deluded about spiritual things. For example, it is possible to enjoy some sort of unique spiritual experience and live in its glow at the expense of *ongoing* spiritual experience and sustained practical obedience. I heard of a man who enjoyed what he took to be a special outpouring of God's blessing upon him. He felt himself transported with Paul to the third heaven. So momentous was the event that he wrote it all up in a paper to which he gave the title, "My Experience." The months slipped past, and he became indifferent to spiritual things. At first he preserved the form, and hauled out his manuscript to show various visitors. But as months turned into years, even the form of godliness was abandoned, and his experience lay forgotten in a dusty drawer. Many years later a minister came calling. The man, thinking to impress his visitor, called upstairs to his wife, asking her to bring down "My Experience." She rummaged around until she found the tattered document, and replied, "I'm sorry, dear, but your experience is rather moth-eaten." Just so: the man had lulled himself into irresponsible spiritual apathy by coasting along on the memory of some past experience.

Another form of self-delusion, however, is evident in Matthew 7:21–23. It is not so much that the false claimant lulls himself into spiritual apathy, as that he mistakes loud profession and supernatural, almost magical formulations and experiences, for true spirituality and genuine godliness. Obedience is neglected. The pressure of the spectacular has excluded the stability of growing conformity to the Father's will. Because he seems to be getting results, immediate results, spectacular results, he feels he is close to the center of true religion. His success indices are soaring: God must be blessing him. Surely God will understand and sympathize if there is not always enough time for prayer, self-examination, or conscious repentance. The results are the important thing. If the truth gets a trifle bent, it's only because the supporters need to hear certain things. And is it wise to run the risk of driving off such supporters by talking about the narrow way? Just as Nixon's closest aides could talk themselves into believing that their cause was more important than their ethics, so these religious extroverts convince themselves that their success-oriented spectacular victories are more important than the nitty-gritty of consistent discipleship.

It is true, of course, that no man enters the kingdom because of his obedience; but it is equally true that no man enters the kingdom who is not obedient. It is true that men are saved by God's grace through faith in Christ; but it is equally true that God's grace in a man's life inevitably results in obedience. Any other view of grace cheapens grace, and turns it into something unrecognizable. Cheap grace preaches forgiveness without repentance, church membership without rigorous church discipline, discipleship without obedience, blessing without persecution, joy without righteousness, results without obedience. In the entire history of the church, has there ever been another generation with so many nominal Christians and so few real (i.e., obedient) ones? And where nominal Christianity is compounded by spectacular profession, it is especially likely to manufacture its own false assurance.

TWO HOUSES
Matthew 7:24–27

Entrance into the kingdom, then, does turn on obedience after all—not the obedience which earns merit points, but which bows to Jesus' lordship in everything and without reservation. Such obedience necessarily blends with genuine repentance, making the two almost one. Within this framework, the issue of obedience is everything. The previous verses have just shown this to be so; and now Jesus draws the Sermon on the Mount to a close with a paragraph introduced by a telling "Therefore." Because only the one who *does* the will of his Father will enter the kingdom, Jesus says—

> [24] *"Therefore*, everyone who hears these words of mine and puts them into practice is like a wise man who built his house on the rock. [25]The rain came down, the streams rose, and the winds blew and beat against that house; yet it did not fall, because it had its foundation on the rock. [26]But everyone who hears these words of mine and does not put them into practice is like a foolish man who built his house on sand. [27]The rain came down, the streams rose, and the winds blew and beat against that house, and it fell with a great crash" (Matt. 7:24–27).

Picture these two houses. There may not be much in their external appearance to enable the casual observer to distinguish between them. Both seem attractive and clean, freshly painted perhaps. One, however, has its foundation resting securely on bedrock; the other has as its foundation nothing more substantial than sand. Only the most severe storm will betray the difference; but granted the storm, the betrayal is inevitable.

The image of the "foundation" is variously used in Scripture. For example, God's personal knowledge of his own people is said to be a divine foundation, providing his people with confidence (2 Tim. 2:19). Good works are a foundation for the coming age, not so much in the sense that they earn life as in the sense that without them there is no life (1 Tim. 6:17–19). But most commonly, Jesus himself is the foundation, a sure foundation. Prophesied in the Old Testament (Isa. 28:16), he comes in the New to be the certain basis of assurance for his people. In this sense, as Peter wisely discerns, there is salvation in none other (Acts 4:12): Jesus Christ himself, in his person and his mission, is the sole foundation.

Nevertheless, Jesus is not the foundation referred to in Matthew 7:24–27. In fact, the focus is not quite centered on the foundations adopted, rock and sand, but upon the two builders and their entire projects. The man who builds his house upon a shifting foundation is likened to the person who hears Jesus' words but who does not put them into practice. The man who builds his house upon a rock is likened to the person who not only hears Jesus' words but also puts them into practice. The difference between the two houses is therefore to be likened to the difference between obedience and disobedience.

The rock in this extended metaphor may well represent Jesus' words: "These words of mine," Jesus twice says, the "of mine" quite emphatic. The expression harks back to the repeated and authoritative refrain, "You have heard . . . but I tell you." Perhaps there is a further nuance. These words are especially Jesus' words in the sense that his own life is perfectly congruent with his words. I who pen these lines may repeat Jesus' words, but I remain a sinner like you who read them. In that sense, Jesus' words are not my words; they are only his. Putting those words into practice, then, is like building a house on a sure foundation. The other man builds a superstructure, and no more.

The violent storm differentiates between the two buildings. In the Old Testament, and also elsewhere in Jewish writings, the storm sometimes serves as a symbol for God's judgment (see Ezek. 13:10ff.), especially God's eschatological judgment, his final judgment. No power was more certain to evoke fear in pre-nuclear man than the unleashed fury of nature's violence—the symbol was therefore apt.

This is the place to pause and reflect on the threats Jesus has been issuing. In 7:13f. he promises destruction for those who travel the broad way. This is followed first by a picture of a fire burning up unproductive branches (7:15–20), and then by a categorical rejection of the disobedient (7:21–23). These are now capped by likening a man who hears Jesus' words and who does not practice them, to a house shattered, pulverized and swept away by a vicious storm. The question will not be restrained: Is Jesus trying to frighten people into the kingdom?

In one sense, of course, the answer must be yes. Some people may well be drawn to Christ because of the attraction of forgiveness; others may feel the first stirrings of desire to follow him when they first glimpse the immensity of his love or the integrity of his life, or when they experience the shame engendered by his scrutiny. But not a few will come only because they see that the issues with which Jesus is concerned are eternal issues—ultimately, nothing less than heaven and hell. Indeed, Jesus' teaching has important things to say about race relations, social justice, and personal integrity; but it cannot be fairly reduced to the temporal concerns of my lifetime here. There is a heaven to be gained and a hell to be shunned.

If you are sleeping soundly in a house desperately threatened by rising flood waters, you may thank me for pounding at your door to rouse you. At the very least, you are not likely to accuse me of frightening you into safety. Frighten you I shall, effect your removal to a safe place I may attempt: but you would not *accuse* me of "frightening you into safety." If you were so attached to your home you could not bear to leave it, you might conceivably choose to stay with it and run the risk of perishing; or if you remained honestly oblivious to the danger you might dismiss me as a fool. But while I tried to frighten you to safety, you would not *accuse* me of doing so.

Similarly, Jesus concludes the Sermon on the Mount by honestly attempting to frighten men and women into the kingdom, into salvation. You may not believe that a hell exists. In that case, you may dismiss Jesus as a liar or a fool. Alternatively, you may be so attached to your sin that even the threat of final and catastrophic judgment may not induce you to leave it. But you will be foolish indeed if you simply accuse Jesus of frightening you into the kingdom.

The real issue is the truth behind Jesus' words, the truth which prompts Jesus' warning. Either there is a hell to be shunned, or there is not. If there is not, then Jesus' entire credibility is shattered, for he himself speaks twice as often of hell as of heaven. The pages of the Bible strain metaphor and exhaust the resources of language in describing the holy delights of the new heaven and the new earth, still to come; but they scarcely do less in outlining the horrors and terrors of hell. It is variously described as the place of outer darkness, the place where the worm will not die, the place of exclusion and rejection, the place of burning and torment, the place where there will be weeping and grinding of teeth. I am not trying to give you hell's coordinates, nor place it on a map. Just as I find myself unable to describe the new heaven and earth except in the metaphors of Scripture, so I cannot describe hell except in the metaphors of Scripture. But those metaphors are staggering.

Whether you accept the existence of hell will depend in large part upon your total estimate of the person and ministry of Jesus. If you can dismiss him, you will have little difficulty dismissing hell. If you claim to follow him, then you cannot with integrity do so in a subjective way which avoids the inconvenient and unpleasant.[1]

My chief concern, however, is not to wax polemical on the subject of judgment and hell, but to assist others in coming to a straightforward understanding of the Sermon on the Mount. The Sermon ends with the threat of judgment. The four sections which make up the conclusion of these three chapters concur in this theme. In fact, these four paragraphs, despite the diversity of their metaphors, each stresses two unyielding themes. The first is that there are only two ways, one which ends in the kingdom of God and the other in destruction. The second theme is that the former way is characterized by obedience to Jesus and practical conformity to *all* his teaching.

These pronouncements ought to instill in us a holy fear. Which one of us stands unashamed beside the precepts of the Sermon on the Mount? Do not these threats of judgment prompt poverty of spirit, which is the first of the kingdom's norms?

We do well to remember that Paul is writing truth when he insists that men are saved only because Christ acted as their substitute and died in their behalf. Christianity is not simply a moralistic religion of high ideals. High ideals—indeed, the highest—it has; but it also presents a crucified yet risen Savior who forgives repentant men and then gives them life to grow to meet those ideals.

We ought not forget that Matthew's record of the Sermon on the Mount must be taken in the context of his entire Gospel. It is not for nothing that his Gospel begins with a prophecy concerning Jesus which stresses his function *as a Savior*: "She [Mary] will give birth to a son, and you [Joseph] are to give him the name Jesus, because he will save his people from their sins" (Matt. 1:21). Within this context, the Sermon on the Mount does not press men and women to despair, still less to self-salvation. Rather, it presses men and women to Jesus. The Sermon on the Mount reflects no malicious glee at the prospect of perdition, no cheer at consigning so many to destruction. The warning is, in fact, entreaty.

May God grant his people a spirit of contrition which petitions him for grace and forgiveness by Jesus Christ, and a growing conformity to the norms and perspectives of the kingdom.

The Sermon ends. "When Jesus had finished saying these things, the crowds were amazed at his teaching, because he taught as one who had authority, and not as their teachers of the law" (Matt. 7:28f.).

The teachers of the law taught derivatively, that is, by referring to the authorities. But Jesus taught with his own authority. All of us are impressed by the man whose skill and knowledge of a subject are so outstanding that he clears away the rubble of misconception and outlines the truth of the matter with sharp, incisive strokes. This was the effect Jesus had on his first hearers.

Those hearers were amazed at Jesus. Perhaps that is part of coming to him, part of the necessary recognition of his authority. May God in his mercy grant that we will not stop at mere amazement, but press on to that deeply rooted commitment which sings:

> Be Thou my Vision, O Lord of my heart;
> Naught be all else to me, save that Thou art—
> Thou my best thought, by day or by night,
> Waking or sleeping, Thy presence my light.
>
> By Thou my Wisdom, Thou my true Word;
> I ever with Thee, Thou with me, Lord;
> Thou my great Father, I thy true son;
> Thou in me dwelling, and I with Thee one.
>
> Be Thou my battleshield, sword for the fight;
> Be Thou my dignity, Thou my delight,
> Thou my soul's shelter, Thou my high tower:
> Raise Thou me heavenward, O Power of my power.
>
> Riches I heed not, nor man's empty praise;
> Thou mine inheritance, now and always:
> Thou and Thou only, first in my heart,
> High King of heaven, my treasure Thou art.

High King of heaven, after victory won,
May I reach heav'n's joys, O bright heaven's Sun!
Heart of my own heart, whatever befall,
Still be my Vision, O Ruler of all.

Ancient Irish hymn
tr. E. H. Hull (1860–1935)
versified by M. E. Byrne (1880–1931)

---

[1]If you need more information about Jesus Christ, or about the New Testament documents which constitute our primary sources concerning him, I recommend two books in particular: *Basic Christianity,* by John R. W. Scott; and *The New Testament Documents: Are They Reliable?,* by F. F. Bruce.

PART TWO

Jesus' Confrontation with the World

Preface

MY PARENTS WERE both born in the United Kingdom: my mother was born a Cockney, my father entered this world just outside Belfast. In the providence of God, I spent several years in doctoral research in England, and at the end of that time, I married an Englishwoman. Owing to the generous sabbatical and study leave system at Trinity Evangelical Divinity School, I have kept returning to Cambridge every so often, drawn not least by the excellent facilities of Tyndale House and the University Library.

One of the strongest attractions to Cambridge for our family, however, is the tie with Eden Baptist Church. In some ways that is our church home. Our family owes our brothers and sisters in that church a debt of gratitude that extends back over a decade and a half. So when we knew we were returning to Cambridge for the 1986–87 academic year, and the invitation came to use the first six weeks of my sabbatical filling the Eden pulpit while its pastor, Dr. Roy Clements, was finishing up his own sabbatical, I was in no position to decline, and was delighted to fill in.

In any case, I was a pastor long before I started pursuing more academic forms of service; and I am deeply persuaded that those of us whose privilege and responsibility it is to study the Scriptures owe the church whatever help we can give at the popular level, quite apart from the responsibility of producing work that attempts to influence teachers and scholars. If the purpose of my sabbatical was to complete a syntactical concordance to the Greek New Testament, there needed to be space as well for something that served the church more immediately.

I first expounded the New Testament chapters treated in this little book, Matthew 8–10, fifteen years ago in the course of pastoral ministry on the west coast of Canada. In the intervening years I have written a full-length commentary on Matthew (in *The Expositor's Bible Commentary*, vol. 8); I hope my grasp of the text is a little firmer now than when I first preached on these chapters. Because I have discussed critical and interpretative questions at some length in that commentary, I have avoided raising such issues here, and for the same reason have not included bibliography and notes. The sermon is not the place for unloading that sort of information in any case. But by comparing the commentary with this exposition, seminary students may obtain some impression of how at least one person tries to move from detailed exegesis to the exposition of the Word of God.

The chapters in this book, then, are sermons that have been reworked for the printed page. Not all traces of the sermon have been removed. In particular, the application of Scripture that characterizes all useful preaching has been retained; but a number of forms suitable to the pulpit have undergone a metamorphosis to become suitable to the written essay. Occasionally I have added a trifle more explanation or other detail than the constraints of the sermons allowed.

I would like to thank Baker Book House for adding this book to the series of expositions they have already published. Not every publisher is willing to print sermons, reworked or otherwise. That they have done so testifies to their awareness of one of the great needs of the church: the need to read the Bible in a way that simultaneously understands what the text is actually saying, and applies it fairly and closely to our own lives and to the world around us. If we lose the first of these two poles, we never hear the Word of God; if we lose the second, the Word never sings or stings.

If this book contributes in a small way to meeting this need, I shall be grateful to God.

Soli Deo gloria.

D. A. Carson
Trinity Evangelical Divinity School

7

The Authority of Jesus

(8:1–17)

[1]When he came down from the mountainside, large crowds followed him.

[2]A man with leprosy came and knelt before him and said, "Lord, if you are willing, you can make me clean."

[3]Jesus reached out his hand and touched the man. "I am willing," he said. "Be clean!" Immediately he was cured of his leprosy.

[4]Then Jesus said to him, "See that you don't tell anyone. But go, show yourself to the priest and offer the gift Moses commanded, as a testimony to them."

[5]When Jesus had entered Capernaum, a centurion came to him, asking for help. [6]"Lord," he said, "my servant lies at home paralyzed and in terrible suffering."

[7]Jesus said to him, "I will go and heal him."

[8]The centurion replied, "Lord, I do not deserve to have you come under my roof. But just say the word, and my servant will be healed. [9]For I myself am a man under authority, with soldiers under me. I tell this one, 'Go,' and he goes; and that one, 'Come,' and he comes. I say to my servant, 'Do this,' and he does it."

[10]When Jesus heard this, he was astonished and said to those following him, "I tell you the truth, I have not found anyone in Israel with such great faith.

¹¹I say to you that many will come from the east and the west, and will take their places at the feast with Abraham, Isaac and Jacob in the kingdom of heaven.

¹²But the subjects of the kingdom will be thrown outside, into the darkness, where there will be weeping and gnashing of teeth."

¹³Then Jesus said to the centurion, "Go! It will be done just as you believed it would." And his servant was healed at that very hour.

¹⁴When Jesus came into Peter's house, he saw Peter's mother-in-law lying in bed with a fever.

¹⁵He touched her hand and the fever left her, and she got up and began to wait on him.

¹⁶When evening came, many who were demon-possessed were brought to him, and he drove out the spirits with a word and healed all the sick. ¹⁷This was to fulfill what was spoken through the prophet Isaiah:

> "He took up our infirmities
> and carried our diseases."

Introduction

I

Certain confrontations inevitably arouse the expectation that there will be an explosion. The media know this best, of course; and that is why whenever they interview a representative of some position or other, they almost invariably try to find a foil, a representative of another position, one that is diametrically opposed to the first. Their aim, of course, is to bring the two positions into confrontation, knowing that the resulting explosion makes good press.

The principle can be grasped intuitively. Take a deeply committed Marxist and an avowed capitalist and ask each to explain to an audience the reasons for the high levels of British unemployment—and what is the result? It is not simply that one side will blame the history of social welfarism and the lack of incentive while the other will point to the economic and social stratification of British society, but that the exchange may generate emotional and colorful charges and countercharges. Maroon a militant atheist and a zealous fundamentalist on a desert island for a few weeks, or put a television camera before an ardent feminist and a reactionary male chauvinist, and you achieve the same result. The confrontation arouses expectations of an explosion, or at least of an extremely revealing encounter.

Something similar can be expected when Jesus confronts the world. I use the word *world* in its larger, theological sense—the created, moral order in rebellion against God its Maker. In the Bible, this sense of "world" is much favored by John. For instance, he warns us, "Do not love the world or anything in the world. If anyone loves the world, the love of the Father is not in him. For everything in the world—the cravings of sinful man, the lust of his eyes and the boasting of what he has and does—comes not from the Father but from the world. The world and its desires pass away, but the man who does the will of God lives forever" (1 John 2:15–17). When Jesus confronts the world in this sense of "world," some kind of explosion can be expected; for Jesus and the world are very different, frankly opposite in their purpose, character, values, and aims. The world is essentially self-centered; Jesus did not come to be served, but to serve, and to give his life a ransom for many (Matt. 20:28). The world is in active rebellion against God; Jesus always pleases his Father (John 8:29). The world (as we have just seen in the quotation from John) is time-bound and temporary; not so Jesus or his kingdom or the person who does his will. The world needs saving, and Jesus comes to save his people from their sins (Matt. 1:21); the world needs judging, and Jesus is the Son of man who comes when least expected and passes the entire world under review (Matt. 24:36–25:46). Jesus and the world are bound to clash with each other.

That is one reason why even those closest to Jesus in the days of his flesh took a long time to understand him: they were much more in league with the world than they understood, so much participants in the world that they did not grasp the nature of the confrontation taking place. Thus when Peter in Matthew 16 confesses Jesus to be the Messiah, he does so only because the Father has revealed the point to him: the implication seems to be that apart from such revelation Peter would have been unable to come to this conclusion. And immediately after his great confession, Peter, confusing Jesus' explanation of this fact with a compliment, thinks he is in a position to correct Jesus as to the nature of his mission, and earns the rebuke, "Get behind me, Satan! You are a stumbling block to me; you do not have in mind the things of God, but the things of men" (Matt. 16:23). Peter was far more attached to the world than he knew.

In the same way, men and women today do not always recognize the nature of the confrontation between Jesus and the world, precisely because they are more deeply bound up in allegiance to the world than they think. Many people, of course, openly admit they have nothing to do with Jesus; but others believe they deserve a very high place in the moral scheme of things and that they are therefore principally in league with Jesus, "Christians," even if they are not, say, churchgoers. These people have not begun to comprehend the gulf that separates them from Jesus; when the claims and demands of the biblical Jesus are pressed on them, they take offense and go away in a huff. Still others are active followers of Jesus, as was Peter, but their allegiance is still warped by exaggerated estimates of their own spiritual insight and wisdom. They are more deeply impregnated by the wisdom of the world than they think. When they find out more about the real Jesus, painful confrontation is part of the price as they examine the foundations once more.

In the three chapters before us, Matthew 8–10, we are presented with a number of things that transpire when Jesus confronts the world. Some of these are quite wonderful: the healings and exorcisms (8:16–17; 9:32–33), and the assurance that Jesus has come to call sinners (9:13). Others are frankly frightening: Jesus' teaching that some who expect to inherit the kingdom are "thrown outside, into the darkness, where there will be weeping and gnashing of teeth" (8:12); his insistence that his mission entails the active disruption of family units as people are forced to choose between family and him (10:34–36). Still others are simply startling: Jesus' rather shocking response to the disciple who wants to suspend following Jesus until he has buried his father ("Follow me, and let the dead bury their own dead" [8:22]). And some are alarming to sincere followers of Jesus, especially the assurance of opposition and persecution (10:16, 22, 37–39). But always there is confrontation, explicit or implicit.

Yet if we think our way carefully through these chapters, they will serve to focus a number of characteristics of Jesus, the way a lens gathers light and focuses it into a beam. The confrontation between Jesus and the world helps to clarify the nature of both Jesus and the world. As a result, we gain understanding of who Jesus is and who we are; we are forced to choose, forced to assess whether our allegiance is to Jesus or to the world, and driven to understand the nature of the confrontation between Jesus and the world two thousand years ago. And in that understanding we find the structures that enable us to comprehend the nature of the confrontation between Jesus and the world today.

II

I have grouped some of the things we learn about Jesus from his confrontation with the world into themes that will be treated chapter by chapter in this book. The first of these concerns the authority of Jesus.

What comes to mind when we use the word *authority?* The answer depends entirely on the context. Consider these six statements:

1. Professor Smith is the world's leading *authority* on the duck-billed platypus.

This does not necessarily mean that Professor Smith is a good man, or that everything he says about the duck-billed platypus is true, or that there is no one who knows more about certain restricted aspects of the platypus than Professor Smith. Rather, it means that no one knows more about the duck-billed platypus than does Professor Smith. Perhaps he has written the major textbook on the subject; all other learning on the topic will be measured by his.

2. The president of the United States has the *authority* to dismiss the secretary of state.

This means that the president, by virtue of the office he holds, can take a certain action (firing the secretary of state). No one can prevent the president from taking this action if he is determined upon it. This authority cannot be contested. Unlike the use of "authority" in the first sentence, this use does not depend on superior knowledge but on rank, a particular office.

3. The prime minister has delegated to her press secretary the *authority* to speak to the media on her behalf.

Here authority is delegated (unlike the first two uses). The person to whom this authority is delegated must use that authority responsibly, or face disciplinary action.

4. All of us love to tweak the nose of the *authorities.*

Here the word *authority* has as its referent not a concept but people—people who exercise certain authority. In this context we conjure up officials who are not as grand or as important as they think they are, and whose pretensions are amusingly burst by some mild fun.

5. His problem is that he likes to stand on his *authority*.

This use is much like the previous one, except that the humor has evaporated to leave the smell of pompous hypocrisy. Here the bureaucrat is confusing personal importance with the rights of office. Such authority depends not on knowledge (use 1) but on an abuse of raw power. It cannot be delegated: indeed, a person who loves to stand on his own authority would not want to delegate it.

6. In the midst of Watergate, President Nixon lost much of his *authority*.

Of course in one sense as long as Nixon remained president he did not lose any of this authority: he enjoyed the full panoply of presidential powers. But in fact he lost a certain *moral* authority. Congress fought him on everything; every statement he made was viewed with grave suspicion and quoted as evidence of his moral delinquency. The kind of authority he lost was not bound up with his office but with his person, with the public perception of his integrity and credibility. A person may enjoy such authority without holding any office; and the authority of office cannot ever replace or be confused with this moral authority.

The reason this discussion is important to the passage before us is that Matthew 8–10 are linked with the Sermon on the Mount (Matt. 5–7) through the crucial verses at the end of chapter 7: "When Jesus had finished saying these things [i.e., the utterances of chaps. 5–7], the crowds were amazed at his teaching, because he taught as one who had *authority*, and not as their teachers of the law" (7:28–29; emphasis added). We must ask what kind of authority Jesus was exercising. The crowds were amazed in part at the *center* of his authority. Many of the teachers of the law proceeded by citing other authorities (not unlike the modern thesis that is no more than a learned recitation of current opinion, complete with endless footnotes); but Jesus said again and again, "You have heard that it was said . . . but *I* tell you . . ." (5:21ff.; emphasis added). In this regard he is not even like an Old Testament prophet who cries, "Thus says the Lord!" He dares to speak with an authoritative "I."

But there is more to Jesus' authority in the Sermon on the Mount than the forms of his speech. He claims to determine who does and who does not enter the kingdom: "Not everyone who says *to me*, 'Lord,

Lord,' will enter the kingdom of heaven, but only he who does the will of my Father who is in heaven. Many will say *to me* on that day 'Lord, Lord, did we not prophesy *in your name*, and *in your name* drive out demons and perform many miracles?' Then *I* will tell them plainly, '*I* never knew you. Away from *me*, you evildoers!'" (7:21–23; emphases added). The true heirs of the kingdom, he insisted, would be persecuted because of their allegiance *to him* (5:11); and indeed *he himself* has come to fulfill the Old Testament law and prophets (5:17–20). They point to *him*, they anticipate *him;* but that means *he* is *in his own perception* greater in significance than they are.

Small wonder that the crowds are impressed with Jesus' self-conscious authority, even if they do not rightly assess it or understand it. But then Matthew, having drawn our attention to Jesus' authority in his teaching ministry, goes on in chapters 8–10 to display Jesus' authority as it is demonstrated in powerful deeds as well as in powerful words. Matthew groups together a series of healings, miracles of nature, the driving out of unclean spirits, and finally even the delegation of some of this authority to his disciples (chap. 10). In this light, then, these three chapters are suffused with Jesus' authority.

And what is the nature of this authority? Here is authority that has a moral center and is always effective. Power is bound up with this authority: there is no mere semblance of vigor, but such awesome capability that even Jesus' words are effective. Like the Sermon on the Mount, those parts of these chapters reflecting Jesus' teaching display the authority of the expert—but unlike Professor Smith of duck-billed platypus fame, Jesus' expertise in the matters he discusses cannot be gainsaid or set aside, for among mortals there is no one qualified to challenge his teaching. At least some of his authority can be delegated to his disciples (10:1); yet he remains qualitatively above them, in his integrity unimpeachable, in his authority peerless. Never is this authority stuffy or arrogant, for its locus is a Savior whose mission is to serve, to die, to help, to heal, to transform. If (ghastly thought) someone should for a dark moment entertain the desire to tweak the nose of this authority, the temptation would quickly be displaced by shame.

The Authority of Jesus

From the first seventeen verses of Matthew 8, we learn five things about the authority of Jesus.

1. The authority of Jesus to heal and transform is implicit in his person and mission (8:1–3). In a general way, this point is best drawn from the array of Jesus' miracles scattered throughout the Gospels. The prophet Isaiah had foreseen a time when the wolf would live with the lamb, when the leopard would lie down with the goat, when the calf and the lion and the yearling would live happily together, and a little child would lead them; when an infant could play safely near a cobra's hole or put his hand into a viper's nest; when no one would harm or destroy others, and when the earth would be full of the knowledge of the Lord as the waters cover the sea (Isa. 11). The Messiah would be sent to preach good news to the poor, to bind up the brokenhearted, to proclaim freedom for the captives and release for the prisoners, to proclaim the year of the Lord's favor, to comfort those who mourn, to bestow on those who grieve a crown of beauty instead of ashes, the oil of gladness instead of mourning, and a garment of praise instead of a spirit of despair—as well as to declare the day of vengeance of our God (Isa. 61). The Old Testament Scriptures preserve many such prophecies, and the miracles of Jesus bring at least some of these prophecies to fulfillment.

When John the Baptist entertains doubts about who Jesus is, Jesus himself replies in words deeply reminiscent of Isaiah 61: "Go back and report to John what you hear and see: The blind receive sight, the lame walk, those who have leprosy are cured, the deaf hear, the dead are raised, and the good news is preached to the poor. Blessed is the man who does not fall away on account of me" (Matt. 11:4–6). In other words, Jesus' ministry of power, displayed in his miracles, constituted evidence of his identity as the promised Messiah. Perhaps the Baptist entertained doubts because while he lay languishing in prison he longed to see a little more of "the day of vengeance of our God"; but whether or not that was the factor that drove him to doubt, the focus of Jesus' response to him is plain enough: the miracles that Jesus performs attest who he is and the mission he was sent to accomplish.

But this general point, which can be deduced from the record of Jesus' miracles as a whole, is greatly stressed in the miracle of healing the leper (8:1–3). The point is made three ways.

First, the disease itself (whether it was what modern medicine calls leprosy [Hansen's disease] or some other skin ailment) was greatly abhorred and feared by the Jews; and its cure was considered a singular mark of God's intervention. Those who contracted the disease were forced to live apart, isolated from human touch and the joys of intimate human contact. To be a leper often meant you were under God's curse (see Num. 12:10, 12; Job 18:13). Healings were rare (see Num. 12:10–15; 2 Kings 5:9–14) and were sometimes thought to be as difficult as raising the dead (2 Kings 5:7, 14). Jesus himself understood the healing of leprosy to be a mark of the dawning of the messianic age (Matt. 11:5). Probably that is why Matthew places this account at the head of his list of healings: it provides a startlingly powerful instance of Jesus' authority at work.

Second, Jesus' act of touching the leper (8:3) is more than a raw historical reminiscence. A leper would not have dared to touch someone who was not a leper; the person who touched a leper was judged ceremonially unclean, quite apart from the danger of contracting the disease. How this leper worked his way through the "large crowds" (8:1), which at this stage dogged every step of Jesus' ministry, is not clear: perhaps he gave warning cries or rang a bell, and the crowd split around him until he could kneel before Jesus. But Jesus "reached out his hand and touched the man." It may have been the first human touch the leper had known for a long time.

Mark explains that Jesus was moved by compassion. He could have healed with a word, avoiding touch; but Jesus touched what others would have found repulsive. Yet the important thing to note is that Jesus does not thereby become unclean, but the leper becomes clean! When Jesus comes in contact with defilement, he is never defiled. Far from it: his touch has the power to cleanse defilement.

Third, the words by which the leper addresses Jesus are immensely significant: "Lord, if you are willing, you can make me clean" (v. 2). Jesus replies, "I am willing. . . . Be clean!" (v. 3). This exchange does not call in question Jesus' general willingness to do good, as if he has to be coerced into kindness. Rather, both the leper's statement and Jesus' response to it frankly recognize that Jesus already has the authority and the power to perform the healing; all that is needed is his decision to act, and the healing takes place. Jesus' authority is here stressed by presupposing it.

This is one of the ways in which Jesus' healing ministry is rather different from that of the Old Testament prophets Elijah and Elisha. They too act and speak with authority; but the total impression deflects attention away from themselves and toward God. Although Jesus is concerned to glorify the Father, nevertheless there is a self-conscious awareness of the center of authority in his own teaching and healings absent from any other person in Scripture. In this passage, the healing of the leper turns on Jesus' will, nothing else: "I am willing"—and the matter is settled. "Go!" he says to the demons (8:32), and they are thereby released to invade the swine. "Your sins are forgiven" (9:2)—and they are remembered no more. "Get up, take your mat and go home" (9:6)—and the paralytic walks.

The authority of Jesus to heal and transform is implicit in his person and mission. The authority is *already* his. He needs only to will the deed, and it is done. Few lessons are more urgently needed in the modern church. Hope for reformation and revival lies not in campaigns and strategy (as important as such things may be), but in the authority of Jesus. His followers must come to him with the attitude of the leper in this account: they must recognize the sweep of his authority and petition him for grace, for a decision to display his authority in their favor.

We can best understand what this involves when we contrast the leper's request for a miracle with requests that Jesus spurns. In Matthew 12:38 and 16:1 certain religious leaders approach Jesus and ask him to perform a miraculous sign; but they earn only rebuke from the Master. They had not asked from the perspective of personal need, nor even from the vantage point of the supplicant. Rather, they ask Jesus for a sign in order that they might come to believe him. They thus set themselves up as judges, not needy folk hungry for grace. There was ample opportunity to witness Jesus' miracles; but they wanted a miracle on demand. If Jesus had complied, he would have been compromised, a trained stuntman programmed to perform tricks on command. The religious leaders would have domesticated him. That is why he rejects their challenge so decisively. The invading power of the kingdom is at *Jesus'* disposal, not theirs. It is *his* will that is decisive, not theirs. To avail oneself of Jesus' transforming power, one must come as a humble petitioner in need—or not at all.

Our generation is in danger of forgetting this. Even with regard to healing, opinion is polarized. One faction is persuaded there can be no miraculous healings today, as if the dawning of the kingdom ceased when Jesus returned to glory, not to be manifest again until he returns. Another faction treats healing as a sovereign right, to be gained by the appropriate manipulation of formulas. Both sides are in danger of trying to domesticate Jesus. I shall return to this subject in the last point of this chapter.

More broadly, the church is closest to heaven-sent revival when it comes to an end of its gimmicks, and petitions the great Lord of the church, who alone has the authority to pour out blessing beyond what can be imagined, who alone opens doors such that none can shut them and shuts them so that none can open them, to use the full authority that is his (Matt. 28:18) to bless his people with repentance and vitality and thereby bring glory to himself. Only his authority will suffice.

2. The authority of Jesus, formally submissive to the law of Moses, in fact transcends it and fulfills it (8:4). Why Jesus forbids the healed leper from telling anyone, Matthew does not make immediately clear. But if we may judge from parallel situations, one of the prime purposes Jesus has in this and similar prohibitions is to discourage the notion that he is primarily a wonder-worker who can be pressed into messiahship by enthusiastic crowds more interested in healings, bread, and trouncing the Romans than in righteousness, repentance, and revelation from the Father. Jesus' authority derives from God alone; it is not dependent on the will of the people. Jesus can never be a democratically elected Messiah. The will of the people is often fickle; and in any case it is usually controlled by what the people think they can get, not by how eagerly they will submit. The parallels (Mark 1:45; Luke 5:15) tell us that the healed leper disobeyed Jesus, and spread the news of his cure far and wide, ultimately hampering Jesus' ministry and forcing him to retire to wilderness areas away from the major centers of population. Those details are not related by Matthew; but he records enough of Jesus' injunctions to be silent that we may be sure he is not unaware of the danger.

But if Jesus will not be submissive to the will of the crowds, it appears at first glance that he is submissive to the Scripture, and to the law of Moses in particular. Leviticus 14 provides detailed information on what the person is to do who believes himself healed of leprosy. The final decision as to whether or not healing has taken place is in the hand of the priest; a lengthy ritual is prescribed involving delay, careful inspection, and finally a sin offering to "make atonement for the one to be cleansed from his uncleanness" (Lev. 14:19). That is the passage Jesus is thinking of when he tells the leper, now cured, "But go, show yourself to the priest and offer the gift Moses commanded" (Matt. 8:4). Indeed, in every particular Jesus was quick to show himself submissive to the written law of God. To use Paul's words, he was "born under law"; and throughout his earthly pilgrimage he remained faithful to that calling.

Nevertheless, the closing words of the verse show there is more to this prescription from the law of Moses than first meets the eye.

"But go," Jesus tells the cured leper, "show yourself to the priest and offer the gift Moses commanded, *as a testimony to them.*" The expression used in the original could be taken to mean "as a testimony *for* them," that is, to help them to come to faith; or "as a testimony *against* them," that is, as a kind of denunciation of their unbelief. Of the places where the expression is used in the synoptic Gospels, however, in only two instances is it clearly negative; usually it is neutral.[1] In other words, Jesus wants the cured leper's obedience to the law to serve as a witness; whether it will prove a positive witness and an incentive to faith, or a negative witness that exposes the depth of unbelief, is not specified in the expression and will be revealed only in the response to the witness.

In fact, debate over whether this witness is meant to be positive or negative has sometimes distracted us from its truly startling feature. *Of what* would this "gift," this sacrifice that the cured leper would offer, serve as a witness? In the context, clearly it would serve as a witness to the fact that the man was healed—and healed by the transforming power of Jesus, who is relating his power to his messianic calling and mission. Thus the law of Moses itself is being used to testify to who Jesus is. In other words, in this context the supreme function of the gift Moses commanded (Lev. 14:10–18) is not as a guilt offering but as a witness to Jesus. In his very act of submission to the law, Jesus makes the law point to himself. If the cured leper pursues the various steps laid out by Moses to attest his purification, then the priest must pronounce him clean; and the pronouncement attests that Jesus performed the miracle that brought about the cleanness. And whereas that does not *prove* Jesus is the Messiah, it does provide attestation that must be taken seriously.

This is a minor but still important example of the way the New Testament writers rather consistently spell out the relationship between Jesus and the old covenant. Already in the Sermon on the Mount Jesus has insisted that he did not come to abolish the law *but to fulfill it*— which does not mean to intensify it, or to show its deeper legal and moral significance, or the like, but quite literally to fulfill it. The presupposition is that the law can be viewed as prophetic; and that to which it points is Jesus and his gospel. The law points to Jesus, prepares the way for him, provides models of sacrifice that find their antitype in him, prescribes morality that finds its apex and best exemplar in him, demands holiness that only he can provide, and generally anticipates him. As Jesus later insists, both the law and the prophets prophesied (Matt. 11:13)—sometimes in propositional forms, sometimes in types, sometimes as part of a matrix that pointed ahead (as Paul in Galations 3, and the writer to the Hebrews throughout his book, insist).

This theme is so pervasive in the New Testament that it would take a very large book even to begin to expound it adequately. But the crucial conclusion from our point of view is that Jesus is presented in the Bible not as an auxiliary figure who complements other notables such as Moses and David and Jeremiah, but as the focal point of God's revelation. As the Epistle to the Hebrews puts it, God had spoken to the fathers by the prophets; but in these last days he has spoken to us in his Son (Heb. 1:1–3). The "word of God" did indeed come to the prophets; but at a deeper level the Son himself is the Word *par excellence,* God's Self-Expression. To use the language of the apostle John, this Word, this Self-Expression of God, has always been with God and is in fact God (John 1:1); but this Self-Expression of God became flesh (John 1:14), enabling us to see his glory. The apex of God's gracious self-disclosure is in Jesus.

As much as it is true that Jesus obeyed the law of Moses, his claims insisted that he stood over it—as its fulfillment (Matt. 5:17), as the Lord of the Sabbath (12:8), as the one to whom the law witnesses (8:4). His authority is astounding, and calls from his followers the reverence of worship and obedience.

3. The authority of Jesus is so sweeping that when Jesus speaks, God speaks (8:5–9). Centurions constituted the military backbone of the Roman Empire. Unlike the senior officers, they went over the wall with their troops. They exercised discipline, trained the recruits, carried out orders from higher up. At this point there were probably no Roman centurions in Palestine. Most likely this one was recruited from a neighboring territory such as Lebanon or Syria. Elsewhere we learn of his Jewish sympathies and friends; in Matthew's brief account, the emphasis is on his race and his faith (8:10–11).

This centurion's approach to Jesus is astonishing in its humility and its display of faith. At the risk of casting slurs, one must admit that centurions do not normally treat representatives of conquered peoples with utmost respect. Yet here is a Roman centurion treating Jesus, one of the conquered Jews, as if he were of a rank so exalted that the humble home of the soldier was not suitable for him. There is no suggestion in the text that the centurion was simply providing a way for Jesus to escape ceremonial defilement. Rather, he felt his unworthiness before Jesus and with becoming humility approached the Master on behalf of his suffering servant. In this attitude he joins with the leper in a stance described by the first beatitude: "Blessed are the poor in spirit, for theirs is the kingdom of heaven" (5:3). Grace answers to unpretentious need, but to neither smug self-confidence nor pretentious and bombastic breast-beating.

But more surprising is the telling power of the illustration the centurion uses when he asks Jesus simply to perform the healing miracle with a word, instead of coming to pray over the servant and perhaps lay hands on him. Just "say the word, and my servant will be healed," the centurion petitions. "For I myself am a man under authority, with soldiers under me. I tell this one, 'Go,' and he goes; and that one, 'Come,' and he comes. I say to my servant, 'Do this,' and he does it" (8:8–11).

The centurion sees himself as simultaneously *under* authority and as one *exercising* authority: "I myself," he says, "am a man under authority, with soldiers under me." In the Roman military system, all ultimate authority was vested in the emperor and was delegated down the military hierarchy. Therefore, because he was a part of this structure, when the centurion commanded a foot soldier to come or go or do something, he was not speaking as one man to another but as a representative of Rome. The centurion was under the authority of his commanding tribune, and so on all the way back to the emperor; but the foot soldier was under him. Therefore when the centurion spoke, so far as those under him were concerned it was Rome that was speaking. Disobedience to the centurion was not mere defiance of a fellow human being, but rebellion against Rome, treason before the emperor, an insult to the empire.

The centurion applies to Jesus this grasp of his own position and authority. Because Jesus is under God's authority, always perfectly conforming to the authority that is exercised over him, the centurion is certain that when Jesus exercises authority it is none less than God's authority. When the centurion speaks, Rome speaks; when Jesus speaks, God speaks. To defy Jesus is to defy God. Jesus' word is invested with God's authority; so he is well able to heal sickness with a word. When the centurion gives commands to those under him, things happen: he does not have to be there to oversee every step of the operation, because he is conscious of the authority vested in him, and his word is sufficient to guarantee that the operation is carried out. He expects no less from Jesus: if when Jesus speaks he exercises the authority of God himself, there is no real need for Jesus to be present or to check up on the result. The word itself is authoritative and cannot be ineffective. If Jesus but commands the sickness to cease, it will cease.

Like all analogies, this one is not perfect; nonetheless, the centurion's argument reveals an astonishing level of faith that recognizes that the powerful deeds Jesus was performing did not turn on magic, ritual, or subterfuge, but on his *authority*, which was nothing other than the authority of God himself. His word would be effective because it was God's word.

4. The authority of Jesus is a great comfort to the eyes of faith, and a great terror to the merely religious (8:10–13). When Jesus heard the centurion's analogy, "he was astonished" (8:10). (Far better to astonish Jesus with our faith, as here, than with our unbelief, as in Mark 6:6.) What astonishes Jesus is the man's faith: "I tell you the truth, I have not found anyone in Israel with such great faith" (8:10). Jesus' fellow Jews were steeped in the Scriptures, and their race had enjoyed centuries of covenantal relationship with God. Jesus seems to imply that if anyone should identify him rightly and approach him with submissive faith it should be the Jew; but here is this Gentile, a centurion from the ranks of the Roman overlord, displaying faith of astonishing vigor and perception. It is possible, of course, that the man had read something of what we today call the Old Testament. But there is no record of Jesus having performed a miracle by word only and from a distance prior to this event (unless John 4:46ff. be judged a separate and earlier healing). Nevertheless the centurion by commenting on Jesus' authority has shown he has penetrated very near the heart of Jesus' identity; and so his faith is both a reflection of an attitude of heart that is right, and a christological confession of some depth. His faith is not only great, it is perceptive; or perhaps it is great because it is perceptive.

The centurion's remarkable faith won the healing of his servant. When Jesus says, "Go! It will be done *just as* you believed it would" (8:13; emphasis added), he does not mean that the miracle performed was *in proportion* to the man's faith, nor even that the miracle was accomplished *because* of the man's faith (i.e., in a strong causal sense that would make faith not only the occasion but also the effective cause of the healing), but rather that the content of the miracle would be *what was expected by* the centurion's faith (similarly 15:28).

But there is more in store for the centurion and for others like him. Jesus insists that many will come from the east and the west (a way of referring to Gentile peoples), "and will take their places at the feast with Abraham, Isaac and Jacob in the kingdom of heaven" (8:11). The picture is that of the messianic banquet, drawn from such Old Testament passages as Isaiah 25:6–9 (cf. 65:13–14) and considerably embellished in later Judaism. The banquet suggests a time of joy and celebration, the consummation of the kingdom; and Jesus here insists that many Gentiles will join in with the Jewish patriarchs on that great occasion. In the context, this can only be because they have responded with the centurion's faith to Jesus. The centurion saw in Jesus' authority the solution to his anguish, and approached him with the eyes of faith. In microcosm that is what men and women have been doing through the centuries: they perceive their need and recognize in Jesus the sole voice of authority that can meet their need, and they come to him in faith.

Not everyone recognizes Jesus' authority; others sense the power but do not respond with faith. Even some who naturally belong to the kingdom, that is, the Jews who had lived under the old covenant and had been the heirs of the promises, turn out to be rejected. They too approach the great hall of the messianic banquet, lit up with a thousand lamps in joyous festivity; but they are refused admission, they are thrown outside into the blackness of night, "where there will be weeping and gnashing of teeth" (8:12). The idea is not that there will be no Jews at the messianic banquet. After all, the patriarchs themselves are Jews, and all of Jesus' earliest followers were Jews. But Jesus insists that there is no automatic advantage to being a Jew. As he later says to those of his own race, "Therefore I tell you that the kingdom of God will be taken away from you and given to a people who will produce its fruit" (21:43). An individual's faith, his or her response to the authority claims of Jesus, will prove decisive. The alternative to entrance into the kingdom is painted in horrible colors: literally *the* weeping and *the* gnashing of teeth, to emphasize the horror of the scene, the former suggesting suffering and the latter despair. The same authority of Jesus that proves such a great comfort to the eyes of faith now engenders terror in the merely religious.

This is not a teaching that is very acceptable to vast numbers in western Christendom today. It flies in the face of the great god Pluralism who holds much more of our allegiance than we are prone to admit. The test for religious validity in this environment is no longer truth but sincerity—as if sincerity were a virtue even when the beliefs underlying it are entirely mistaken. Teaching about hell is unpopular for another reason: it seems cruel to the modern mind, in which, unlike Scripture, it is popular and easy to believe in the love of God and difficult to make much sense of his holiness and wrath.

I must not stop and give this difficult subject the treatment it deserves; I hope to do so shortly in another publication. Nevertheless a few lines many not be out of place. Perhaps the most startling thing to observe is that Jesus says far more about hell than anyone else in the Scripture. If he speaks as the meek and humble teacher (Matt. 11:28–30), he also appears as the final judge (7:21–23) who sends some to eternal punishment and other to eternal life (25:31–46). It is impossible to accept a partial Jesus; for one would be buying into a domesticated Jesus, one shaped by our predilections, not one who can command us or demand anything of us we are unprepared to give. Second, from the few images of hell presented in the Scripture, there is nothing to suggest that its residents ever repent. Just as a great sinner who dies a lingering and painful death may be consumed not by remorse but by bitterness, so it is quite possible that hell continues on and on because the rebellion of its citizens continues on and on. Hell becomes a continuation of a life orientation on this side: "Let him who does wrong continue to do wrong; let him who is vile continue to be vile" (Rev. 22:11). And third, probably most of us entertain a thoroughly inadequate understanding of sin. The heart of sin is not so much discrete acts of moral degradation, concrete steps of hardened rebellion, as an attitude of life that is foundationally self-centered. That is the nature and measure of our sin. Endemic to this horrible situation is our utter inability to assess the matter rightly: how can self-centeredness assess self-centeredness, except by criteria already utterly compromised? The only hope is for God to speak to us from outside our selfishness. Once grant that he has done so in Scripture and supremely in Christ, and even our slowness to accept God's assessment of our need and of our destiny apart from him becomes a numbing judgment on our sinfulness.

In the immediate context, the alternatives—the messianic banquet or the darkness characterized by weeping and gnashing of teeth—become starker precisely because those assigned to each destiny are not drawn from the polarities of what the world would judge to be moral behavior. Jesus does not set up a contrast between the ancient world's equivalent of Hitler and Francis of Assisi, or Idi Amin and Augustine, or Stalin and Mother Theresa. Those thrown outside are religious people, "good" people, religiously privileged people. The only difference between them and those like the centurion who come from the east and the west to sit with the patriarchs at the messianic banquet is *faith*—the kind of faith displayed by the centurion, the faith that approaches Jesus in the posture of a supplicant and sees in him the sufficient answer to our need. Such revelation recognizes the unique authority of Jesus, and hungers above all that Jesus might use such authority to help us in ways we cannot help ourselves. Satisfied self-centeredness, even of a religious sort, is inimical to transforming faith. And that is why on the long haul the authority of Jesus will prove a great comfort to the eyes of faith, and a great terror to the merely religious.

This is the *kind* of faith we must exercise by God's help, when, on this side of the cross, we understand, even better than the centurion, the purpose of Jesus' coming, and sing:

> *Not the labour of my hands*
> *Can fulfill thy law's demands;*
> *Could my zeal no respite know,*
> *Could my tears for ever flow,*
> *All for sin could not atone,*
> *Thou must save, and thou alone.*
>
> *Nothing in my hand I bring,*
> *Simply to thy cross I cling;*
> *Naked, come to thee for dress;*
> *Helpless, look to thee for grace;*
> *Foul, I to the fountain fly;*
> *Wash me, Saviour, or I die!*

Augustus M. Toplady
(1740–1778)

And that brings us to the final lesson to be learned about the nature of Jesus' authority as it is displayed in this passage.

5. The authority of Jesus is a function of his work on the cross (8:14–17). These first two healings (8:1–13) are capped by a brief account of the healing of Peter's mother-in-law (8:14–15), and a generalizing statement that lays to rest any suspicion that these were only occasional displays of power (8:16–17). Peter, of course, was married (cf. 1 Cor. 9:5); apparently his mother-in-law was living with Peter and his wife in Capernaum, the town which Jesus had also made his headquarters at this point (Matt. 4:13). The nature of the woman's illness is unclear: in those days the fever itself was viewed as a malady, not just a symptom. But Jesus healed her with a touch, even though Jewish tradition forbade touching persons with many kinds of fever. As in verse 3, Jesus' touch does not defile the healer but heals the defiled. The mother-in-law immediately got up and began to wait on Jesus: the point is made to attest the effectiveness and instantaneity of Jesus' healing power. He needs only to exercise his authority, and the deed is done.

But these healings are merely examples of a great host of healings and exorcisms he performed. On into the evening the needy came—a point that attests the pace of Jesus' ministry (although the parallels, Mark 1:32–34 and Luke 4:40–41, point out that the day was a Sabbath, and some may have wished to wait until sundown and the end of the Sabbath before venturing to carry their sick to Jesus, since carrying a burden was considered a forbidden act of work). He "drove out the spirits with a word and healed all the sick" (Matt. 8:16). All this took place, we are told, to fulfill what was spoken through the prophet Isaiah: "he took up our infirmities and carried our sorrows" (53:4).

This quotation is from the well-known passage of Scripture sometimes called the fourth Servant Song (Isa. 52:13–53:12). On the face of it, that passage seems to present the Servant as a sacrifice substituted that others might be spared: for example, "But he was pierced for our transgressions, he was crushed for our iniquities; the punishment that brought us peace was upon him, and by his wounds we are healed" (53:5). In the New Testament this Servant Song is constantly linked to Jesus' death on the cross—not least by Matthew himself (20:28 [Isa. 53:10–12]; 27:12 [Isa. 53:7]; 27:57 [Isa. 53:9]; and elsewhere, e.g., Acts 8:32–33; 1 Peter 2:24). But here, apparently, Matthew is saying that Jesus' healing ministry, not his atoning death, is the way he "took up our infirmities and carried our diseases." This has prompted not a few scholars to suggest that Matthew here quotes Isaiah rather out of context.

In fact, the point of connection is profound. Both Scripture and Jewish tradition understood that all sickness is caused, directly or indirectly, by sin. When the direct connection is operative, a particular sin issues in a particular illness; and in that case healing of the illness cannot occur unless the sin is dealt with. But not every illness is the direct result of a specific sin. Sickness may reflect the fact that all of us live this side of the fall, under the curse, limited by mortality. Such sickness will plague us until the consummation of the kingdom, when there will be "no more death or mourning or crying or pain" (Rev. 21:4), when the curse itself will have been overthrown (Rev. 22:3). In this larger sense, sickness is still connected with sin; but the connection is indirect, and finally remedied only by the return of Christ at the end of the age.

The New Testament recognizes both the direct and the indirect connections. In John 5, the man who had been paralyzed for thirty-eight years is told not to sin lest a worse thing befall him—which presupposes that the paralysis was the direct result of a specific sin. By contrast, in John 9, when the disciples ask Jesus whether the man born blind or his parents had sinned that he should be so afflicted, Jesus says neither option is correct: this situation came about for the glory of God. Outside the Gospels, some Christians in Corinth had fallen ill, and others had actually died, because of their improper approach to the Lord's Supper (1 Cor. 11:17–30). But in Galatians 4, Paul testifies that the reason he brought the gospel to his readers in the first instance was because of an illness: apparently when he arrived at the southern coast of what is now Turkey he contracted a fever, possibly malarial, and so headed north into the hills to escape the fetid atmosphere and to regain his health. There is no suggestion whatsoever that Paul was suffering on account of some specific sin in his life, still less that he was miraculously healed. Far from it: the illness was the Lord's providential means of bringing the gospel to the Galatians. The same Paul who on occasion performs healing miracles can on other occasions mention that he has had to leave Trophimus behind, ill; or that Timothy should take a little wine for his frequent infirmities.

Much more evidence could be gathered, but the heart of the matter can be summarized this way. First, all sickness is the result of the condition of sinfulness in which we find ourselves, but only some sickness is the direct result of immediate and specific sin. That perhaps suggests that illness ought to serve as an occasion for the thoughtful person to engage in a little quiet self-examination. Second, whatever the immediate cause, some sickness is healed in the Scripture, and some is not. Modern voices that suggest God cannot or does not heal miraculously today have little exegetical warrant to support their stance; but equally, those modern voices that insist God inevitably grants healing provided only that there is adequate faith have forfeited the balance of Scripture and pursued a reductionism that once again tries to domesticate God. The God who allows James to be killed by Herod while providing escape for Peter is the God who arranges for Paul to be ill while granting Dorcas life.

Now we are in a better position to understand why Matthew cites these lines from Isaiah. Matthew, after all, understands that Jesus came to save his people from their sin: he emphasizes that point in his first chapter (1:21). The same authority that heals also forgives sin, as Matthew emphasizes (9:1–8). And it is Jesus' death that inaugurates the new covenant, which deals so effectively with sin (26:27–29). The ultimate undoing of sin will result in the abolition of illness; in the consummated kingdom, as we have seen, there will be no more suffering of any sort, but a bliss of righteousness and an end to all suffering, savagery, and tears—as the prophets themselves anticipated. When Isaiah 53 tells us that the Servant bears our infirmities and carries our sicknesses, it is the context of the Servant Song, as well as the understood connection between sin and suffering, that show us that the *way* the Servant bears the sicknesses of others is through his suffering and death, by which he deals principally with both sin and suffering.

Granted, then, that the New Testament writers, including Matthew, understand Isaiah 53 in this way, why does Matthew 8 draw the connection between Isaiah 53 and Jesus' healing ministry? There can be only one reason. Matthew understands that Jesus' healing miracles were not simply acts of power, but were performed as a function of Jesus' atoning death still to take place. Because even within Jesus' ministry, before the cross, the kingdom was being inaugurated and demonstrated, it was appropriate that healings and exorcisms should be performed in anticipation of the great day when sickness and demonic power would be forever removed from God's people; but because all such benefits stem from Jesus' atoning death, those same healings can be understood to point beyond the authority of Jesus to the cross of Jesus. They are signs not only of Jesus' authority but also of his servanthood. As they are the anticipation of the consummated kingdom still awaited, so also are they the fruit of the cross-work of Jesus not yet performed. Matthew, writing *after* the death and resurrection of Jesus and therefore easily perceiving the connection, draws attention to it by citing Isaiah 53 in connection with Jesus' healing ministry. When Jesus healed Peter's mother-in-law, the centurion's servant, the leper, and all the others, he did so not merely out of the abundance of power rightly his, but because he was to absorb in his own person, in his own act as a willing, atoning sacrifice, the sin bound up with suffering. Precisely because the healings were done in anticipation of Calvary, they fulfilled what was spoken through the prophet Isaiah: "He took up our infirmities and carried our diseases."

Two general conclusions must be drawn. First, it is important that Christians should not think of the benefits they have in Christ Jesus *apart from thinking about his atoning death*. When the structures of New Testament thought are put together, the death and resurrection of Jesus stand at the heart of everything else. The canonical Gospels move toward Jesus' death and resurrection; the apostles and others in Acts preach in Jesus' death and resurrection the remission of sins; the Epistles presuppose the atonement and build upon it. Even the blessed Holy Spirit, given to us as the downpayment of the promised inheritance, has been bequeathed to us in the wake of Jesus' triumph on the cross and subsequent return to his Father. *Jesus' powerful, transforming acts, whether in the days of his flesh or today, must never be abstracted from his work on the cross.* Nowhere, perhaps, is this truth more clearly enunciated than in Colossians 1:15–20; but already it receives subtle support in Matthew's Gospel.

Second, we must inevitably conclude (to use the modern jargon) that "there is healing in the atonement." But this clause has been much abused. One party insists that, because there is healing in the atonement, therefore Christians must expect to be healed today. The atonement has already provided this benefit, as it were; so if Christians are not healed, it cannot be the fault of Jesus or of his atonement, but of our unbelief. The opposing party, struggling to avoid this unsettling conclusion, argues therefore that there is no healing in the atonement: that is something that is provided for only at the consummation. But in fact, both sides have set the categories wrongly. The truth of the matter is that there *is* healing in the atonement; but the atonement provides God's people with *all* benefits that ultimately come to them. In that sense, there is also a resurrection body in the atonement; but no one uses that point to argue that all believers should today be sporting resurrection bodies, and failure to do so betrays a formidable lack of faith. The question is *not* whether or not the atonement stands as the basis for all blessings that come to God's children, but which of those benefits are applied *now*, and which of them can be counted on *only later*. Healing, judging by some of the passages already briefly adduced, is one of those benefits that has been secured by the cross, occasionally applied now, and promised for the new heaven and the new earth. If in God's mercy he grants healing now, whether by "normal" or "miraculous" means, we must be grateful; but we have no right to *claim* the benefit *now* simply because it has been secured by the work of Jesus on the cross.

In short, the authority of Jesus must never be seen in independence of his atoning sacrifice; it is always a function of his work on the cross. That simple truth ought to drive us back to basics again and again.

Conclusion

When Jesus confronts the world, his *authority* soon emerges as one of the crucial and most disputed storm centers. This is not an accidental result: if our sin is at root a defiance of God's authority, a deeply rooted self-centeredness at enmity with God and his claims, and in love with ephemeral dreams of autonomy, it cannot be surprising that when Jesus confronts the world his authority, the authority of God himself, soon erupts as one of the focal points of debate.

May all of us who read these pages pledge ourselves anew to submit joyfully to Jesus' authority, to come to him in full recognition that only he can meet our needs and sustain us both in this life and in the life to come, and give him thanks that all of his transforming power, whether exercised now or hereafter, stems from the immeasurably great sacrifice he underwent on our behalf.

> *Thine arm, O Lord, in days of old,*
> *Was strong to heal and save;*
> *It triumphed o'er disease and death,*
> *O'er darkness and the grave.*
> *To thee they went—the blind, the dumb,*
> *The palsied, and the lame,*
> *The leper with his tainted life,*
> *The sick with fevered frame.*
>
> *And, lo, thy touch brought life and health,*
> *Gave speech, and strength, and sight;*
> *And youth renewed and frenzy calmed*
> *Owned thee, the Lord of light.*
> *And now, O Lord, be near to bless,*
> *As mighty as before,*
> *In crowded street, by restless couch,*
> *As by Gennesaret's shore.*
>
> *Be thou our great Deliverer still,*
> *Thou Lord of life and death;*
> *Restore and quicken, soothe and bless,*
> *With thine almighty breath;*
> *To hands that work and eyes that see*
> *Give wisdom's heavenly lore,*
> *That whole and sick, and weak and strong,*
> *May praise thee evermore.*
>
> Edward H. Plumptre (1821–1891)

---

1 The expression εἰςμαρτύριον αὐτοῖς occurs in the Synoptics only here and at 10:18; 24:14, Mark 1:44; 6:11; 13:9; Luke 4:14; 9:5; 21:13.

8

The Authentic Jesus

(8:18–34)

[18]When Jesus saw the crowd around him, he gave orders to cross to the other side of the lake.

[19]Then a teacher of the law came to him and said, "Teacher, I will follow you wherever you go."

[20]Jesus replied, "Foxes have holes and birds of the air have nests, but the Son of Man has no place to lay his head."

[21]Another disciple said to him, "Lord, first let me go and bury my father."

[22]But Jesus told him, "Follow me, and let the dead bury their own dead."

[23]Then he got into the boat and his disciples followed him.

[24]Without warning, a furious storm came up on the lake, so that the waves swept over the boat. But Jesus was sleeping.

[25]The disciples went and woke him, saying, "Lord, save us! We're going to drown!"

[26]He replied, "You of little faith, why are you so afraid?" Then he got up and rebuked the winds and the waves, and it was completely calm.

[27]The men were amazed and asked, "What kind of man is this? Even the winds and the waves obey him!"

[28]When he arrived at the other side in the region of the Gadarenes, two demon-possessed men coming from the tombs met him. They were so violent that no one could pass that way.

²⁹"What do you want with us, Son of God?" they shouted. "Have you come here to torture us before the appointed time?"

³⁰Some distance from them a large herd of pigs was feeding. ³¹The demons begged Jesus, "If you drive us out, send us into the herd of pigs."

³²He said to them, "Go!" So they came out and went into the pigs, and the whole herd rushed down the steep bank into the lake and died in the water. ³³Those tending the pigs ran off, went into the town and reported all this, including what had happened to the demon-possessed men.

³⁴Then the whole town went out to meet Jesus. And when they saw him, they pleaded with him to leave their region.

Introduction

Very frequently our experience of something is different from our expectations. The experience itself may be far happier or far sadder than what we anticipated; but the difference between the two is marked.

For instance, we plan a family holiday with a detailed itinerary, and look forward to the two weeks with visceral enthusiasm. But if many of the planned excursions depend on fine weather, and if we endure two solid weeks of drizzle, our experience during those holidays will be radically different from our expectations. Someone may look forward to marriage with a dreamy-eyed, romantic perspective that believes marriage to be a universal panacea, the fulfillment of life's purposes and the ultimate solution to certain temptations. Marriage itself may then prove something of a disappointment: monumental quarrels can develop over the decision to squeeze or to roll the tube of toothpaste. Painful clashes recur until differing values and perspectives are resolved. Living at close quarters with another human being inevitably demands adjustments, give and take, forbearance, and a lot of hard work. Temptations do not seem much alleviated, merely refocused. On the other hand, it is also possible for someone to view marriage with a certain dread, based perhaps on painful memories of a shattered home, of a drunken and abusive father, or a crabby and selfish mother; and then as the years roll by, one is suddenly struck by how peaceful this marriage has been, how rewarding, how fulfilling, how beneficial to both parties.

Christian work can also generate false expectations. A prospective missionary may anticipate the mission field with a romantic, even sentimental notion of service: standing under the shade of a palm tree, preaching powerfully to vast throngs of men and women who hang on your every word, counseling with profound biblical wisdom many national leaders who are overwhelmingly grateful for your leadership, building churches that are evangelistic and spiritually mature. Reality may prove disappointingly different. The missionary arrives in the designated country, and may find the food unpalatable and the flies prolific. The ordinary administrative details of life—shopping, going to the bank, securing a driver's license, repairing a puncture—take three or four times as much energy and time as at home. A year or two is devoted to gaining a still rudimentary knowledge of the new language. Nationals may have very mixed feelings about your presence; and the personality conflicts you faced at home are magnified under the stresses of an alien culture. You may be assigned for lengthy periods of time, not to preaching to great crowds, but to bookkeeping or running a school for missionary children. Alternatively, you may serve the Lord for years in a part of the world where there is very little fruit, and then suddenly and unpredictably enter a period of immense fruitfulness, tremendous joy, and almost breathless growth. Either way, expectations are shattered by reality.

When Jesus confronts the world, many of the world's expectations are destroyed. This was true during Jesus' earthly ministry. Many of his contemporaries were looking forward to a messiah who would turf out the Romans, raise the nation of Israel to supreme prominence in the international community, and introduce not only prosperity but a global centrality to Jerusalem such that foreigners would flock to her, bring tribute, and acknowledge that the God of the Jews was the true God. But not many focused much attention on the need for repentance, on the many promises of Scripture that anticipated thoroughgoing righteousness. And no one, so far as we know, clearly connected the promised messianic king with the promised suffering servant, and understood that one person would take up both strands in himself. Even Jesus' closest disciples failed to make these connections until after the resurrection. The world's expectations turned out to be too narrow, too partisan, too limited, and sometimes just plain wrong. The authentic Jesus outstripped the expectations.

When Jesus confronts the world today, similar misconceptions must often be cleared away. When an individual first begins to draw near to Jesus, he or she often carries along an assortment of expectations urgently in need of modification. Perhaps the would-be convert thinks that Jesus is a spiritual "fix" worth trying, a fine source of spiritual fulfillment—without raising questions about sin, truth, obedience, or the like. In some communities, family or cultural pressures teach that profession of faith in Jesus is a step to local acceptability, always provided, of course, that religion is not taken too seriously. When someone from that sort of background first reads the Bible with real understanding, and finds out what the authentic Jesus is like, it can produce something of a jolt.

One of the points of friction that develops when Jesus confronts the world is the sheer authority of Jesus. That theme of Jesus' authority continues in the verses now before us. Whoever dares make allegiance to family secondary to allegiance to him (8:22) is either a lunatic or someone with authority nothing less than divine; for only to God could such supreme loyalty be rightly due. In the next paragraph, Jesus demonstrates his authority over the forces of nature (8:23–27); and in the final section of Matthew 8, not only does he display his power over the world of demons, but also the demons recognize both his right and his power to do so, especially "at the appointed time" (8:29—presumably the end of the age).

But I shall not pursue the theme of authority in this chapter. Instead, I shall cast the confrontation between Jesus and the world in wider terms, to show that the authentic Jesus, the real Jesus, regularly turns out to be unforeseen, unpredictable, unnegotiable, and (in any real encounter with him) unavoidable. I do not mean to suggest that everyone finds him unavoidable: in this life, that is demonstrably untrue, for many do not even hear of him. But where there is a genuine encounter between Jesus and an individual or a group of people, when Jesus does in fact confront the world, then who and what the authentic Jesus really is becomes unavoidable.

What, then, are some of the characteristics of the real Jesus that are often overlooked? From these verses we may observe four of them.

Some Characteristics of the Authentic Jesus

1. The authentic Jesus makes demands that are personal and costly (8:18–22). Two people are introduced in this pair of vignettes—a teacher of the law (8:18–20), traditionally called a scribe, and another man, simply designated a disciple (8:21–22). Some see a contrast between the two: scribes are always opponents of Jesus, and so this one is simply put off, whereas the disciple is told to follow Jesus.

In fact, this interpretation is artificial. Jesus does not have *categories* of opponents (e.g., "All scribes are enemies of Jesus"); rather, he assesses men and women as they divide around him. The "teacher of the law" category can be applied to *Christian* teachers (13:52; 23:34; the same word in Greek). This one in 8:19 approaches Jesus respectfully: even though scribes were first and foremost teachers themselves, he addresses Jesus as "teacher," and there is nothing in the context to suggest his approach is anything but sincere. The opening words of verse 21, "another of his disciples," mean that Matthew viewed the teacher of the law as a disciple and the second man who is mentioned as "another of his disciples." After all, the term *disciple* does not mean, despite arguments to the contrary, that a firmly committed "Christian" is in view. Applied to the ministry of Jesus, it customarily refers to a broad spectrum of people who are at that point following Jesus. That following can be quite physical: after all Jesus was an itinerant preacher, and some folk *followed* him from place to place in order to glean more from his teaching and become one of his intimates. Similarly John the Baptist had "disciples" (Matt. 11:2) who followed him. Such followers, such disciples, were more likely to be sincerely pursuing Jesus' teaching than at least some others who would not or could not find the time to do so; but their number also included Judas Iscariot. Thus both the men in Matthew 8:18–22 are disciples of some sort. If Jesus uses the words *follow me* only to the second, it is not because only he is a true disciple, but because only he is planning *not* to follow Jesus at that point, and needs to be told to reverse his commitments.

The basic point of these verses is simple enough. Two disciples (in the sense I have just explained) promise some kind of allegiance to Jesus, and in some measure Jesus rebuffs them both. But there is a difference between the two. The first is too quick in promising; the second is too slow in performing.

At first glance the words of the first seem promising: "Teacher, I will follow you wherever you go." We might be reminded of the unconditional promise of Ittai to David when the king, facing a revolt, counseled him to change his allegiance. Ittai responds, "As surely as the LORD lives, and as my lord the king lives, wherever my lord the king may be, whether it means life or death, there will your servant be" (2 Sam. 15:21). We might also think of the peerless determination of Ruth when Naomi tries to dissuade Ruth from following her: "Don't urge me to leave you or to turn back from you. Where you go I will go, and where you stay I will stay. Your people will be my people and your God my God. Where you die I will die, and there I will be buried. May the LORD deal with me, be it ever so severely, if anything but death separates you and me" (Ruth 1:16–17). But Jesus detects in this man less the commitment of an Ittai and a Ruth than the overconfidence of a Peter, who would later boldly promise, "Even if all fall away on account of you, I never will. . . . Even if I have to die with you, I will never disown you" (Matt. 26:33, 35)—only to disown his master shamefully, even with oaths.

Jesus' reply tests the scribe's commitment, but probably reveals what Jesus diagnosed his problem to be. "Foxes have holes and birds of the air have nests," Jesus responds, "but the Son of Man has no place to lay his head" (8:20). This response stresses not so much Jesus' poverty as his homelessness. Apparently he detected that the teacher of the law envisaged a connection with Jesus that would secure stability, perhaps even privilege. After all, if Jesus is the Messiah (he may well have thought), and if the Messiah is to rule in a powerful and wealthy kingdom supremely blessed by God, then it would be wise to become a close follower of Jesus now, in order to get on the inside track when the day of glory dawns. Alternatively, his motives may not have been so crass. Perhaps he liked much of what he saw and heard in Jesus, and decided to follow him more closely, but without giving much thought to the kind of itinerant ministry Jesus was actually exercising, and to the difficulties and privations such work entailed.

Whatever the case, the hurdle Jesus erects for the man establishes an important point. As one commentator puts it, "Nothing was less aimed at by our Lord than to have *followers*, unless they were genuine and sound; he is as far from desiring this as it would have been easy to obtain it." Little has done more to harm the witness of the Christian church than the practice of filling its ranks with every volunteer who is willing to make a little profession, talk fluently of experience, but display little of perseverance. Too often the old maxim proves true: Soon ripe, soon rotten. This is not to deny that conversion may take place quickly, nor is it to suggest that early profession of allegiance to Christ is invariably spurious. Rather, it is to insist that part of a genuine closing with Christ at some point entails counting the cost, and coming to grips with the fact that loyalty to Jesus brings with it demands that may be costly.

The second man, another of Jesus' disciples, utters a request which, on the surface of things, seems reasonable: "Lord, first let me go and bury my father" (8:21). Commentators have wavered between two opinions: either the man was asking for the time needed to bury and mourn for his father, recently deceased; or else his father was aged, and the man was waiting for him to die and be buried before he would consider following Jesus more closely. Either way, this man was reflecting Jewish Palestinian piety: sons were expected to look after their parents, and to bury them when the time came.

Jesus' answer is stunning: "Follow me, and let the dead bury their own dead" (8:22). The utterance is, of course, paradoxical: "Let the (spiritually) dead bury the (physically) dead"; but it is no less biting for that. It cannot mean that Jesus is encouraging chronic disrespect for parents, when elsewhere he can berate those who used the temple contribution system to withhold from their parents the support that was their due. Nowhere does the New Testament set aside the emphasis of Deuteronomy 27:14, 16: "The Levites shall recite to all the people of Israel in a loud voice: . . .'Cursed is the man who dishonors his father or his mother.' Then all the people shall say, 'Amen!'"

In fact, this is a powerful way of getting at the point Jesus will later make explicit: "Anyone who loves his father or mother more than me is not worthy of me; anyone who loves his son or daughter more than me is not worthy of me; and anyone who does not take his cross and follow me is not worthy of me. Whoever finds his life will lose it, and whoever loses his life for my sake will find it" (Matt. 10:37–39). Jesus' concern in 8:22 is not so much to forbid all who would follow him from attending the funerals of near relatives, as it is to expose the danger of merely qualified discipleship. Indeed, sometimes Jesus purposely uses language that is rather shocking, not because it is meant to be taken literally, but because it most tellingly makes the point. For example, in Matthew 5:27–30 Jesus insists that the eye that lusts is best plucked out; the hand that touches what is forbidden is best cut off. One of the early church fathers took this literally, and castrated himself; but in one sense even self-castration is simply not radical enough. Jesus' point is not that self-mutilation is an effective way to deal with sin, but that sin must be dealt with radically, at its root, even if such dealings are costly. Similarly in Matthew 8, the point is not so much that people should not be concerned for their parents, but that if concern for parents becomes an excuse for not following Jesus, or for delay in following Jesus, then concern for parents, as important as it is, is being too highly valued.

Some who read these lines have made difficult and costly decisions regarding their families. A colleague from a wealthy family was disinherited when he went into the ministry. A close friend, when she became a Christian, was bombarded by emotional barrages from her unbelieving family: "Don't you think we are good enough? Didn't we bring you up right? Are you now saying that you are better than we?" Indeed, the division can become more acute as the months pass, and the new convert recognizes that his or her goals and values are in certain respects no longer in line with those inherited from the family.

The two vignettes in these verses, then, teach us that the authentic Jesus makes demands that are often personal and costly. That is why Jesus can elsewhere tell parables the point of which is that would-be disciples *ought* to count the cost before they promise too much (Luke 14:25–35).

Certainly Paul understood that following Jesus entailed costly decisions. They may not be the same for every Christian; but for him they involved shame, pain, suffering, privation, and large-scale rejection (1 Cor. 4:8–13; 2 Cor. 11:21–33)—even being considered "the scum of the earth, the refuse of the world."

This point is frequently misunderstood by evangelicals, precisely because we have (rightly) stressed the importance of justification by grace, the freedom of God in giving salvation. Our works do not save us; we can be acquitted before the bar of God's justice and declared righteous in his presence solely on the basis of God's grace given us in Christ Jesus. But does that mean there is no cost for us to consider at all?

The kind of misapprehension that frequently occurs cropped up recently when a friend of mine was witnessing to a lady of the Jehovah's Witnesses persuasion. She asked, rather suspiciously, what he thought the way of salvation was; and he replied with a more or less traditional evangelical presentation, stressing the grace of God. She replied with words to this effect: "That's what I thought you would say. But I couldn't bear a religion that costs me nothing."

Her misunderstanding was profound; in fact, her response betrayed a double misunderstanding. She needed to come to grips with the fact that in the Scripture salvation turns on God's free gift. In that sense she could contribute nothing but her sin; and if that is the kind of religion she could not stand, she was rejecting the biblical revelation. So in the first place, she misunderstood the nature of salvation in the Scripture. But on the other hand, those elementary truths do not mean that there are no costs at all, no personal demands. Biblical salvation is paid for by someone else: in that sense it is free. But individual appropriation of it entails repentance, personal death to self-interest, principial submission to the lordship of Jesus Christ. These are not meritorious acts. They are, finally, evidence of the grace of God in the Christian life, but they are no less personal or costly for that. So she displayed a second misunderstanding: she failed to see that salvation that has been paid for, and is therefore free, nevertheless works in our lives so powerfully that it transforms us, confronts our will, demands our devotion and allegiance, and calls forth our deepest commitment.

In concrete terms, the "costs" Christians pay in the West, as compared with those paid by many Christians in the world, are very small. Principially, however, they are exactly the same for all Christians: death to self-interest, a daily "dying" that can be quite painful. But it is precisely that attitude that breeds a Borden of Yale, who abandoned great wealth and status to prepare for ministry in the Middle East. Only a short time after his arrival, he contracted the disease that killed him; and as he lay dying, with others bemoaning the "waste," his conclusion was firm: "No reserve; no retreat; no regrets." In one sense, our salvation costs us absolutely nothing; in another, it costs us not less than everything. The former is true because Jesus paid it all; the latter is possible because Jesus enables us to respond to his upward call. Those who stress the latter and neglect the former may never learn that salvation is by grace alone; those who stress the former and neglect the latter may buy into a cheap facsimile of grace that knows little of the biblical gospel and less of biblical holiness.

The authentic Jesus makes demands that are personal and costly.

2. The authentic Jesus is far more wonderful than even his most intimate followers suspect (8:23–27). Over the centuries some pretty fantastic interpretations of this miracle have been advanced. Tertullian argued that the boat stands for the church: those who are in the church with Jesus can weather any storm, for he will protect them. That old interpretation has been dressed up again in modern garb: this section betrays the dangers facing Matthew's church, and the point is that as the disciples who *followed* him into the boat were safe, so those who *follow* Jesus in true discipleship are safe.

But this will not do. The verb *to follow* is not a technical one that invariably refers to true discipleship. It can be used to describe the action of the crowd, not the disciples (Matt. 4:25; 8:1, 10; 12:15); indeed, in 9:19 Jesus and his disciples *follow* the ruler (the same verb in Greek) to his home—which certainly does not mean that Jesus had become a genuine disciple of the ruler! The point of the account is not so much focused on the nature of discipleship as on the person of Christ: it ends with the ejaculation, "What kind of man is this? Even the winds and the waves obey him!" (8:27).

Sudden, violent squalls are not uncommon on Galilee, which lies six hundred feet below sea level. Hot, steamy air can start to rise, drawing in a rush of air from the desert that churns the surface of the lake into a violent cauldron. Here men cry out in alarm; and Jesus (as one commentator rather quaintly puts it) "does not chide them for disturbing him with their prayers, but for disturbing themselves with their fears." "You of little faith," he cries, "why are you so afraid?"

The words *little faith* may not so much refer to quantity of faith as to its impoverished nature (as in 17:20, where faith like the grain of a mustard seed is not *large* faith but a certain *kind* of faith). Jesus presupposes that proper faith would drive out fear; he rebukes the disciples in that in their case fear has driven out faith. Clearly they have enough faith to turn to him for help; but the desperation of their cry and their astonished remarks after the miracle show their faith is not very mature. Their attitude is something like that of a crowd toward an illusionist, a modern magician: they believe he is going to do something remarkable, but gasp in surprise when it is done. In the case of the disciples, the situation is heightened by the danger of their situation (which does not of course apply to the crowd watching a magician).

Modern Christians will sympathize with the disciples a little when we remember our own prayers. We sometimes fall into difficult straits, and cry to God for help. Our credal stance is that God is a prayer-hearing and prayer-answering God; we believe he can resolve the difficulty both for his glory and for our good. But such is the poor quality of our faith that in many instances when God has answered, often in ways vastly superior to what we expected, we are greatly surprised. It is then that we lift our voices with renewed understanding:

> *Sometimes a light surprises*
> *The Christian while he sings;*
> *It is the Lord who rises*
> *With healing in his wings.*
> *When comforts are declining,*
> *He grants the soul again*
> *A season of clear shining,*
> *To cheer it after rain.*
>
> *In holy contemplation,*
> *We sweetly then pursue*

The theme of God's salvation,
And find it ever new:
Set free from present sorrow,
We cheerfully can say,
E'en let the unknown morrow
Bring with it what it may.

It can bring with it nothing
But he will bear us through;
Who gives the lilies clothing
Will clothe his people too;
Beneath the spreading heavens,
No creature but is fed;
And he who feeds the ravens
Will give his children bread.

Though vine nor fig-tree neither
Their wonted fruit should bear,
Though all the field should wither,
Nor flocks nor herds be there,
Yet, God the same abiding,
His praise shall tune my voice;
For, while in him confiding,
I cannot but rejoice.

William Cowper (1731–1800)

But the most serious deficiency of faith displayed by the disciples lay in their failure to recognize who Jesus really is. If they had truly come to terms with the kind of messiah Jesus was, could they really have thought that a squall on Galilee could swamp the boat and take the life of the heaven-sent Redeemer whose mission was to die in shame and rise in triumph for the salvation of his people? Could a storm snuff out the life of him who is the agent of creation? That is the point Matthew is making when he records the final exclamations of the disciples: they have *not* come to grips yet with who he is; and that is precisely why their faith is so beggarly.

The lesson is well put in a song by Mary A. Baker that I remember my mother singing, a song no longer well known in the church. It pictures the disciples crying out:

Master, the tempest is raging;
The billows are tossing high!
The sky is o'ershadowed with blackness,
No shelter or help is nigh!
Carest thou not that we perish?

> *How canst thou lie asleep,*
> *When each moment so madly is threat'ning*
> *A grave in the angry deep?*

To which Jesus replies:

> *The winds and the waves shall obey my will:*
> *Peace! Be still!*
> *Whether the wrath of the storm-tossed sea,*
> *Or demons, or men, or whatever it be,*
> *No water can swallow the ship where lies*
> *The Master of ocean, and earth, and skies.*
> *They all shall sweetly obey my will:*
> *Peace! Be still! Peace! Be still!*
> *They all shall sweetly obey my will:*
> *Peace. Peace. Be still.*

Jesus is always better than our fears. Moreover, our faith will be most stable *if we center it on who Jesus is.* Faith urgently needs to know, not so much what Jesus will do or what promises he may have made that are applicable to this or that situation, but *who Jesus is.* The Christian must learn that knowing the authentic Jesus better is what strengthens faith the most. We discover with increasing delight that Jesus is always far more wonderful than we had anticipated.

Indeed, all three of the portions that constitute the section of Matthew we are studying in this chapter (8:18–34) include some paradoxical aspects of Christ's nature. In the first, Jesus says that *the Son of Man* has no place to lay his head (8:20). The expression was ambiguous in Jesus' day. It could be used as a simple self-reference; it was sometimes associated with the sufferings of the Messiah; but it could also signal the glories of the Messiah, in direct allusion to Daniel 7:13–14, where one *like a son of man* receives a kingdom from God himself, the Ancient of Days (cf. Matt. 26:64). Here in 8:20, there is a simple self-reference, with overtones of privation ("no place to lay his head"); but Christians after the resurrection would not be able to avoid the connection with Daniel 7, and marvel that in Jesus there was combined kingly authority and the heart of a servant. In the second paragraph, Jesus is asleep in the boat, exhausted from the exertions of his ministry; yet he remains Lord of nature, muzzling the storm by his word, exercising the authority of God himself who controls and stills the seas (Job 38:8–11; Pss. 29:3–4, 10–11; 65:5–7; 89:9; 107:23–32). In the third, he is recognized even by the demons as the one who has final authority on the day of judgment; but the Gadarenes implore him to leave their territory, and he quietly leaves without exercising any judgment at all.

But these paradoxical features in Christ's nature are the very things that give us such confidence in him. He knew by experience the loneliness of homelessness, the sleep of exhaustion, and the rejection of thoughtless people; yet he was the glorious Son, the Lord of nature, the Judge of all in earth and heaven. Small wonder the writer of the Epistle to the Hebrews delights to remember that our champion has been touched with the feelings of our infirmities; but because he is the Lord, he has the capacity to provide all the succor we need. This is the authentic Jesus.

3. The authentic Jesus puts spiritual and human realities before other considerations (8:28–34). Some wag has suggested that when the disciples asked what kind of man Jesus was (8:27), the demons went out to tell them (8:28–29). That may have been the result; but it was certainly not the demons' intention, and it is doubtful that the disciples saw it that way at the time.

Nevertheless, although the passage is not particularly aimed at giving us a detailed knowledge of demons, it may be worth reflecting a little on what it does suggest about them. In the Western world, there are still many who prefer to demythologize demons: demons, they say, are not real, spiritual beings but popular projections of evil. Only the inroads of philosophical materialism could read that conclusion into the New Testament evidence; only those completely ignorant of spiritual warfare, not only in parts of the world under the influence of animism but now also increasingly in occult centers in the West, could voice such skepticism with so much confidence and condescension.

In the account before us, the demons are able to dissociate themselves from the men they possess (8:32). They recognize Jesus; in that sense they know him better than the disciples do. They know that Jesus is the unique Son of God; yet they are demons still. As one writer puts it, "He is the firstborn of hell, that knows Christ, and yet hates him, and will not be subject to his law." They are even aware of their ultimate fate (cf. Jude 6; Rev. 20:10), and that Jesus is the one who will consign them to it; but that knowledge in their case breeds taunts, violence, and hatred, not repentance. What distinguishes saints from demons is loving obedience, not naked knowledge.

These demons can animate other beings than humans. Why they should beg to be sent into the herd of pigs (Mark 5:13 says there were about two thousand animals) is not self-evident. Some have suggested that demons like to clothe themselves in bodies; but if so, why should their first action after being dismissed to the swine be the destruction of their new home? More likely, their hatred of the Creator extends to his creation. Whatever will do damage, especially against people (as in the destruction of herds people own), will be desirable to them.

But one of the points of the story is that Jesus has matchless, unassailable authority over *all* powers of darkness and evil spirits. Later on, the disciples would be stymied by a case of demon possession with which they tried to deal (Matt. 17:14–20); but Jesus is never so limited. The present incident takes place in the Decapolis area, largely inhabited by Gentiles; and the herd of pigs, which no self-respecting Jew would keep or tend, equally betrays the Gentile cast of the context. But Jesus is not limited in his authority to a Jewish environment. He is not bound by geography or race, who commends the Gentile centurion, who can leash the forces of nature, who can multiply five loaves and two small fishes, who can heal the sick and raise the dead, and who can turn sinners into saints.

But the account does not end with reflection on Jesus' authority. After Jesus' miracle, those tending the pigs run off and tell the town folk what had happened—"including what had happened to the demon-possessed men" (8:33). The news was startling: a large herd of swine had been destroyed, and with it the wealth and livelihood of many people; and two demoniacs, well-known and universally avoided as dangerous, were now restored. So the whole town goes out to meet Jesus; but instead of focusing on the marvelous transformation of the two men who had been possessed, instead of asking further if Jesus might help others in their number, they apparently focus on the fiscal losses, and plead with him to leave their region (8:34).

Some human beings prefer pigs to people. People are fine—but not if they adversely affect my pocketbook. Why Jesus allowed the demons to possess and destroy the pigs is not clear. At one level their loss becomes part of the entire sweep of disasters, illnesses, storms, sorrows, and death that are part of the human condition this side of the new heaven and the new earth. Why Jesus granted the demons their request when he could have done something else is merely one of a thousand similar questions: Why did he not stop the injustices of Rome? Why did he heal only the one paralytic by the pool (John 5), and not all who were present? Why were not more raised from the dead? This kind of question I do not propose to address here;[1] but whatever answers we give, it is clear that the least that must be said of this account is that Jesus puts spiritual and human realities above other considerations. The release of the two men who had been demon-possessed is clearly of more importance to him than the loss of the two thousand pigs; the limitation of demonic activity is of greater moment than fiscal considerations.

This is of a piece with many biblical emphases. It is easy for us to devote much of our thought and energy to matters that, in the light of eternity, are of *relative* unimportance. Politics, sport, entertainment, the daily administration of family matters, clothes, health, education, and the like all enjoy varying degrees of importance; but compared with the really basic questions these subjects fade into insignificance—or, more accurately, these subjects find their true significance *only when they are seen as subsets of the really fundamental concerns.* Such concerns include righteousness, knowing God savingly both now and for all eternity, growing in thoughtful obedience to Jesus Christ, freedom from sin and from demonic power, displaying the love of Christ in lives transformed by the Spirit he has bequeathed.

The priorities we set, consciously or unconsciously, betray what we judge to be important. This question is raised in many different ways in the Bible. One of the most intriguing is found in 1 Corinthians 7, where Paul is talking about marriage, divorce, and related matters. After discussing various combinations of problems, his line of thought takes an important turn:

> [25]Now about virgins: I have no command from the Lord, but I give a judgment as one who by the Lord's mercy is trustworthy. [26]*Because of the present crisis* [emphasis added], I think that it is good for you to remain as you are.
> [27]Are you married? Do not seek a divorce. Are you unmarried? Do not look for a wife.
> [28]But if you do marry, you have not sinned; and if a virgin marries, she has not sinned. But those who marry will face many troubles in this life, and I want to spare you this.
> [29]What I mean, brothers, is that the time is short. From now on those who have wives should live as if they had none;
> [30]those who mourn, as if they did not; those who are happy, as if they were not; those who buy something, as if it were not theirs to keep;

[31]those who use the things of the world, as if not engrossed in them. For this world in its present form is passing away.

These verses are often misunderstood in one of two ways. Some understand the words *the present crisis* to refer to a bout of persecution. Because of this crisis, it is argued, it might be best for Christians contemplating marriage to put the idea on hold. Oppressive forces can apply horrible pressure by making family members the targets of their attacks. Living singly may then provide the best opportunity for serving Christ without compromise or distraction. But this interpretation really will not do. There is not a shred of evidence that the Corinthian church was undergoing persecution at that point in its history; indeed, a strong whiff of persecution might have done it a great deal of good. Besides, this interpretation does not really explain verses 30–31: what exactly is the connection between this alleged persecution and mourning or being happy? And is Paul in verse 29 really advocating celibacy for married folk, when in the opening verses of the chapter he has so strongly insisted that partners in marriage must *not* abandon sexual activity, except under very restrictive conditions?

The second false interpretation argues that "the present crisis" refers to Paul's belief that the Lord Jesus was going to come so soon, within a few years at most, that the Corinthian Christians should live their life in the light of that impending event. I am not persuaded, on broader grounds, that this is a fair interpretation of Paul; and in any case it leaves us with the unavoidable conclusion that Paul was wrong, since almost two thousand years have elapsed without the Savior's return.

What Paul is referring to by his words *the present crisis* is the entire period between the first advent of Christ and the second. This entire age is characterized by crisis, however long or short it may be. During this period, called "the last hour" by John (1 John 2:18), this world in its present form is passing away (1 Cor. 7:31). The emphasis is not on the *shortness* of the time left for this world, but on the *transitoriness* of this world. During this period between the advents, Christians must learn to live "as if not": *everything* linked exclusively to an age that is passing must fall under the judgment of God's "as if not." Christians are so linked with the age to come, they so live with eternity's values in view, that the joys and sorrows and realities that are part of this age cannot be allowed to dominate their lives. Marriage is important here; but in the new heaven and the new earth, there is neither marriage nor giving in marriage. The wise Christian will learn to view marriage "as if not"—that is, marriage will no longer be a dominating category, but viewed from the eternal perspective. Within this framework, marriage is still perfectly acceptable (7:28); but it can no longer be viewed as the goal of life, the promise of perfect bliss, the fulfillment of all human aspirations. The same is true of *whatever* makes the children of this world happy, or mourn; it is true of *everything* that is bought and sold. All is placed under God's "as if not": Christians live with the perspectives of the new age so deeply embedded in their minds and hearts that the foci of this age are held more loosely, *"as if* they do *not"* have permanent validity or ultimate importance—precisely because *they do not!*

In short, just as the authentic Jesus puts spiritual and human realities before other considerations, his followers must do the same. We may rejoice in all that God gives us here, so richly to enjoy; but we must never confuse the blessings he gives us that are irretrievably linked to this passing age with the blessings he gives us that will last for all eternity.

4. The authentic Jesus consistently overturns many common expectations. This point emerges not from a particular verse or section in the chapter before us, but from the flow of the argument both in this chapter and throughout the Gospels. One of the most self-evident aspects of Jesus' ministry is its flexibility. Here is someone who has exactly the *right* word for the harlot, the tax collector, the priest, the teacher of the law, the common laborer, the would-be disciple, the Pharisee, the crowds of common folk, the smooth-tongued interrogator, the Roman official, the soldier, the grieving sister, the blind, the poor.

But there is more than mere flexibility here. Any polished person, skilled in public relations, can make small talk with all and sundry. Jesus' flexibility is not characterized by gifted small talk. In every recorded conversation he gets to the heart of the other's being. Exposed to view are the needs, values, selfishness, weakness, hurts, or pride that chiefly characterize the individual now being addressed.

In addition to the insight displayed by Jesus in this chapter, we might briefly mention a number of other instances. When a well-instructed Pharisee by the name of Nicodemus respectfully but hesitantly approaches, Jesus immediately turns to Nicodemus's area of expertise: the Scriptures. Nicodemus is apparently probing Jesus to find out if he is the Messiah; but Jesus' response drives Nicodemus, himself "Israel's teacher" (John 3:10), to reflect on Old Testament promises that under the new covenant there would be clean, Spirit-renewed hearts—what Jesus calls a "new birth." To the rich young ruler whose god was his wealth, Jesus prescribes that he give away his possessions (Matthew 19:16–30). To the disciples who were jockeying for position (Matthew 18), Jesus makes appeal to a child as the standard of what proper response is like in the kingdom. And to religious leaders more concerned to trap Jesus in his words and to tear down his ministry than to bow before him and acknowledge him as Lord, Jesus not only responds with sharp replies on a case-by-case basis (Matthew 22), but also delivers a blistering yet grieving denunciation (Matthew 23). To Zacchaeus (Luke 19), Jesus' presence and personal interest seem to have been enough to bring about restitution.

One interesting dimension about all this diversity is what Jesus does *not* say in each of these instances. He may tell the rich young ruler to sell all he has; he does not lay down this requirement to Nicodemus, nor to the disciples, nor even to Zacchaeus. The "new birth" predicted under the new covenant stands as part of the Old Testament Scriptures; but only Nicodemus is berated for not having grasped it. The model of a child's responsiveness and simple faith is not applied by Jesus to Zacchaeus, Nicodemus, or the rich young ruler.

What, then, is the commonality in all of this, other than Jesus' flexibility and peerless skills in spiritual diagnosis? The answer comes clear in the wake of two reflections. First, the gospel of Jesus Christ is a massive structure that can be applied to tremendously diverse circumstances. Second, it is wisely applied in most cases in ways that stand *directly opposite* to the circumstances of the individual.

To take a couple of unambiguous instances: Paul writes, "For he who was a slave when he was called by the Lord is the Lord's freedman; similarly, he who was a free man when he was called is Christ's slave" (1 Cor. 7:22); and James insists, "The brother in humble circumstances ought to take pride in his high position. But the one who is rich should take pride in his low position, because he will pass away like a wild flower" (James 1:9–10). The damage that could be done if these points are applied in inverse array is incalculable. If the slave is told again and again that as a Christian he is still a slave, and nothing more, while the free man is told that the gospel of Christ is a liberating thing, and he is privileged to share in the rich heritage of Christ, the declarations, though true, are at best serious misapplications of the gospel, and at worst morally and spiritually catastrophic. The slave may indeed have to be told that conversion does not necessarily bring with it an automatic change in his physical position; but he must also be told that in the light of Christ's crosswork, and in the light of the prospect of Christ's return, his status before God (which on the long haul is what counts) is immensely different from what it was. Slave he may be; but he is now a child of God, an heir of God and a joint heir with Jesus Christ. Meanwhile the free man may need to have some of his arrogance before the slaves curtailed; and in that sense he is wise to think of himself as a fellow slave—a slave of Jesus Christ. Similar sensitivity must be shown in the application of the gospel to the rich and to the poor, as James shows.

In other words, the gospel is not only big enough to be applicable to highly diverse circumstances, but also is most fittingly applied in ways that fly in the face of the individual involved. The reason is not hard to find. The complex diversity of the human condition has at its core a handful of rudimentary commonalities. Among these is our sinfulness. Apart from grace, we rebel against God in some fashion— whether in social rebellion, religious perversion, moral delinquency, sheer arrogance, aped humility, or some other form. When Jesus confronts the world, he confronts sinners. Some are crushed, profoundly aware of their guilt, hungry for the forgiving word. Others are oppressed, guilty no doubt, but also discouraged, defeated, and eager to hear the reassurance that there is justice in the universe and that we may live with a longer-range vision than the contemporary political or economic climate permits. Still others are so full of themselves and their accomplishments, so little aware of the favor that has been shown them in the circumstances of their birth, upbringing, education, and material advantages that the only religion they want is a domesticated variety; but what they need is rebuke, the sharp exposure of their danger and real need.

Among those who read these words will be persons of good birth and high breeding; there will also be some who do not know who their fathers are, and who spent much of their lives in foster homes. Some will be quite wealthy; others could not possibly afford the price of this book, and are reading it only because they managed to borrow a copy from a friend or a library. Some will have been reared in Christian homes, and may not even be sure of the date of their conversion; others will have been skid-row alcoholics or drug addicts who were converted and marvelously and publicly transformed. It is important for all of us who are Christians, regardless of our backgrounds, to recognize that although the gospel applies to us, the particular elements that must be *stressed* in each case, the particular elements that we must apply to ourselves most strenuously, are precisely those elements most at variance with our position.

In short, the gospel can be applied with such flexibility precisely because the needs turn out to have more commonalities behind them than a casual glance might suggest. That is also the reason why Jesus consistently overturns so many common expectations. Our expectations are inevitably bound up with who we are; who we are is bound up with our ignorance of and rebellion against God. Despite our diversity, that is what Jesus and his ministry inevitably confront. Small wonder then that Jesus overthrows our categories and our expectations; for if he did not, he could not possibly be the one who was sent to save his people from their sins (Matt. 1:21).

The same truth has a bearing on modern discussions about contextualization—the need for the gospel to be shaped in large part by the culture in which it is being promulgated. In large part, the insights from recent treatments of contextualization are valid and important. Indeed, that is why John's Gospel does not sound exactly the same as Luke's: not only was John a different writer, but also he was ministering to a different audience, with different needs and categories. But the point can be pushed too far. Although the gospel must be presented to any group in terms of the categories and felt needs of that group, just as Paul wisely shapes his presentation of the gospel to the Athenians to take into account their intellectual history and structures (Acts 17), *it must always press on to the point where it is in some measure subverting and overthrowing the categories of that culture.* It must do so because *all* cultures are in some degree and particulars in rebellion against God, and will be judged by him. If the presentation of the gospel remains entirely congenial to any culture, it can only be because the gospel has been eviscerated, stripped of its stark independence—hopelessly tamed, like a pet poodle, to do the bidding of that culture.

Examples are not hard to find. In much of the West, many people are looking for a sense of fulfillment. If the gospel is presented as something that meets this need, well and good; for in a sense, as Augustine discovered, our souls are restless until they find their rest in God. But if this theme is constantly reiterated without any mention of servanthood and death to self-interest, we become guilty of nurturing the very narcissism and hedonism that have corrupted so much of Western culture and that stand as glaring indications of our rebellion against God. Again, because society in India is still so highly stratified, believers from the lower levels tend to relate to others in terms of petition and begging, while Christians who are promoted to senior ranks tend to exercise authority in peremptory ways. If the latter group stresses all the texts about heeding the authorities and obeying those who watch for the souls of others, their cultural blind spot will not be healed. They must also listen to injunctions about not lording it over others, about serving as an example, about being the least of all.

Ready examples are easy to find in *every* culture; and Christians in every culture must thoughtfully discover just where their lives have been too greatly shaped by the pervasive influence of their surroundings, rather than by Jesus Christ and his truth. The authentic Jesus consistently overturns many common expectations. Any other Jesus is a sham.

Conclusion

When Jesus really does confront the world, he does so on his own terms; and those terms are not negotiable. People, cultures, movements, values—all are subject to immense change. But the authentic Jesus, however flexible, cannot be pocketed or brought to heel. He makes demands that are personal and costly; he puts spiritual realities before other considerations; he overturns many common expectations; but, thank God, he is always far more wonderful than even his most intimate followers suspect.

> *My song is love unknown,*
> *My Saviour's love to me;*
> *Love to the loveless shown,*
> *That they might lovely be.*
> *O, who am I,*
> *That for my sake*
> *My Lord should take*
> *Frail flesh, and die?*
>
> *He came from his blest throne*
> *Salvation to bestow;*
> *But men made strange, and none*

The longed-for Christ would know.
But O! my Friend,
My Friend indeed,
Who at my need
His life did spend.

Sometimes they strew his way,
And his sweet praises sing;
Resounding all the day
Hosannas to their King.
Then Crucify!
Is all their breath,
And for his death
They thirst and cry.

They rise and needs will have
My dear Lord made away;
A murderer they save,
The Prince of life they slay.
Yet cheerful he
To suffering goes
That he his foes
From thence might free.

In life, no house, no home
My Lord on earth might have;
In death, no friendly tomb,
But what a stranger gave.
What may I say?
Heaven was his home;
But mine the tomb
Wherein he lay.

Here might I stay and sing,
No story so divine;
Never was love, dear King!
Never was grief like thine.
This is my Friend,
In whose sweet praise
I all my days
Could gladly spend.

Samuel Crossman (1624–1683)

---

[1] The immediate context of the destruction of the swine provides at least a little perspective. He who is Lord of nature (Matt. 8:23–27) is also its ultimate owner, to

dispose of it as he wishes (8:28–34). Apparently to banish the demons entirely would be to breach the "appointed time" (8:29). Moreover the stampede of swine, whatever else it achieved, dramatically demonstrated that the demoniacs had been released (and what they had been released from!), and exposed the highest values of the surrounding people.

9

The Mission of Jesus

(9:1-17)

¹Jesus stepped into a boat, crossed over and came to his own town.

²Some men brought to him a paralytic, lying on a mat. When Jesus saw their faith, he said to the paralytic, "Take heart, son; your sins are forgiven."

³At this, some of the teachers of the law said to themselves, "This fellow is blaspheming!"

⁴Knowing their thoughts, Jesus said, "Why do you entertain evil thoughts in your hearts? ⁵Which is easier: to say, 'Your sins are forgiven,' or to say, 'Get up and walk'? ⁶But so that you may know that the Son of Man has authority on earth to forgive sins. . . ." Then he said to the paralytic, "Get up, take your mat and go home." ⁷And the man got up and went home.

⁸When the crowd saw this, they were filled with awe; and they praised God, who had given such authority to men.

⁹As Jesus went on from there, he saw a man named Matthew sitting at the tax collector's booth. "Follow me," he told him, and Matthew got up and followed him.

¹⁰While Jesus was having dinner at Matthew's house, many tax collectors and "sinners" came and ate with him and his disciples.

¹¹When the Pharisees saw this, they asked his disciples, "Why does your teacher eat with tax collectors and 'sinners'?"

¹²On hearing this, Jesus said, "It is not the healthy who need a doctor, but the sick.

[13]But go and learn what this means: 'I desire mercy, not sacrifice.' For I have not come to call the righteous, but sinners."

[14]Then John's disciples came and asked him, "How is it that we and the Pharisees fast, but your disciples do not fast?"

[15]Jesus answered, "How can the guests of the bridegroom mourn while he is with them? The time will come when the bridegroom will be taken from them; then they will fast.

[16]"No one sews a patch of unshrunk cloth on an old garment, for the patch will pull away from the garment, making the tear worse.

[17]Neither do men pour new wine into old wineskins. If they do, the skins will burst, the wine will run out and the wineskins will be ruined. No, they pour new wine into new wineskins, and both are preserved."

Introduction

It has been well said that if you aim at nothing you are likely to hit it. That is why parents, for instance, encourage their children to set goals for themselves. People without goals, people without various kinds of purpose, tend to drift from experience to experience, even from crisis to crisis. Their aimless life is easily dissipated in fruitless or even harmful directions, since they have no goals that establish priorities and thereby preserve them from some follies. The best companies and organizations quickly discover the same truth. Any corporation or institution can survive for a little while on the unarticulated dream of the founder or on the surge of the economy; but before long it will fade into irrelevance, if not bankruptcy, unless it repeatedly formulates and reviews its goals.

But goals provide more than aim and incentive. They also provide a set of criteria by which to measure performance. Organized people know this. They carry slips of paper in their pockets with lists of what they intend to do today, or this week, or this month; and as they work through the list, they cross off the completed tasks one by one. This simple action generates enormous satisfaction; but it also provides a kind of check that ensures energy is being *and has been* used wisely. A senior evangelical scholar, known for his prolific pen, carries a list of his current writing projects with him— whether books, articles, or book reviews—and marks them off as he completes them. A father of ten in one of the northern states in

America disciplined his children to prepare such lists daily, in order to encourage them to use their time in a disciplined manner. This practice also helps to eliminate false expectations: a few weeks of preparing lists that are extravagantly long and never completed by the day's end soon fosters more realistic goals. Similarly, companies that check what they are doing from time to time against stated goals soon learn to eliminate distracting and time-consuming profit-absorbing sidelines.

In some measure these relations between goals and performance hold true even in the spiritual arena. Of course, one can go too far. I am always a little nervous when I hear of a church setting a goal of, say, 30 percent growth over the next period of time. Doubtless such goals can be set forth in a genuinely spiritual fashion, but too often they are formulated so starkly that it appears the leaders do not believe that conversion is at the end of the day a work of God. It is almost as if the Holy Spirit could get up and walk out and not be missed: the fine machinery would continue to clank on and meet the stated goals.

But before we laugh too hard at these activists, we need to remember that we are morally responsible beings. We have choices to make and priorities to set. For instance, often much praying is not done, whether corporately or by the individual Christian, simply because there has been no real *intention* of praying, no real *plan* to pray. One does not simply drift into a disciplined prayer life. Much evangelism has not been done because we have not aimed to do it. We have not intended to share our faith with our neighbors, or set a goal of getting to know the family across the back fence during the next six months, with the express purpose of loving them for Christ's sake and presenting Christ to them. Something similar could be said about Bible reading. Moreover, to have goals in these areas helps to provide us with criteria by which we can in some measure assess the discipline of our spiritual progress.

Goals, then, are powerful things. It is precisely because of these relationships between goals and performance that when someone wants to take over or redirect a movement or even an individual career, one of the first things he or she does is to meddle with the goals of that movement or career. You see this sometimes in a political party that has lost its way and fallen into considerable disfavor. Then along comes a bright spark who senses the public's mood and decides to capitalize on it. One of the first things he or she may try to do is to restate the party's goals in order to bend the organization to the new mood. Often the organization is willing to go along: the bright spark gains by being supported by the established political machine, and the party gains by being rejuvenated and brought in line with popular concerns.

The same kind of manipulation of goals was attempted in the first century. According to John 6:14–15, some of Jesus' hearers intended to appoint Jesus king by force. They perceived in someone with his miraculous powers the ideal person to take on the Roman overlords and reestablish the kingdom to its long-lost splendor. If they could *force* his hand by appointing him king, even without his formal approval, their agenda would necessarily become his. Once king, he would attract the anger of the ruling overlords; and then he would have to use all of his miraculous powers to extricate himself and the people from the opposition that would ensue.

Satan himself, according to Matthew 4 and Luke 4, attempted to co-opt Jesus by offering him the kingdoms of the world without the pain of the cross. When Peter in Matthew 16 insists that Jesus will never go the way of suffering and death, Jesus recognizes the same source, and responds, "Get behind me, Satan! You are a stumbling block to me; you do not have in mind the things of God, but the things of men" (Matt. 16:23). The attempt was to foist on Jesus a modified set of goals, a revised mission that eliminated suffering and the cross. But Jesus saw the attempted takeover for what it was, and rejected it with some heat.

There are attempted takeovers of Christianity today as well. If someone wants to bless a movement with the powerful influence of the church, then the first thing to be attempted is a redefinition of the church's mission that turns out, wonder of wonders, to be lined up with the aims of the movement. Marxists have been known to appeal to Acts 2 to show that what Christianity is really about is communal sharing. Marxism is therefore the rightful heir to Christianity. Of course one does not then mention that the sharing of Acts 2 was achieved by the power of transformed lives, and that power was generated by the atonement of Christ and the Spirit he subsequently bequeathed; Marxist sharing depends on what comes out of the end of a machine gun. Right-wing economic and political agendas also try to shanghai the gospel. Did not Jesus say that the truth would set men free, and that he came to give them the abundant life? Jesus is obviously for freedom; the principle extends to the marketplace. That may or may not be good economics; it is a horrible abuse of Scripture. More recently, liberation theology appeals to the exodus as the archetypal freeing of slaves, and Jesus' concern for the poor, to tell us what the Bible is really about. But one wonders why the exodus is chosen. Why not Jeremiah's insistence that the remnant should not rebel against the Babylonian empire? And for all that Jesus displays immense compassion on the poor and the downtrodden, it is remarkable that poverty is never for him the decisive division between those who are accepted and those who are not. When he clears out the temple, for instance, it is not the religious authorities who are chased out but the sellers *and buyers.* The latter certainly included many of the poor—all those who were there to buy the doves, as opposed to the more expensive sacrificial animals.

There have been countless attempts to co-opt the gospel to a cause that, however meritorious, was not itself the proclamation of the gospel. So it becomes extremely important for us to listen to Scripture and to try to articulate the gospel as accurately as possible, to articulate the mission of Jesus. If we succeed in listening to the Scripture on these points, we shall be preserved from the vagaries of every passing theology; more, we shall better grasp the very heart of the faith we profess.

In this series I have been examining what happens and what we may learn when Jesus confronts the world. In this chapter I want to suggest that the passage before us helps answer the questions: What was Jesus' mission? Why did he come? If the answers it provides are not exhaustive, at least they are crucial.

Why Did Jesus Come?

1. Jesus came to forgive sin and transform sinners; this was foundational to the rest of his ministry (9:1–8).[1] When the people of Gadara pleaded with Jesus to leave their region, preferring pigs to people and wanting swine more than healing (8:34), Jesus acquiesced: he stepped back into the boat he had so recently used, crossed over Galilee, and "came to his own town" (Matt 9:1). This, of course, was Capernaum (4:13), right on the lake in an area of fairly high-density Jewish population; so he was immediately plunged back into the vortex of ministry. Matthew does not describe the crowd at this point, nor mention that the only way the friends of the paralytic could reach Jesus was through the roof of the house where he was speaking; typically, he focuses on what is essential to his own narrative. Accordingly he picks up themes that are interwoven throughout these chapters. For instance, the emphasis on Jesus' authority returns (9:6, 8; cf. 7:29; 8:9, 15, 27, 29). Similarly, the emphasis on faith—the faith of the centurion (8:10) and the lack of faith among the disciples (8:26)—appears in new guise in the faith Jesus perceives in the friends who carry the paralytic to him (9:2). Jesus "saw" their faith: that is, he saw their actions in bringing the victim to him, and their actions testified to their faith. Because of *their* faith, Jesus confers great blessings on *the paralytic*—just as today the prayers of faith a believer offers in behalf of another person may benefit the other person.

But the startling new turn in this story that sets it apart from other healing miracles and ties it thematically to the sections that follow begins in verse 2, where Jesus first addresses the paralytic. To the surprise of the onlookers, and probably of the paralytic and his friends, Jesus says, "Take heart, son; your sins are forgiven."

The words were unexpected. Here was a paralytic who, on the face of it, came to Jesus to be healed of his paralysis; and Jesus' response seems at best tangential to the man's obvious needs. But closer reflection shows that there are more connections than first meet the eye. Jesus perceives at least two ailments that needed his touch: the paralysis and the sin. Of the two, he clearly judges the latter to be the more important or the more urgent in some way. Sickness is the consequence of sin—sometimes directly, more commonly indirectly. That is why Jesus' healing ministry pointed to the cross, which deals with sin supremely (8:16–17). But that Jesus should tell this paralytic to take heart from his words strongly suggests that this man's paralysis was the direct result of a specific sin—and the man knew it and labored under terrible pangs of guilt. Jesus' gentle "Take heart, son," as a preface to his "Your sins are forgiven," would have been unbearably cruel if the man was aware of no guilt and wanted only to be free of paralysis. But if profound guilt compounded the unutterable weakness, then Jesus' opening words offered the brightest hope. They showed Jesus really understood the man's condition, and was dealing with the deepest hurt. And if the paralysis and some specific sin were so connected, then Jesus' words dealing with sin brought hope that the physical ailment would also be remedied.

But the religious authorities mutter to themselves and entertain dark thoughts about blasphemy (Matt. 9:3). The verb rendered "is blaspheming" (βλασφημέω [*blasphēmeō*]) normally means "to slander"; but when the one who is slandered is God, the meaning is very close to the modern "to blaspheme," and hence the translation here. Some leaders in Jesus' day thought blasphemy occurred only when God's name was invoked and used in an inappropriate way; clearly that is not the case here. In this context, however, the principle is being expanded a little to include demeaning God by claiming to do what God *alone* can do. If I claim to be able to do what only God can do, then I am belittling him by comparing myself with him, and thereby dragging him down to my level.

If this principle applies anywhere, it applies to the question of who may forgive sin. After all, in the last analysis sin is always primarily an affront against God. Others may be hurt, but he is the one whom the rebellious action has most deeply offended. David understood the point: "Against you, you only, have I sinned and done what is evil in your sight, so that you are proved right when you speak and justified when you judge" (Ps. 51:4). God himself declares, "I, even I, am he who blots out your transgressions, for my own sake, and remembers your sins no more" (Isa. 43:25; cf. 44:22). Yet here is Jesus, boldly saying "your sins are forgiven," though in the eyes of his critics he is certainly not a priest giving absolution and even more certainly not God himself.

Whether Jesus knew their thoughts (Matt. 9:4) by some supernatural perception of his own, or simply from the rather obvious shuffling and muttering, makes little difference. Either way he detects the malignant intent of their whispered criticism: "Why do you entertain evil thoughts in your hearts?" he asks (9:4). It is not so much that their concern to preserve the holiness of God was wrong, as that their inability to grasp Jesus' true identity was in part a moral failure. Then Jesus asks them the question that they should have asked themselves: "Which is easier: to say, 'Your sins are forgiven,' or to say, 'Get up and walk'?"

The alternatives can easily be misunderstood. What is easier or more difficult is not determined by modern skepticism but by the peculiar brand of skepticism represented by the teachers of the law whom Jesus is confronting. To a modern skeptic, it is doubtless easier to say, "Your sins are forgiven" than to say, "Get up and walk"; for the results of the former cannot be tested, whereas the results of the latter will be plain to all. To a contemporary skeptic, talk is cheap. Anyone can absolve another from sin: it is all meaningless. But to command a paralytic to walk again offers the prospect of empirical results to authenticate the potency of the utterance. The teachers of the law in Jesus' day, however, saw the matter in quite another way. They would have immediately insisted that it is far easier to say "Get up and walk," than to say, "Your sins are forgiven." After all, their own Scriptures offered numerous examples of the kind of person who could say the former. Miracles were credited to Moses, Aaron, Elijah, Elisha, and many, many others. Some of them had even raised the dead. But not one of them had ever granted absolution from sin in so authoritative and unmediated a fashion. That was the more difficult thing by far; for to forgive sin is God's prerogative, and his alone.

In other words, by the rhetorical question Jesus asks, he is claiming to do the more difficult thing, the thing that is God's prerogative. He argues, in effect, that his antagonists should have seen this, and been a little more cautious about accusing him of resorting so easily to blasphemy. But if his utterance was *not* blasphemy, then it is a claim of startling clarity.

If, however, they are unable to make these connections themselves, he offers them a more direct one. "But so that you may know that the Son of Man has authority on earth to forgive sins . . . ," he begins, then turns to the paralytic: "Get up, take your mat and go home" (Matt. 9:6). Matthew tersely comments, "And the man got up and went home" (9:7). Jesus thus uses the less difficult thing to attest the authority of the more difficult thing. Doubtless the healing was not only a wonderful relief to the paralytic, but also a confirming sign that his sins had indeed been forgiven. To the religious opposition, however, the same miracle is cast as something of a rebuke. They could not credit Jesus' claim to do the harder thing by their direct perception; perhaps they will be able to absorb the point by this less significant display more suited to their capacity. The presupposition is like that found in John 9:30–31: if Jesus had in fact blasphemed when he assured the paralytic that his sins were forgiven, then how could God possibly be granting him the authority to perform this lesser but still spectacular deed? Conversely, if Jesus has the authority to restore a paralytic to full health, even after having assumed the prerogatives of God to forgive sin, then who is to say that the authority he is claiming in the more difficult arena is not also rightfully his?

Even Jesus' use of the "Son of Man" title is designed to prompt reflection. Like the use in Matthew 8:20, it is purposely obscure: it could simply be a self-reference. But for anyone who remembers that one "like a son of man" receives a kingdom from God, the Ancient of Days, in Daniel 7, there is at least the potential of link-ing that promised kingdom with the authority to forgive sin. Certainly Christians made the connection after the cross and resurrection; at this point, the use of the title was pregnant with meaning and vaguely troubling, but still too opaque for Jesus' hearers to comprehend.

The crowds responded intuitively. They were filled with fear (not simply "awe," as in the NIV). They were right to be afraid: we *ought* to fear the one who has the authority to forgive sins. They praised God in terms better than they understood: they praised God, Matthew records, "who had given such authority to men" (9:8). They see in Jesus a man; and they are right. They see in him a man who exercises God's authority to forgive sins; and again they are right. Exempt from the theological hang-ups of the more sophisticated teachers of the law, they intuitively draw some correct conclusions. But Matthew's readers know more than the crowds he is describing. Unlike the crowds, the readers know that this particular man was virgin-born, engendered of the Holy Spirit, and called Emmanuel, "God with us," in fulfillment of prophecy (Matt. 1). They know that his purpose in coming was to "save his people from their sins" (1:21). Jesus is all the crowds said—and much more. God had indeed given this authority to men—not by simply delegating it to a particular mortal, but by sending his Son, virgin-born, to become Emmanuel.

So Jesus did not come simply to heal, or to reign, or to raise people from the dead. He came to forgive sin, and to transform sinners. The earlier connection (8:17) between healing and the atonement confirms that this sin-forgiving, sinner-transforming ministry was central to everything else that he did. The same point is spelled out in the next two segments of Matthew 9; and it is decisively confirmed by the obvious fact that the movement in all four Gospels is toward the cross and the empty tomb.

Before we press on to the next sections to learn how this thought is developed, however, it is worth pausing to reflect how *radical* Jesus' approach really is. During the "radical sixties," when Western universities were aflame with many groups of "radicals" (most of whom have now become yuppies!) telling the world how to sort out all its problems, the president of one Canadian university dropped in from time to time on one or another of the discussion groups sponsored by these "radical" organizations. At one such meeting, the president, a devout Christian, listened carefully to the presentation and discussion; and to his surprise, at the end of the hour he was asked if he wanted to respond in any way. He replied affirmatively; then he rose, and said that he had hoped to hear some genuinely radical solutions, but was profoundly disappointed to hear nothing but tired old clichés.

That was a profoundly Christian evaluation. Truly *radical* solutions must go to the *radix*, the root of the problem. The sad fact is that as important as it is to attempt political and economic reforms, for example, they are at best temporary, frequently superficial, sometimes merely cosmetic. The Marxist revolution in China has doubtless succeeded in eliminating many of the immense disparities between the haves and the have-nots; but in the process, a new and totalitarian oligarchy has been formed that has been responsible for between twenty and fifty million deaths. No political or economic order can wipe out corruption: what is required is a moral transformation so that society at large judges corruption to be a hideous evil. Then there will only be isolated cases of the problem. Simplistic solutions are not radical; they are reductionistic. Those who advocate a return to nineteenth-century market freedom forget the robber barons, the thousands of immigrants who died building railroads across America, the starvation wages and abysmal conditions in British mines. Marxist theorists, on the other hand, trying to explain the human condition in purely economic terms, keep predicting that once revolutionary man has done his destructive work, the "new" man of Marxist theory will emerge. He hasn't shown up yet, and he never will; for the theory is wrong. What is at the heart of the human tragedy is not economic injustice but sin. Economic injustice is merely a symptom; and both capitalists and Marxists focus on symptoms and never get near the *radix* at all.

But Jesus does. He is the purest radical. He came to forgive sin, and transform sinners. Where he does his work in abundance, there society is largely transformed.[2] If the next generation, or the one after that, forgets him and knows little of his grace, Christ's people will be reminded of their dependence on him, and recognize afresh that the ultimate solution draws near only when Jesus returns and deals with sin and sinners decisively and finally. Until then the most radical transformations in society take place where Jesus does his pardoning and transforming work.

Jesus came to forgive sin and transform sinners; and this was foundational to the rest of his ministry. That is why Christians, who have begun to appreciate the immense liberty in experiencing God's pardon, sing lustily:

Great God of wonders! all thy ways
Are worthy of thyself, divine;
And the bright glories of thy grace
Among thine other wonders shine:
  Who is a pardoning God like thee?
  Or who has grace so rich and free?

Pardon from an offended God!
Pardon for sins of deepest dye!
Pardon bestowed through Jesus' blood!
Pardon that brings the rebel nigh!
  Who is a pardoning God like thee?
  Or who has grace so rich and free?

O may this glorious, matchless love,
This God-like miracle of grace,
Teach mortal tongues, like those above,
To raise this song of lofty praise:
  Who is a pardoning God like thee?
  Or who has grace so rich and free?

Samuel Davies (1723–1761)

2. Jesus' central ministry, the forgiveness of sin, meant that he came to call the despised and disgusting elements of society (9:9–13). The first event in this section is the call of Matthew. The "tax collector's booth" at which he sat was probably a customs and excise booth at the border between the territories of Herod Antipas and Philip, not far from Capernaum. Tax collectors were not held in high esteem. The tax-farming system meant corruption was widespread; and to many politically conservative Jews, tax collectors were almost traitors since they were serving the ends of the overlords, not the Jewish people themselves. Moreover the higher echelons of Jewish tax collectors would necessarily have dealings with their Gentile superiors, and this would almost certainly put them in situations where they would be contaminated by ceremonial uncleanness. But Jesus called Matthew to follow him; and Matthew obeyed. It has been pointed out, rightly, that Matthew's post meant he had to be fluent in Aramaic and Greek, and accustomed to keeping accurate records—characteristics that later stood him in good stead when, so far as we can tell from the external evidence, he kept notes on Jesus' ministry and eventually penned this Gospel.

The focus of interest in this verse, however, is not on Matthew's scribal habits, but on the resulting dinner at which many tax collectors and "sinners" joined Matthew and Jesus. The quotation marks around the word *sinners* in the New International Version is a way of drawing attention to the fact that these people were sometimes so designated by the Pharisees and others, even when they were simply common folk who did not share all the Pharisees' ceremonial scruples. But the term also included other, more disreputable people—harlots, shysters, renegades on the outskirts of Jewish life. They are all lumped together in the mind of the Pharisees, who are deeply offended that Jesus and his disciples should actually be eating with them. Jesus and his followers could scarcely do so without risking ceremonial defilement; but just as bad, they were keeping company with the wrong sort of people. Can you not tell a person's character by the company he keeps? Isn't it true that if you live with garbage you will smell like garbage? Besides, when the Messiah comes, won't he side with the righteous and the good, build them up and promote them, and purify the land and nation of its disgusting elements?

Jesus' response brings us to the heart of the dispute between him and some of his chief opponents. "It is not the healthy who need a doctor, but the sick" (9:12), he says; and then he adds to his case by citing Scripture. The expression he uses to introduce the quotation, "go and learn," was a rabbinic formula used in a slightly sardonic way to administer a gentle rebuke to those who needed to go and study the text of Scripture further. Jesus' opponents, who prided themselves in their knowledge of Scripture and their own conformity to it, needed to "go and learn" what it meant.

The quotation itself is from Hosea 6:6: "I desire mercy, not sacrifice." In the context of Hosea's day, God was telling the religious leaders and nobles through his prophet that although they continued the temple ritual at full tilt they had lost the center and heart of their God-given religion. From God's perspective, they were apostate, despite their observance of religious formalities. They had forgotten that the God whom they claimed to serve was the compassionate God who had delivered them from Egypt, graciously given them the covenant at Sinai, disclosed himself to them in countless ways, provided a sacrificial system by which their sin might be atoned for, cared for them and disciplined them as they learned the lessons of obedience and gradually took possession of the Promised Land, and promised them a deliverer, a Messiah, who would bring to pass all of his rich promises to them. God in mercy had sought them, called them, and constituted them a nation. Now, Jesus says, he too has come with the same heart: "I have not come to call the righteous, but sinners" (9:13). What this means, of course, is that Jesus by quoting this passage is not simply saying that the Pharisees ought to be more compassionate, but that he aligns them with the apostates of ancient Israel. Like those whom the prophet Hosea condemned, Jesus' opponents have in his view preserved the shell and lost the core. Their attitude to tax collectors and "sinners" simply proves the case. This also means that when Jesus says "I have not come to call the righteous, but sinners," he is *not* suggesting that the Pharisees are genuinely righteous and without need of him. He is not dividing the world's population into righteous and unrighteous, and insisting he came only for the latter. After all, he has just lumped these "righteous" Pharisees with Israel's apostates! That Jesus does not think the righteousness of the Pharisees to be adequate is made clear elsewhere in this book, when Jesus insists that to enter the kingdom one must possess righteousness that *exceeds* that of the Pharisees and teachers of the law (Matt. 5:20).

The point of verse 13b is not to divide humanity into two groups, the righteous and the unrighteous, but to disavow one image of what the Messiah would be and do, and replace it with another. The saying gives us the essential nature of Jesus' messianic mission as he himself saw it. His mission was characterized by grace, by a pursuit of the lost. Contrary to the expectations of some of his opponents, he did not come to establish the righteous and destroy the sinners (as they established these categories), but (still using their categories) to win sinners. By implication, those who do not understand Jesus' mission as he himself does, and who therefore exclude themselves from the list of "sinners" because they see themselves as "righteous," can have no part in the messianic bounty Jesus is beginning to introduce.

In short, Jesus' central ministry, the forgiveness of sin, meant that he had to entangle himself with sinners. He came to call the despised and disgusting elements of society. When today those who promote themselves as righteous view religion through the prism of their self-justification, Jesus says in effect that he did not come for them. Their understanding of what the Christian religion is all about is so warped that the only way he can even begin to make them understand is to insist that he came for the very people whom they despise and find repugnant. Against the broader canvas of Jesus' thinking, however, including the powerful rebuke that links these self-righteous people with ancient apostates, what this means is that, if they but realized it, these "righteous" people are really nothing of the kind.

It turns out that the people who think they are *worthy* of Messiah's *attention* are no more worthy than the socially repulsive people whom they dismiss. And both kinds of people are in *need* of his *mercy,* even if they are not *worthy* of his *attention.* From this perspective, when we say that Jesus came to call the despised and disgusting elements in society, it turns out that no one is exempt. Christ came, as Calvin puts it, "to quicken the dead, to justify the guilty and condemned, to wash those who were polluted and full of wickedness, to rescue the lost from hell, to clothe with his glory those who were covered with shame, to renew to a blessed immortality those who were debased by disgusting vices." But then, is any of us exempt? And if we think we are, we face not only the conclusion that Christ did not come for us, but also the intense rebuke that aligns us with the apostates of old.

There are at least three practical lessons to be drawn from this passage.

First, Christians must learn profound gratitude for the salvation that has won them. Contrary to popular opinion, genuine Christians do not think of themselves as better than other people. Indeed, many converts discover, within a few short weeks of their conversion, that their hearts are more deceptive and sinful than they ever thought possible. That is a common aftermath of conversion: the euphoria (if there was any) gradually dissipates, to be replaced by a puzzling and growing sense of sin. The reason is obvious to more mature Christians: growing conformity to Jesus Christ, the powerful work of the Spirit within us, soon shows up the level of our self-centeredness. Attitudes and reactions we display that never troubled us in the past now appear as abominations. But there is an immense benefit. Our growing awareness of the magnitude of our sin can only result in growing thankfulness for the richness of the pardon we have received. When we are reminded that Jesus said, "I have not come to call the righteous, but sinners," far from being offended, we are relieved.

Second, Christians will also learn from Jesus' example. We will not develop a posture of supercilious self-righteousness toward those whom society dismisses; for we know that Jesus came to call the despised and disgusting elements of society. Not only so, we know that includes us; and as we get to know our own hearts better, we begin to realize that there is scarcely a sin we cannot conceive of committing ourselves, if only our circumstances, parents, upbringing, and the like had been different, if only we had not tasted the elixir of forgiveness from our pardoning God.

There is a story of a Christian woman who visited a condemned Nazi officer after Nuremburg. That officer had been responsible for the brutal deaths of her parents and siblings, and for her own torture. She had heard that he was deeply repentant; and when she approached him he wept and begged her for forgiveness. Her initial reaction was bristling rage: How dare he ask for forgiveness when his crimes were so heinous? Would his pathetic tears bring back her family? Was forgiveness so cheap?

And then she remembered that forgiveness is never cheap. If the grace of God could not extend to this Nazi officer, then it was insufficient for her; and she needed it as much as he. Because she had been forgiven, she also frankly forgave.

Christians can never afford to adopt haughty stances toward other sinners. They are never more than poor beggars telling others where there is bread.

Third, there is immense hope in this passage for the person who would like to follow Christ, but who does not feel good enough. The simple truth is that if you feel good enough for Jesus he does not want you. He came for the sick and the sinful, the broken and the needy. He invites sinners to him; and he forgives them and transforms them. He does so because he died and rose again *for sinners.* That is why the church sings:

> *Come, ye sinners, poor and needy,*
> *Weak and wounded, sick and sore;*
> *Jesus ready stands to save you,*
> *Full of pity, love, and power:*
> *He is able,*
> *He is willing; doubt no more.*

> *Now, ye needy, come and welcome;*
> *God's free bounty glorify:*
> *True belief and true repentance,*
> *Every grace that brings you nigh,*
> *Without money,*
> *Come to Jesus Christ and buy.*

> *Let not conscience make you linger,*
> *Nor of fitness fondly dream;*
> *All the fitness he requireth*
> *Is to feel your need of him:*

This he gives you—
'Tis the Spirit's rising beam.

Come, ye weary, heavy-laden,
Lost and ruined by the Fall;
If you wait until you're better,
You will never come at all;
Not the righteous—
Sinners Jesus came to call.

View him prostrate in the garden,
On the ground your Maker lies!
On the awful tree behold him,
Hear him cry before he dies.
It is finished!
Sinner, will not this suffice?

Lo, the incarnate God, ascended,
Pleads the merit of his blood;
Venture on him, venture wholly,
Let no other trust intrude:
None but Jesus
Can do helpless sinners good.

Joseph Hart (1712–1768)

And while the church sings this, the person who under the crush of guilt hungers for forgiveness and relief, hears that Jesus came for sinners and sings:

No, not despairingly
Come I to thee;
No, not distrustingly
Bend I the knee:
Sin hath gone over me,
Yet is this still my plea,
Jesus hath died.

Ah, mine iniquity
Crimson hath been,
Infinite, infinite,
Sin upon sin:
Sin of not loving thee,
Sin of not trusting thee,
Infinite sin.

Lord I confess to thee
Sadly my sin;

All I am tell I thee,
All I have been:
Purge thou my sin away,
Wash thou my soul this day;
Lord, make me clean.

Faithful and just art thou,
Forgiving all;
Loving and kind art thou
When poor ones call:
Lord, let the cleansing blood,
Blood of the Lamb of God,
Pass o'er my soul.

Then all is peace and light
This soul within;
Thus shall I walk with thee,
The loved Unseen;
Leaning on thee, my God,
Guided along the road,
Nothing between.

Horatius Bonar
(1808–1889)

3. As part of his effective dealing with sinners, Jesus came to set up a new structure that could embrace the profound reality he was introducing (9:14–17). Doubtless John the Baptist himself was free from petty jealousy when he saw how superficially popular Jesus and his ministry became. Unfortunately, there is ample evidence that not all of John's disciples were so large-hearted. Sometimes they complained to him (John 3:26–36); sometimes, as here, they approached Jesus himself and found fault with his ministry, making common cause with the Pharisees in the process. In one sense, it was easy for them to do so on this point; for their master, the Baptist himself, had clearly been an ascetic, so on matters of fasts the Baptist's disciples and the Pharisees enjoyed a more or less common perspective.

Jesus' answer is profoundly christological—that is, its validity depends entirely on who he himself is. "How can the guests of the bridegroom mourn while he is with them? The time will come when the bridegroom will be taken from them; then they will fast" (Matt. 9:15).

What kind of person can say, in effect, "Be happy; for I am here!"? I know of a little girl who, when she was about two and a half, went to visit a home for senior citizens that she and her mother had visited before. Remembering how happy many of these senior folk had been to see her the last time, she burst into the common room, flung wide her arms, and cried, "I'm here!" The extraordinary self-centeredness of a child is forgiven, even indulged, precisely because, ironically, it is so ingenuous. But an adult could not take the same approach, except perhaps on a slapstick comedy show. Yet here is Jesus adopting just such a stance.

In fact, the implicit christological claim is even stronger than it first appears, because of the metaphor of the bridegroom to which he appeals. According to the fourth Gospel, John the Baptist had applied the same metaphor to Jesus: John himself was the best man (to use modern terminology), while Jesus was the bridegroom (John 3:29). But the roots of the metaphor go back to the Old Testament. Commonly it is applied to God himself, in his relationship with his covenant people: "For your Maker is your husband—the LORD Almighty is his name—the Holy One of Israel is your Redeemer; he is called the God of all the earth" (Isa. 54:5; cf. 62:4–5; Hos. 2:16–20). Jews in Jesus' day sometimes applied the metaphor to the long-awaited Messiah; and the messianic banquet that marked the full coming of the messianic age was this bridegroom's wedding feast. That notion is picked up in the New Testament (e.g., Matt 22:2; 25:1; 2 Cor. 11:2; Eph. 5:23–32; Rev. 19:7, 9; 21:2). The language Jesus uses is cryptic enough that probably not even his closest disciples fully understood what he was talking about until after the resurrection; yet in fact he was claiming to be the Messiah, and that his presence marked the dawning of the messianic age. That, he says, is reason enough why his disciples should not fast.

There was another enigma built into his saying. Jesus says that the time will come when he will be taken away; and then it will be appropriate for his disciples to fast. Of course, this side of the cross and the resurrection, we understand what he meant, and we remember the tears that were shed by the early band of disciples until they found the tomb was empty and then touched and saw and ate with their Master. But at the time Jesus said these words, when no one around him, not even his most intimate followers, understood that though he was king of Israel yet his mission would take him to the cross, Jesus' saying recorded in this verse must have been almost incomprehensible. Just when even the opponents might suspect that Jesus was making a messianic claim, he spoke of being taken away, and causing his disciples grief. But would the genuine Messiah be taken away? Would the disciples of the genuine Messiah begin their experience with him in joy, and end it in sorrow? Like so many of Jesus' utterances, this one too was necessarily cast in somewhat veiled terms that would be fully explained only after the cross and resurrection had become history.

But if Jesus is the Messiah, what difference would it make so far as fasting and other Jewish religious practices are concerned? Verse 15 shows it ought to make a *personal* difference: that is, his very presence is cause for joy and a suspension of some religious practices of a mournful nature. But verses 16–17 show that in addition to these personal differences there will also be large *structural* differences introduced to the practice of religion. The lesson is spelled out in two parables, each a slice of life. The first takes place in the sewing room: "No one sews a patch of unshrunk cloth on an old garment, for the patch will pull away from the garment, making the tear worse" (Matt. 9:16). To repair a large rent in an old and well-shrunk cloth, it is necessary to use a patch that is similarly well-shrunk. The two parts must be compatible.

The second parable takes place in a wine cellar: "Neither do men pour new wine into old wineskins. If they do, the skins will burst, the wine will run out and the wineskins will be ruined. No, they pour new wine into new wineskins, and both are preserved" (9:17). Skin bottles for carrying various fluids were normally made by killing and skinning an animal, sewing up all orifices, fur side out, after tanning the skin with special care to reduce the possibility of disagreeable taste in the liquid to be stored. Eventually such a skin bottle became brittle. If new wine, still fermenting, were stored there, the fermentation gases could easily exert enough pressure to split the bottle. New wine was therefore placed in new wineskins, if at all possible, because they would still be pliable and somewhat elastic, and therefore less likely to split open.

What this means, of course, is that the new wine Jesus is introducing simply cannot be stored in the old wineskins of the structures of Judaism. The old structures could not stand the pressure. New structures would have to be used in conjunction with this new wine.

The dimensions of this claim are nothing less than astonishing. Here is someone who is proposing to overturn the prevailing structures of Jewish religion, on the ground that they are inadequate to contain the new revelation and the new situation he himself is introducing. The contents of the new revelation are not here spelled out; but they are not hard to deduce, partly from the rest of this Gospel, and partly from the way other New Testament writers have fleshed out the skeleton. Matthew's Gospel has already been at pains to show that Jesus and the kingdom he is introducing are the *fulfillment* of Old Testament expectations, promises, and structures. Elsewhere we are told that if Jeremiah promises a *new* covenant (Jer. 31:31ff.), we are driven to the conclusion that even some Old Testament writers recognized the principial obsolescence of the Mosaic covenant (Heb. 8:13). If the Psalms promise a new priest who does not spring from the tribe of Levi, but who is a messianic figure serving in the order of Melchizedek (Ps. 110:4), then necessarily there is envisaged an overthrow of the Mosaic legislation as it then stood; for the Levitical priesthood is so interwoven with that legislation, its tabernacle (later temple) rites, its sacrificial system and feasts, that a new priesthood unavoidably means a new covenant (Heb. 7). Paul insists that in any case the gospel he preaches is in direct line with and fulfillment of the covenant with Abraham, a covenant that was not overturned when the Mosaic law was introduced centuries later. The Mosaic covenant was in certain respects a training period until the promised Redeemer arrived (Rom. 4: Gal. 3). Acts 2 insists that Pentecost is the fulfillment of Joel's prophecies about the universal distribution of the Spirit; and this expectation, both in Joel and elsewhere (e.g., Ezekiel 36), marks the end of the tribal, representative nature of the old covenant, and the beginning of a new age and arrangement between God and his people. Jesus himself elsewhere insists that the time was at hand when the focal point for worship would no longer be Jerusalem (John 4); and if not Jerusalem, then not the temple; and if not the temple, then not the sacrificial system. Without the sacrificial system, the Mosaic covenant is necessarily transmuted into something unrecognizable. Indeed, Jesus insists that *he* is the temple, the new and real meeting place between God and man (John 2:19–22; cf. Matt. 26:61).

Now of course little of this is spelled out in detail in Matthew; still, the careful reader cannot help but spot adumbrations of this structure even within the teaching of Jesus. When he instituted what we call the Lord's Supper he spoke of the blood of the new covenant. He repeatedly claimed, sometimes with greater and sometimes with lesser clarity (largely dependent on the circumstances in which he found himself), to be the promised Son of man, the predicted Messiah, the fulfillment of prophetic hopes and expectations. And though he himself was born under the written law and took pains to obey it, he not infrequently spoke in ways that anticipated its obsolescence.

In short, the verses before us (Matt. 9:14–17) insist that Jesus came to bring revelation and introduce a situation so new that the very structures of antecedent revealed religion would change. It will not do to suggest, as some have done, that because Jesus says, at the end of this parable, that "both are preserved" that he envisages the legitimate preservation of *both* Judaism *and* the new religious structures he is introducing. For in the categories of the parable, the "both" that are preserved are not the *old* wineskins and the *new* wine, but the *new* wineskins containing the *new* wine. In other words, Jesus envisages the preservation of the new revelation that he himself was introducing, and the new structures, the new forms of religious expression, the new covenantal relationships, that would embrace it.

Jesus is not simply another Abraham or Moses, another Elijah or Jeremiah. All of biblical revelation comes to its focus in him. Nor is this a conclusion of the later church, foisted back on him—a theological conclusion of which he was blissfully unaware. Far from it: in the Gospels he operates out of a profound self-awareness that understood his own authority to be nothing less than divine, that understood his own mission to be the culmination of centuries of revelatory preparation. This is the authentic Jesus; unless we see him in this light, and obey him and worship him as he is presented to us in Scripture, we shall be guilty of manufacturing a false Jesus, a Jesus with different goals and purposes from the ones the authentic Jesus actually held and exemplified.

Conclusion

What was Jesus' mission? Why did he come? He came to save his people from their sin; he came to transform sinners. He did not come to call the righteous, but sinners. And this mission required the establishment of new forms of religious expression, changes to the existing covenantal structure between God and his people, to accommodate the new reality being introduced. No longer would priests offer daily, weekly, monthly, and yearly sacrifices that covered sin over; now one sacrifice would deal finally and effectively with sin. No longer would the meeting place between God and man be localized in a temple in Jerusalem; now it would be "localized" in the person of God's Son. No longer would the Spirit be poured out only on the leaders of the covenant community; now all the heirs of the new covenant would know the Spirit's work for themselves. And if the final fruition of Jesus' mission must await his return, then at least we may rejoice that the principial dealing with sin has already taken place in Jesus' initial mission—even if the consummation of his work awaits his return.

Suppose you heard of a medical doctor who discovered an infallible cure for cancer. Would you not want to bring to him anyone you knew who was suffering from this dreaded disease? Suppose, further, that he could heal Alzheimer's disease, reverse all cardiopulmonary disease, and eliminate dependence on alcohol. Suppose in addition he were a brilliant economist who, quite demonstrably, advanced solutions that removed tensions between the haves and the have-nots, but did so in such an equitable way that all sides were pleased. Suppose, further, that he was so politically astute and forceful that he advanced satisfactory solutions to the most intractable problems: Northern Ireland, Afghanistan, the Middle East. Would you not think the world would beat a path to his door?

But quite apart from the fact that many would not want his solutions if they adversely impinged on their own selfish desires, we must conclude that this mythical person cannot hold a candle to Jesus and all that he provides. For Jesus is eventually going to do all these things anyway. He will one day introduce a new heaven and a new earth, where there will be no more disease, no more war or injustice. But he will do so *because he has already dealt foundationally with the root problem, the problem of sin.* That is why the various attempts to domesticate Jesus by redefining his mission in order to swing the weight of the church behind some contemporary cause are so pathetic. The resulting Jesus is not authentic, merely an idol. The resulting solutions are not stable, but at best temporary and at worst ephemeral. The resulting religion is without power to transform, but is merely formal. And the resulting expectations are invariably dashed.

Not so the real Jesus. He came to forgive sin and transform sinners; he founded the church as the ongoing display of his covenant people and the agent to proclaim his truth and manifest his power; and he comes again to bring his sin-cleansing, life-transforming work to completion. That is God's plan; that is the mission of Jesus.

Blessed be God, our God!
Who gave for us his well-beloved Son,

The gift of gifts, all other gifts in one—
Blessed be God, our God!

What will he not bestow,
Who freely gave this mighty gift unbought,
Unmerited, unheeded, and unsought—
What will he not bestow?

He spared not his Son!
'Tis this that silences each rising fear;
'Tis this that bids the hard thought disappear—
He spared not his Son!

Who shall condemn us now?
Since Christ has died, and risen, and gone above,
For us to plead at the right hand of love,
Who shall condemn us now?

'Tis God that justifies!
Who shall recall the pardon of the grace,
Or who the broken chain of guilt replace?
'Tis God that justifies!

The victory is ours!
For us in might came forth the Mighty One;
For us he fought the fight, the triumph won—
The victory is ours!

Horatius Bonar (1808–1889)

---

[1]The sequence of events in Matthew 9 is rather different from that in the parallels. I have discussed these relations at some length in my commentary on Matthew (in *The Expositor's Bible Commentary*, edited by Frank Gaebelein, vol. 8 [Grand Rapids: Zondervan, 1984]), pp. 220ff., and will not raise such matters here.

[2]I shall not here discuss the view, common in some quarters, that it is possible to know Christ's pardon without displaying any evidence of its effect in one's life. This contemporary return to pagan perspectives, adopted in the name of defending grace and Christian assurance, understands neither grace nor assurance.

10

The Trustworthiness of Jesus

(9:18–34)

¹⁸While he was saying this, a ruler came and knelt before him and said, "My daughter has just died. But come and put your hand on her, and she will live." 19Jesus got up and went with him, and so did his disciples.

²⁰Just then a woman who had been subject to bleeding for twelve years came up behind him and touched the edge of his cloak.

²¹She said to herself, "If I only touch his cloak, I will be healed."

²²Jesus turned and saw her. "Take heart, daughter," he said, "your faith has healed you." And the woman was healed from that moment.

²³When Jesus entered the ruler's house and saw the flute players and the noisy crowd, ²⁴he said, "Go away. The girl is not dead but asleep." But they laughed at him.

²⁵After the crowd had been put outside, he went in and took the girl by the hand, and she got up.

²⁶News of this spread through all that region.

²⁷As Jesus went on from there, two blind men followed him, calling out, "Have mercy on us, Son of David!"

²⁸When he had gone indoors, the blind men came to him, and he asked them, "Do you believe that I am able to do this?"

"Yes, Lord," they replied.

²⁹Then he touched their eyes and said, "According to your faith will it be done to you"; ³⁰and their sight was restored. Jesus warned them sternly, "See that no one knows about this."

[31]But they went out and spread the news about him all over that region.
[32]While they were going out, a man who was demon-possessed and could not talk was brought to Jesus.
[33]And when the demon was driven out, the man who had been mute spoke. The crowd was amazed and said, "Nothing like this has ever been seen in Israel."
[34]But the Pharisees said, "It is by the prince of demons that he drives out demons."

Introduction

Like many parents with young children, we read quite a lot to our two. *What* we read varies from the sublime to the ridiculous, or at least to the humorous. Standing rather closer to the latter side than to the former is a little book called *Alexander and the Terrible, Horrible, No Good, Very Bad Day.*[1] I cannot hope to convey the marvelous pictures to you; but let me cite a few paragraphs:

> I went to sleep with gum in my mouth and now there's gum in my hair and when I got out of bed this morning I tripped on the skateboard and by mistake I dropped my sweater in the sink while the water was running and I could tell it was going to be a terrible, horrible, no good, very bad day.

> At breakfast Anthony found a Corvette Sting Ray car kit in his breakfast cereal box and Nick found a Junior Undercover Agent code ring in his breakfast cereal box but in my breakfast cereal box all I found was breakfast cereal.

> I think I'll move to Australia.

> In the car pool Mrs. Gibson let Becky have a seat by the window. Audrey and Elliott got seats by the window too. I said I was being scrunched. I said I was being smushed. I said, if I don't get a seat by the window I am going to be carsick. No one even answered.

> I could tell it was going to be a terrible, horrible, no good, very bad day.

> At school Mrs. Dickens liked Paul's picture of the sailboat better than my picture of the invisible castle.

At singing time she said I sang too loud. At counting time she said
I left out sixteen. Who needs sixteen?

I could tell it was going to be a terrible, horrible, no good, very
bad day.

I could tell because Paul said I wasn't his best friend anymore.
He said that Philip Parker was his best friend and that Albert
Moyo was his next best friend and that I was only his third best
friend.

I hope you sit on a tack, I said to Paul. I hope the next time you
get a double-decker strawberry ice-cream cone the ice cream part
falls off the cone part and lands in Australia.

There is much more along this vein. I shall not spoil the book for
you by telling you how it turns out. Certainly Alexander was learning, among the myriads of life's little tragedies, that friends are frequently fickle. School alignments shift and shift again. Especially
when people move around are old alliances broken and new ones
formed. The other day I was trying to think of one person with whom
I was reasonably close when I was an undergraduate at McGill University, who is still a close friend today. I could not think of one. The
person with whom I was closest preceded me to seminary. We often
prayed together, and worked at evangelism and Bible studies together.
But in time our ways parted. He subsequently apostasized, and then
later tragically committed suicide.

Often enough in the business arena the same dislocation of friendship occurs. Perhaps a friend is promoted, and suddenly becomes
supercilious, condescending, or aloof. Even marriage, a God-ordained
institution that ought to generate the most marvelous intimacy, sometimes turns friends into acquaintances, acquaintances into enemies.
Friends are not always trustworthy.

Indeed, this question of trustworthiness is not tied exclusively to
friendship. How often do we idolize someone, raise him to the pro-
portions of majestic statuary, only to discover the statue has clay
feet. We marvel at our idol's integrity and candor, and then discover
he cheats on his income tax. We praise his courtesy and charm, and
find out he is abusive to his wife. We admire her beauty, mature
restraint, and competence, only to learn she is making a cuckold of
her husband.

Even in the best of circumstances, we are likely to be disappointed. Long-time and cherished friends and spouses can still cause hurt. Indeed, part of maturity as a human being is learning how to accept human frailty.

And then suddenly, with chagrin, we recognize that human frailty begins with *us;* we remember with shame the many people whom *we* have disappointed or otherwise hurt. And we wonder if genuine trustworthiness can be predicated of anyone.

But Christians rightly sing:

> *One there is above all others,*
> *Well deserves the name of Friend;*
> *His is love beyond a brother's,*
> *Costly, free, and knows no end:*
> *They who once his kindness prove,*
> *Find it everlasting love.*

John Newton (1725–1807)

In our study of Matthew 8–10, we have been considering what happens when Jesus confronts the world. I want to suggest to you now that one of the things that stands out whenever this confrontation occurs is the sheer trustworthiness of Jesus.

This is not what happens in many other confrontations. Too often both sides sacrifice their integrity on the altar of victory. Political manipulation becomes more important than honesty; it is not only in war that truth is the first victim. In academic confrontation, a thesis may be followed by antithesis, which is then followed by personal abuse. Teenagers in a family start a squabble, and pretty soon each side is looking around for weapons that will really hurt. He yells, "Pimple face!" and she yells back, "Fatty!"

But there is in Jesus a center, an integrity, a fidelity that makes him utterly trustworthy. I shall sketch in:

Four Facets of Jesus' Profound Trustworthiness

1. Jesus is trustworthy with respect to the purposes for which he came. After all, one cannot be trustworthy in the abstract. One must be trustworthy with respect to an assignment, a mission, a responsibility, an obligation. Jesus is trustworthy, then, with respect to the purposes for which he came, the mission that we surveyed in the last chapter.

The point is made by several features in Matthew's presentation of Jesus' miracles. The sequence of miracles in chapters 8–9 is, of course, topically arranged, as is clear by comparing the parallel reports in the other synoptic Gospels. Together, as we have seen, they underline several important themes, including the authority of Jesus and the mission of Jesus. But the last three miracles reported in these chapters, the ones we shall now look at more closely, bear their own special importance. The first is a miracle of resurrection from the dead (9:18–19, 23–26), to which the healing of the woman with the hemorrhage is attached (9:20–22); the second is the healing of the blind men (9:27–31); and the third is the exorcism and consequent healing of the mute (9:32–34). But these three kinds of miracles—raising the dead, healing the blind, and making the dumb speak—are specifically taken up just a couple of chapters later. There, John the Baptist, languishing in prison and troubled that Jesus is not taking strong action to bring about justice in the land, sends envoys to Jesus to ask him if he is the one who was to come, or if they should expect someone else (11:2). Jesus replies with words evocative of Isaiah 35:5–6 and 61:1, but referring specifically to the miracles he has already performed: "Go back and report to John what you hear and see: The blind receive sight, the lame walk, those who have leprosy are cured, the deaf hear, the dead are raised, and the good news is preached to the poor. Blessed is the man who does not fall away on account of me" (Matt. 11:4–6).

Clearly, then, the miracles of Matthew 8–9, and not least these last three, have prepared the way for Jesus' response. In a sense, therefore, they supply us with some of Jesus' messianic credentials. He performs them, and they are recorded, to demonstrate that Jesus is indeed the one predicted by Old Testament prophets. Jesus must prove trustworthy in meeting the strictures of that role.

This same rather simple but no less important point is made by the way Matthew condenses the account of the healing of the ruler's daughter (Matt. 9:18–19, 23–26). If we compare the parallel account in Mark 5:21–24, 35–43, we discover far more details. The ruler was a synagogue ruler by the name of Jairus. There were crowds of people all around; and when Jairus first approached Jesus, his daughter had not yet died. A little farther on, after the healing of the woman with the hemorrhage, some men came from Jairus's house with the news the girl was dead. We are provided with an exact list of which persons were permitted to accompany Jesus to the dead girl's side and witness the miracle. Jesus' exact words in Aramaic are preserved. But little of this is found in Matthew, who eliminates the details of little interest to the principal point he wishes to make. Even with respect to the little girl's death, Matthew condenses, as one author puts it, "so as to present at the outset what was actually true before Jesus reached the house"—a standard of reportage common enough in the Gospels. But Matthew preserves the details about the mourners, since they serve as witnesses that the girl is in fact dead. In that culture, even a poor family was expected to provide a couple of flute players and at least one professional wailing woman to set the right tone for the loud lamentations that testified to the passing of the dearly beloved. The synagogue ruler's daughter, clearly, was dead—in fact, so clearly was she dead that the crowd laughed at Jesus when he seemed to suggest otherwise (9:24).

With this clean, stripped-down account of the miracle, then, there is not much left except the miracle itself—which of course is one way of focusing attention on that miracle. Jesus as the Messiah is doing what some Old Testament prophets said the Messiah would do.

The same emphasis is almost certainly bound up with the "Son of David" title used by the blind men when they called out to Jesus for help: "Have mercy on us, Son of David!" (9:27). That title is used by Matthew in the very first verse of this Gospel: Matthew begins with a record of the genealogy of "Jesus Christ *the son of David,* the son of Abraham" (1:1; emphasis added)—clearly a messianic title. But many of the occurrences of the title throughout the book are bound up with healings and exorcisms. In addition to the one here in Matthew 9, we find a substantial list. The Canaanite woman cries to Jesus, "Lord, Son of David, have mercy on me! My daughter is suffering terribly from demon-possession" (15:22). In 20:30, we read of two more blind men crying, "Lord, Son of David, have mercy on us!" Other occurrences are no less clearly messianic. In Matthew 21, the children cry in exuberant praise, "Hosanna to the Son of David!" (21:9, 15); and in 22:41–46, in a discussion with the Pharisees over the meaning of Psalm 110, Jesus clearly presupposes that the Messiah is both the Son of David and David's Lord.

In all of these instances, then, the people who were addressing Jesus in this way were petitioning him *as the Messiah.* The blind men in the chapter before us, for instance, may not have had a very nuanced theological understanding of the Old Testament; but their

need drove them to confessions that might not have been attempted
if they were both whole and sophisticated. Perhaps they reasoned like
this: We have heard of the wonderful healings this man from Nazareth
has performed. Perhaps he is indeed the Messiah. Do not the Scriptures look forward to a time when the eyes of the blind will be opened
and the ears of the deaf unstopped (Isa. 35:5)? What have we got to
lose by asking him for help? If he ignores us, we shall not be worse
off than we already are. If he hears us and heals us—ah, then we shall
have our heart's desire!

And so their desperation drove them, as the exuberance of the children in Matthew 21 drove *them*, to appeal to Jesus as the Son of David.
Though blind, they "saw" better than some who could see only with
their eyes. Need and desperation, like poverty of spirit (Matt. 5:3), are
often the first steps in the pathway of faith.

That is the sort of reasoning that the blind men probably adopted;
but Matthew himself is less interested in their psychology than in the
christological confession itself. His point is simple: these blind men
rightly addressed Jesus as the Son of David, the Son of David introduced in the very first verse of this book; and Jesus then performed
the miracle that confirmed the attestation. Just as the healing of the
paralytic confirmed that Jesus has authority to forgive sins (9:1–8),
so here the healing of the two blind men confirms that Jesus is the
promised Son of David, the Messiah, who brings with him the blessings of the kingdom. Jesus is faithful to discharge all the functions
that are bound up with his mission. Failure to do so would mean he
was untrustworthy in the mission for which he was sent. And that is
Matthew's elementary and repeated point.

That simple truth—that Jesus truly is the promised Messiah, and
is utterly trustworthy in discharging all that is bound up with that
mission—should be a marvelous encouragement to believers today.
If he came to save his people from their sin (1:21), will he not do so?
If his purpose as the Messiah is to bring in the blessings of the consummated kingdom, will he not achieve it? If even now his mission
is to give foretastes of what it will be like when both sin and the effects
of sin are removed by his life-transforming authority, shall we not
witness such foretastes ourselves? He is utterly trustworthy in meeting the purposes for which he came; and those purposes are bound
up with the good of his people.

2. Jesus is trustworthy even in the face of scorn and slander.
On the face of it, this is a rather easy and obvious point; but it is one
with some important ramifications for us.

The scorn is found in the laughter of the crowds when Jesus tells them, "Go away. The girl is not dead but asleep" (9:24). Doubtless they thought the great healer had come too late. Intoxicated by his success, he would try out his skills on a corpse, and make a fool of himself. In fact, Jesus' words are very important; and even if they were not well understood at the time, they became much clearer after his own resurrection. "Sleep" is not infrequently a euphemism for death (Dan. 12:2; John 11:11; Acts 7:60; 1 Cor. 15:6, 18; 1 Thess. 4:13–15; see also 2 Peter 3:4); but since sleep is here *contrasted* with death, something more must be meant. If "sleep" in this context is precisely the equivalent of death, then Jesus' statement reduces to something like, "Go away. The girl is not dead but dead." Nor will it do to suppose that Jesus was referring merely to the physical reality: everyone else had thought she was dead, but they were wrong, for in reality she was, quite literally, only asleep. If that were all that was meant, this miracle would hardly have been special, and Jesus would have been ill placed to list, among his credentials, that "the dead are raised" (11:5).

The least that Jesus meant by this contrast between sleep and death was that in this instance the real death of the girl was not as final as the mourners thought. In his presence, before his authority, death itself must flee. Death is reduced to not much more than sleep. Implicitly there may also have been a criticism of the Sadducean view that said there was no resurrection (cf. 22:23). In any case, Jesus' statement can be understood only if we see that he is less interested in making a medical diagnosis than in making a christological claim. When Jesus confronts our last, great enemy, death itself, death is the loser. It is stripped of its power and reduced to sleep.

Like many of Jesus' utterances, this one was guarded, even mysterious, in its initial context. The mourners exhibited neither the spiritual discernment nor the emotional sympathy that might have pierced through to Jesus' meaning. What it earned him at the time was scorn. Yet this does not deter him from his course. Another might have withdrawn in a huff, offended by the coarse rejection, and unwilling to serve in a context of such skepticism; but not Jesus. Indeed, part of his mission *was to be rejected!* Even his perseverance under attack becomes a microcosm of the suffering of the cross that lay ahead.

Something similar must be deduced from the slanderous attacks recorded at the end of this section of Scripture. After Jesus had driven the demon out of the mute, the "crowd was amazed and said, 'Nothing like this has ever been seen in Israel'" (9:33). Unfortunately, there was another opinion: "the Pharisees said, 'It is by the prince of demons that he drives out demons'" (9:34). In short, their official view was that if Jesus could control demons, he was in cahoots with them.

From the point of view of the Pharisees, this was a comforting explanation. The claims of Jesus could then be dismissed; even the evidence of the wonderful works he performed could be ruled out. Satan himself might be prepared to suffer a few tactical losses for a greater strategic end. Doubtless that was why the same criticism was leveled against Jesus again and again. In chapter 12, for instance, when some are asking if Jesus could indeed be the Son of David (12:23), the Pharisees argue: "It is only by Beelzebub [one of the names given to Satan], the prince of demons, that this fellow drives out demons" (12:24). Jesus' answer, in part, is that Satan can hardly afford to continue in this vein; for he would in fact be destroying his kingdom, his household. And in any case, Jesus puts the alternative explanation of his miraculous power in straightforward terms: "if I drive out demons by the Spirit of God, then the kingdom of God has come upon you" (12:28). His point is that if the Pharisees' dismissive charge does not stand up, there is really only one alternative; and that alternative entails the conclusion that the promised kingdom of God has dawned. It has arrived and is operating among the people. It "has come upon you."

Thus Jesus' opponents sometimes directly misrepresented his motives and maligned his miracles. He came from the Father; they said he came from the devil. His authority was God's; they said it was demonic. He came in fulfillment of Scripture; they believed he was perverting Scripture. For most of us, it is very hard to persevere with calm integrity when we are so thoroughly misunderstood, so systematically slandered. However, Jesus not only proved trustworthy in the face of scorn and slander, but also did so precisely because it was part of his mission to do so. The movement is toward the cross.

What we must recognize, however, is that this pattern of behavior is not to be dismissed as relevant only in the case of Jesus, but is something we too are called to emulate. It is to this very slander—that Jesus was the agent of the prince of demons—that he refers in 10:24–25: "A student is not above his teacher, nor a servant above his master. It is enough for the student to be like his teacher, and the servant like his master. If the head of the house has been called Beelzebub, how much more the members of his household!"

The point, of course, is that as followers of Jesus we cannot expect to be treated better than he was. It would be unreasonable to think otherwise. If the world judges us narrow, bigoted, or mad, that is only to be expected. At least the world does not usually accuse us of being in cahoots with the devil! Part of our growing trustworthiness as Christians will be reflected in our ability to handle opposition, scorn, and slander in the same way that Jesus did.

3. Jesus is trustworthy, whether the faith of others to apprehend him be great or small—provided only that it issues from need and is focused on him. Doubtless this point needs explaining; but once understood it becomes an immensely stabilizing factor in a Christian's faith.

We may begin by observing that faith has already played a fairly important role in these three chapters. The centurion (8:5–13) displayed *great* faith. He understood, as we saw in the first chapter, that Jesus stood between God and man in much the same way that a centurion stood between Rome and the common foot soldier. Because of the chain of authority in both cases, when the centurion spoke, Rome spoke; and when Jesus spoke, God spoke. The analogy may not have been perfect; but the centurion had penetrated deeply into the nature of Jesus' authority, so much so that Jesus himself was surprised by the greatness of the man's faith.

On the other hand, in 8:25–26 we saw an example of poor faith, bankrupt faith. Here the disciples cry in desperation as the ferocious storm threatens to capsize their boat; and they are so undiscerning that they can actually entertain the supposition that Jesus the Messiah might die in a squall. Surely if their faith had penetrated, even a little, to who he really was, they would have recognized how impossible it was for the Lord from heaven to have his mission destroyed by a freak boating accident! Their faith was very poor. Yet even so, Jesus performed the miracle that calmed their fears.

When we turn to the passage before us, we find two more references to faith; and in both instances faith is portrayed in a somewhat novel guise. In the first (9:20–22), we encounter the woman with the hemorrhage. Once again Matthew strips the story down to its essentials. The seriousness of the woman's condition is briefly noted: she has suffered for twelve long years. If the bleeding was from her womb, then according to Jewish law she would have been considered unclean for that entire period. Strictly speaking, she should not have been in this crowd, where she could be contaminating many others; and most certainly she should not have been touching Jesus. Her faith is min-

gled with superstition: she thinks touching a piece of cloth can heal
her. She is like the people in Acts 5 who think that they will receive
some special blessing or miraculous help if only Peter's shadow could
pass over them.

Mingled with superstition or not, her faith is honored, and she is
healed. Indeed, Jesus draws attention to her faith: "Take heart, daughter," he says, "your faith has healed you."

Finally, in the healing of the two blind men (9:27–31), Jesus asks
the men if they really *believe* he is able to meet their request (9:28):
presumably this is a device to increase and focus their faith. When
they reply in the affirmative, Jesus says, "According to your faith will
it be done to you" (9:29); and their vision is restored. This cannot
mean that the miracle would be executed *in proportion* to their faith—
as if Jesus were saying, "So much faith, so much sight; 50 percent
faith, 50 percent sight. Believe wholly and 20/20 vision will be restored
to you." The "according to" language does not deal with proportion-
ality here, but with factuality: in line with your faith, which believes
I can restore your sight, let your sight be restored.

The diversity of these exhibitions of faith drives us to an important conclusion. In one sense, it is not faith that heals, that saves, that
transforms. It is Jesus who does that. He is the one who has the authority; he is the one who is inaugurating the kingdom. The faith is effective only as a *means* is effective. In that sense, Jesus rightly says to
the hemorrhaging woman that her faith has healed her. But he does
not mean that it is faith in and of itself, irrespective of faith's object.
The faith that saves is the faith whose object is Jesus; and in reality
it is Jesus who saves.

Now it is clear why the different degrees and kinds of faith mentioned in these chapters prove effective. Whether it is the great faith
of the centurion, or the bankrupt faith of the disciples, or the super-
stitious faith of the hemorrhaging woman, or the hopeful messianic
faith of the two blind men—in each case the faith *is directed toward
Jesus, and is an expression of need.* Such faith is necessary to apprehend the blessings Jesus brings; at the end of the day, it is not so
much the strength or purity of the faith that is at stake, but whether
or not faith issues from self-acknowledged need, and is directed to
the one who has the power to meet that need, the Lord Jesus Christ
himself.

After all, there is little virtue in faith in the abstract. If my faith
has as its object Krishna, or the sacred mushroom, or Marxist hope
for a better world completely free of struggle and injustice, then by

all biblical evidence my faith is worthless. It may have some power to drive my life in a unified direction and give it some kind of sub-jective meaning; but because its object, in the light of biblical rev-elation, is unworthy of such faith, the faith itself is not commend-able. Faith must be founded on fact: the truthfulness of the revelation of Jesus Christ is everywhere presupposed. Elsewhere, when the Corinthians seem to be calling in question the resurrec-tion of Jesus Christ, Paul goes so far as to say that if they are right then our Christian faith is futile (1 Cor. 15:17). He will not acknowl-edge as valid that faith whose object is not real, true, and in con-formity with the revelation that Jesus Christ is and brings. On the other hand, as James 2:19 points out, if faith has a proper object but is merely credal, then the devils themselves can be said to believe—but with no benefit to them. Faith not only must have a proper object, but also must issue from need and be characterized by genuine trust and obedience.

Faith in some merely abstract sense, then, is not presented in Scrip-ture as an unqualified virtue, any more than sincerity is. Doubtless sincerity is better than insincerity; but one may be simultaneously sincere and entirely mistaken. There is no reason to doubt the sin-cerity or the faith of the prophets of Baal who opposed Elijah, crying out and cutting themselves to win their god's attention.

The real virtue, then, is not in faith itself so much as in that which faith rightly apprehends. That is why the varieties of faith displayed in the chapters before us all produce fruit: at least they have this in common, that they issue from need and turn to Jesus for help. And Jesus, the object of faith, provides the help. That in turn means the crucial element is not the strength of our own faith, *but the trust-worthiness of Jesus*. To reiterate the main point: Jesus is trustworthy, whether the faith of others to apprehend him be great or small—pro-vided only that it issues from need and is focused on him.

An example from the Old Testament will clarify the point. It is the night of the first Passover. Mr. Smith and Mr. Jones, two Israelites who have observed the succession of plagues that have befallen Egypt and sometimes spilled over into the land of Goshen where most of the Israelites lived, are having a conversation over the back fence.

Mr. Jones confesses his deep worries over the coming night: "Of course I'm concerned. Shouldn't I be? God has sent waves of plagues: flies, frogs, darkness, water turning to blood. But this latest announce-

ment is frankly terrifying. The loss of the firstborn in every household in Egypt! The nation will be shattered."

"But haven't you done what Moses said, and daubed the side posts
and lintel with blood from the paschal lamb?"

"Of course. I'm an Israelite, just like you. But a bloodstain or two
seems a strangely weak way to stop the ravages of the angel of death.
I'm terrified for my son, and I don't know what else I can do to ensure
his safety."

Mr. Smith sighs. "You've done all you need to, all you can do. You
know that I've got a son, too, and I'm perfectly confident that he is
safe. God has promised through Moses that in households where the
blood has been applied as stipulated, the firstborn male will be safe.
Don't you think God will keep his word? Where is your faith?"

When Mr. Jones replies, he is hesitant and troubled. "Please don't
give me moralizing sermons about faith. I'm scared, and that's all
there is to it. I've sprinkled blood around, just as God said; but I'm
frightened for my son, and I wish I could do something to guarantee
his safety."

That night the angel of death passed through the land. In most
houses there was loud weeping and wailing, as the firstborn males
died in huge numbers throughout the land. Now the question is this:
Which man, Mr. Smith or Mr. Jones, lost his firstborn son?

The answer, of course, is: Neither. Mr. Smith had great faith; Mr.
Jones displayed rather anemic faith. But both had shown enough
faith to daub the blood on the door posts and lintel. Beyond that, the
outcome depended utterly on the reliability of the promises of God.

Something very similar is portrayed in the Gospels, and especially
in these three chapters. We do not wrench blessings from Jesus by
somehow increasing the intensity of our faith. Granted we have any
genuine faith at all, what is far more important is the faithfulness of
Jesus. And ironically, when we focus on that we find our own faith
strengthened as we come more greatly to appreciate the one on whom
our faith rests.

**4. Jesus is trustworthy, even when some seek to sidetrack his
mission.** There were always enough people around who, wittingly or
unwittingly, were trying to sidetrack that mission.

In Matthew 8:4, Jesus enjoined silence on the man he cured of his
leprosy. With miracles as spectacular as this, it was not always possible to keep things quiet. News of the raising of Jairus's daughter,
we are told, "spread through all that region" (9:26). Perhaps it was

because of his spreading fame as a miracle-worker that Jesus refrained from dealing with the two blind men until they were all indoors (9:28), away from the fervent enthusiasm of the crowd. Reports of privately performed miracles would of course leak out; but such reports were less likely to excite uncontrolled enthusiasm than those done in full view of a large and expectant audience—in much the same way that reports of a favorite rock group will prove less exciting to a vast crowd of teenagers than a performance by the gyrating pop stars themselves. Concern that he *not* be perceived as simply another miracle-worker, concern that his messiahship *not* be reduced to many of the popular expectations of the day, was doubtless the primary reason Jesus enjoins silence on the two healed men who had been blind (9:30). Their discourtesy and disobedience in spreading the news about him "all over that region" (8:31) cannot obliterate the fact that Jesus himself took concrete steps to forestall misrepresentation of his ministry, which could have warped it and steered it off in another direction, sidetracked from the mission on which the Father had sent him.

This is not a case of reading too much out of too little; for the danger of being sidetracked is one Jesus recognizes at the outset of his public ministry, one that he has to confront again and again. The heart of the temptations dangled before him by the devil himself (Matt. 4:1–11) was the prospect of kingly rule *without continued submission to the Father's plan, including the path to the cross.* That is why Jesus responded so firmly when Peter had the audacity to suggest that the cross should have no part in Jesus' agenda (16:21–23). Gethsemane itself was nothing but the agonizing desire to escape the cup he was committed to drink (26:39). Even on the cross itself, in the midst of the most awful shame and rejection, Jesus was buffeted with the temptation to escape the pain and ignominy, and prove his credentials, by the jeers of bystanders who "hurled insults at him, shaking their heads and saying, 'You who are going to destroy the temple and build it in three days, save yourself! Come down from the cross, if you are the Son of God!'" (27:39–40).

But if popularity and the attendant acclaim of the masses could not seduce Jesus or veer him from his course, neither could shame, mockery, and the self-conscious attempts to sidetrack him from his mission. As his ministry progresses and the opposition mounts, Jesus becomes more and more set on the course he is pursuing.

How unlike much of our own drift! There are few religious leaders who are not spoiled by acclaim, and even fewer who keep their perspectives and integrity when under intense fire. But Jesus proves utterly trustworthy, even when some seek to sidetrack his mission.

Conclusion

Now all of these observations lead to one final point of great importance. The pattern of Jesus' trustworthiness is displayed in one way or another in all the Gospels, and sometimes referred to in other New Testament books (e.g., Heb. 3:1ff.). Behind this pattern stands one cardinal truth: *Jesus Christ is trustworthy first and foremost because he is faithful to his Father.*

Implicitly, of course, we have recognized this truth when we have said that Jesus is always faithful to his mission; for his mission is not simply *his* mission, as if it were something he rather willfully decided to take up on his own, but *the Father's* mission entrusted to him. He came, above all, to do the Father's will. Even the dark hour in Gethsemane does not find Jesus crying, "Help me to love these sinners more! Help me to prove trustworthy to them!"—but rather, "My Father, if it is possible, may this cup be taken from me. Yet not as I will, *but as you will*" (Matt. 26:39; emphasis added).

The same pattern is found elsewhere. In John's Gospel, for example, Jesus says, "The one who sent me is with me; he has not left me alone, for I always do what pleases him" (John 8:29). Even more stunning is John 14:31: "the world must learn that I love the Father and that I do exactly what my Father has commanded me."

This does not mean that Jesus and his Father are engaged in some sort of private transaction in which the interests of humanity are of little concern. The point is that the mission of the Son is to save sinners. God *so loves* the world that he sends his Son; the Son comes to give his life a ransom for many. But it does mean that we ought not weigh the trustworthiness of Jesus purely in terms of what he does for us, nor purely in terms of his personal relationship with his Father, but in the profound truth that the interpersonal relationships of the Godhead, so far as we know them, are directed toward the redemption of men and women from every tongue, tribe, people, and nation. It is in the context of his redemptive purposes that we experience Jesus' great love for us. To continue the words of the poem by John Newton that introduced this chapter:

> *Which of all our friends to save us,*
> *Would consent to shed his blood?*
> *But our Jesus died to have us*
> *Reconciled in him to God:*
> *This was boundless love indeed!*
> *Jesus is a Friend in need.*
>
> *When he lived on earth abased,*
> *Friend of sinners was his name;*
> *Now, above all glory raised,*
> *He rejoices in the same:*
> *Still he calls them brethren, friends,*
> *And to all their wants attends.*
>
> *Could we bear from one another*
> *What he daily bears from us?*
> *Yet this glorious Friend and Brother*
> *Loves us, though we treat him thus:*
> *Though for good we render ill,*
> *He accounts us brethren still.*
>
> *O for grace our hearts to soften!*
> *Teach us, Lord, at length to love;*
> *We, alas, forget too often*
> *What a Friend we have above!*
> *But when home our souls are brought,*
> *We shall love thee as we ought.*

Nevertheless, that trustworthiness and redemptive love of Jesus that we enjoy is displayed as a function of Jesus' fidelity to his Father's redemptive plan. If we know that his love for poor sinners is utterly trustworthy, it is because Jesus' love for his Father is perfectly trustworthy.

> *O, the deep, deep love of Jesus!*
> *Vast, unmeasured, boundless, free;*
> *Rolling as a mighty ocean*
> *In its fulness over me.*
> *Underneath me, all around me,*
> *Is the current of thy love;*
> *Leading onward, leading homeward,*
> *To my glorious rest above.*
>
> *O, the deep, deep love of Jesus!*
> *Spread his praise from shore to shore;*

> *How he loveth, ever loveth,*
> *Changeth never, nevermore;*
> *How he watches o'er his loved ones,*
> *Died to call them all his own;*
> *How for them he intercedeth,*
> *Watcheth o'er them from the throne.*
>
> *O, the deep, deep love of Jesus!*
> *Love of every love the best:*
> *'Tis an ocean vast of blessing,*
> *'Tis a haven sweet of rest.*
> *O, the deep, deep love of Jesus!*
> *'Tis a heaven of heavens to me;*
> *And it lifts me up to glory,*
> *For it lifts me up to thee.*

S. Trevor Francis (1834–1925)

And that brings us to the subject of the next chapter.

---

[1]Judith Viorst, *Alexander and the Terrible, Horrible, No Good, Very Bad Day,* illustrated by Ray Cruz (New York: Atheneum, 1972).

11

The Compassion of Jesus

(9:35–10:15)

³⁵Jesus went through all the towns and villages, teaching in their synagogues, preaching the good news of the kingdom and healing every disease and sickness.

³⁶When he saw the crowds, he had compassion on them, because they were harassed and helpless, like sheep without a shepherd.

³⁷Then he said to his disciples, "The harvest is plentiful but the workers are few. ³⁸Ask the Lord of the harvest, therefore, to send out workers into his harvest field."

¹He called his twelve disciples to him and gave them authority to drive out evil spirits and to heal every disease and sickness.

²These are the names of the twelve apostles: first, Simon (who is called Peter) and his brother Andrew; James son of Zebedee, and his brother John;

³Philip and Bartholomew; Thomas and Matthew the tax collector; James son of Alphaeus, and Thaddaeus;

⁴Simon the Zealot and Judas Iscariot, who betrayed him.

⁵These twelve Jesus sent out with the following instructions: "Do not go among the Gentiles or enter any town of the Samaritans.

⁶Go rather to the lost sheep of Israel.

⁷As you go, preach this message: 'The kingdom of heaven is near.'

⁸Heal the sick, raise the dead, cleanse those who have leprosy, drive out demons. Freely you have received, freely give.

⁹Do not take along any gold or silver or copper in your belts;

[10]take no bag for the journey, or extra tunic, or sandals or a staff; for the worker is worth his keep.
[11]"Whatever town or village you enter, search for some worthy person there and stay at his house until you leave.
[12]As you enter the home, give it your greeting.
[13]If the home is deserving, let your peace rest on it; if it is not, let your peace return to you.
[14]If anyone will not welcome you or listen to your words, shake the dust off your feet when you leave that home or town.
[15]I tell you the truth, it will be more bearable for Sodom and Gomorrah on the day of judgment than for that town."

Introduction

Little is more tiring than constant service to people—even constant exposure to people. When we have not mixed with people for a while, we long to be with them; when we have been with too many people for too long, we need to be by ourselves. That is one reason why families that live in the country, sometimes many miles from their nearest neighbor, tend to be open and eager to welcome the passing stranger. The hospitality of country folk is proverbial. But if you live in the heart of London or New York, you will see thousands and thousands of people on the streets every day, and be aware of millions more; and then your tendency will be to treat your flat as an enclave that visitors may approach only with care. If the Englishman's home is his castle, the city-dweller's home is his private, fortified castle. The person who arrives unannounced and unexpected is not likely to be given a warm reception.

The same problem of too much exposure to people is likely to bedevil the couple where one spouse spends most of the day with hordes of people and the other spends the day largely alone. Come evening, the first wants to stay home or, at the most, spend a quiet evening with intimate friends; the other wants to talk, socialize, invite friends in, go to a party perhaps.

In one sense, the burnout we feel when we hear of yet more suffering, famine, and disaster on the nightly news stems from the same sort of exposure. Before the advent of the mass media, the ordinary family was called upon to worry about local conditions and affairs, and only occasionally about national and international matters—for instance, when one of the men was called up to serve in the military.

The news normally received about international events was months or even years late. But today, a few shots can be fired anywhere in the world, and we are called to worry about them that evening on the news. We become tired; our compassion seems to dry up as we are called upon to exercise it again and again, with no seeming change in the nature of the news. We harden ourselves a little, and find it easier to philosophize about evil and suffering than to weep over it or do much about it.

Anyone who has engaged in extensive public ministry knows that emotional burnout is a great danger. When it takes place, genuine ministry is traded for mere professionalism. The high goals with which we began may dissolve in the acid bath of sheer need. We may become more proficient; but we may also become more mechanical, less compassionate.

Jesus faced the same pressure. He "went through all the towns and villages" of Galilee, we are told (9:35), "teaching in their synagogues, preaching the good news of the kingdom and healing every disease and sickness." According to Josephus, a Jewish historian writing about a generation after Jesus, there were 204 cities and villages in Galilee, each with no fewer than fifteen thousand persons. Even if the latter figure is applicable only to the walled cities, and not to the villages (which is not what Josephus says), a conservative estimate points to a very large population, even if smaller than the three million that Josephus's figures indicate. If Jesus were to speak in two towns or villages a day, it would still take about four months to canvass the lot. Quite apart from the sheer energy needed to keep up such a pace was the emotional drain of serving more and more people who pressed to hear him and see him. This pressure was at least part of the reason why on another occasion he felt it necessary to withdraw from the crowds and attempt to escape by boat across the lake—only to be thwarted in this plan by the crowds of people who ran around the north end of the lake, crossed at the fords, and met him as he disembarked. Whatever the success or failure of this attempt to retire for a while, Jesus certainly recognized the need for rest.

Nevertheless, Jesus' basic stance toward the vast numbers of people who pressed in on him was compassion. Immediately after the summary of Jesus' strenuous ministry, Matthew recalls: "When he saw the crowds, he had compassion on them" (9:36).

I began to understand what this attitude looks like about twenty years ago, when I was trying to begin a church in the west end of

Ottawa. The work was slow and discouraging, and there were times I wanted to get away from it. The pastor who was supervising me, a chap called Ken Hall, suggested one evening that we go for a swim at a lake nearly forty miles back in the hills. I eagerly anticipated the evening. The water was always clean, there were seldom many people up there, and a raft was tethered several hundred yards out that made a convenient target for a lazy swim. To my horror, when we arrived we found the beach covered with hundreds of teenagers. They were having a very noisy beach party to celebrate high-school graduation. High-decibel sound equipment belted out the latest rock music so forcefully that residents in Ottawa probably had to shut their windows in self-protection. Not a few of the young people were already drunk, and the combination of celebration, booze, and bathing suits guaranteed that the public necking would be only a shade less than obscene.

Deeply disappointed that my evening's relaxation was being shattered by a raucous party, I was getting ready to cover my disappointment by moral outrage. I turned to Ken to unload the venom, but stopped as I saw him staring at the scene with a faraway look in his eyes. And then he said, rather softly, "High school kids—what a mission field."

In one sense, he had seen and heard exactly what I did; in another sense, we had not seen and heard the same things at all. The difference was not in the objective reality, but in his compassion. I had much to learn.

Of course, rest is necessary. But Christians can never treat the relationship between ministry and rest in the same way that the world treats the relationship between work and holidays. Many see vacations as the *end* or *purpose* of work, and even of life itself. Their work *earns* a holiday; they then *deserve* a vacation. When they return from their two or three weeks, they hate the thought of going back to work; and they can hardly wait for the next set of holidays. By contrast, the Christian loves to serve. Ministry of all kinds is the *end*, the *purpose*; holidays are simply a means to that end. Far from serving in order to earn a rest, we take rests now and then in order to serve the better. That means, of course, that if a planned rest doesn't work out just as we had expected, and more ministry intervenes, we cannot be frustrated or bitterly disappointed. Our times are in the Father's hands; he well knows the rest can be delayed a little if there is need for urgent ministry.

In other words, compassion in ministry is not so much the characteristic of a certain type of personality, as the characteristic of the person with a certain set of *priorities*. If we forget that our task is to minister *to people*, compassion will no longer be the characteristic of our life, but a quality we try to turn on and off depending on whether or not we think we should be "on duty."

When Jesus confronts the world, one of the features that stands out most starkly is his compassion. In the verses before us we shall notice several aspects of this compassion.

Reflections on the Compassion of Jesus

1. Compassion is Jesus' fundamental response to varied human needs. When Jesus saw the crowds, we are told, "he had compassion on them, because they were harassed and helpless, like sheep without a shepherd" (9:36).

It is important to see, first, that Jesus seems to be especially touched by the masses and their needs precisely *because* they are leaderless, harassed, bullied, bruised, helpless. Like sheep without a shepherd, they are exploited, adrift, moving as a flock but rarely knowing why or where. The activity that we might berate as mindless he sees as the result of being leaderless. The mass fads and hysteria that we write off as immature and ignorant he can therefore treat with compassion. The resentments, rebellion, diverting amusements, foolish pastimes, raw hooliganism, and stupid habits can be condescendingly dismissed by the elite of society; but Jesus' diagnosis implicitly puts not a little of the blame on those who are so dismissive. Behind the objectionable behavior, indeed the sinful behavior, lie frustration, exploitation, unarticulated despair at not knowing which way to turn. Where, then, are the leaders? The sad truth is that they are often in the same state as the led—which is another way of saying they are not real leaders at all. In other instances they are too busy worshiping themselves; in still others, far from helping or leading the masses, they contribute to the sheer harassment of the people.

That is what Jesus sees when he contemplates the great crowds; and according to Matthew, that is why he is moved to compassion. It is a commonplace of Scripture that God brings comfort to the downcast and succor to the downtrodden. "He has brought down rulers from their thrones but has lifted up the humble. He has filled the hungry with good things but has sent the rich away empty" (Luke 1:52–53). This ties in rather tightly with Jesus' summary of his own mission: "It is not the healthy who need a doctor, but the sick" (Matt. 9:12). It is almost as if Jesus is drawn to those who are most put upon, those who are suffering and exploited, those who are most aware of their needs and who hope that he can meet them. Is it not the poor in spirit who inherit the kingdom of God?

I am preparing these lines in England, to which I have returned after an absence of a couple of years. As I settle down to reading the newspapers and hearing the television news readers, I detect a subtle change in the atmosphere. That change is marked by the decay of hope.

Two years ago, British commentators recognized, of course, many of the problems that confront the country: rising racial tensions, high unemployment, loss of standing in the world community so far as productivity, trade balances, and standard of living go; rising cultural pluralism that threatens to rend the fabric of the nation, continuing strife in Northern Ireland—and, at the time, a coal miners' strike of breathless hate and barely suppressed violence. But even so, sturdy British resilience was not far beneath the surface. Britain has weathered storms in the past: it can handle this one as well.

Now the commentators are not so sure. Pessimism surfaces as Britain falls lower in the ranks of the European Economic Community, as its educational system produces too few scientists and engineers (and too many of the best of their ranks cannot find adequate employment and therefore emigrate). There are so few heroes, notes *The Times*, that there is a moment of national rejoicing when Botham rejoins the cricket team against New Zealand, following his suspension for smoking marijuana. More and more editorials sound bleak. Hope is gradually dying.

But in one sense, this may provide Christians with an opportunity that comes only where there is a sense of loss and ferment. It is rare that Christians earnestly seek the Lord's face when things are going swimmingly, when material blessings abound and we seem to be protected from the vicissitudes faced by others. But in the blackness of discouragement, when we are harassed and downcast, we may indeed turn to the Lord and acknowledge our helplessness apart from his grace; we may do so knowing that God is a compassionate God, and that Jesus' compassion was particularly directed toward the harassed and the helpless.

But second, it is no less important to see that in the context of the Gospel of Matthew Jesus, by exercising his compassion, in no way relinquishes his moral stance. With us, it is so often the case that compassion and moral outrage prove incompatible: the one devours the other. The compassion generates excuses for those to whom the compassion is directed, and the high ground of holiness is somehow lost. Or the expression of concern for holiness, rightly refusing to make excuses for sin, wrongly refuses to be compassionate as well, and falls headlong into self-righteousness.

But with Jesus it is not so. If we place this passage within the context of all of Matthew, we discover with delight that Jesus recognizes the prevalence and vileness of sin, yet is compassionate. The book as a whole pictures Jesus coming to save his people *from their sin* (1:21). In the Sermon on the Mount, Jesus simply assumes that people are evil: for example, "If you, then, though you are evil, know how to give good gifts to your children, how much more will your Father in heaven give good gifts to those who ask him!" (7:11). Even Jesus' healing ministry, as we saw in the first chapter of this book, was exercised as a function of his principial handling of the problem of sin (8:17); for he did not come to call the righteous, but sinners (9:13). Jesus dares to articulate moral outrage (see especially Matt. 23); but the same Jesus weeps over the city of Jerusalem.

Third, Jesus' compassion is here cast in a metaphor that betrays more than compassion. The people, Jesus laments, are "like sheep without a shepherd" (9:36). The language calls to mind the rich array of Old Testament passages in which either God or God's promised Messiah is the compassionate shepherd who will come to lead, feed, and protect God's people. At one point, God promises, "'I will place over them one shepherd, my servant David [written hundreds of years after David's death, so the reference must be to great David's greater Son], and he will tend them; he will tend them and be their shepherd. I the Lord will be their God, and my servant David will be prince among them. I the Lord have spoken. . . . You my sheep, the sheep of my pasture, are people, and I am your God, declares the Sovereign Lord'" (Ezek. 34:23–24, 31; cf. 37:24). Matthew himself cites Micah 5:2: ". . . out of you will come a ruler who will be the shepherd of my people Israel" (Matt. 2:6). Again, in connection with his death, Jesus cites Zechariah 13:7: "'I will strike the shepherd, and the sheep of the flock will be scattered'" (Matt. 26:31). Preserving the same metaphor, Jesus in the passage before us sends the disciples "to the lost sheep of Israel" (10:6).

Inevitably, then, biblically literate Christian readers, thinking through the report of Jesus' words after the fact, detect not only compassion but another messianic allusion. Jesus' very compassion toward "sheep without a shepherd" qualifies him as the shepherd they need, the shepherd long promised in Scripture who (as Matthew has carefully noted) would be born in Bethlehem and truly tend the flock of God.

In short, compassion is Jesus' fundamental response to varied human need. This compassion is not diluted by other responses equally fundamental, and complementary to his profound compassion. Rather, it rises the more starkly to the fore, and serves to authenticate his messiahship as faithfully and powerfully as any miracle.

2. The compassion of Jesus issues in a call to pray. "When he saw the crowds," we are told, "he had compassion on them. . . . Then he said to his disciples, 'The harvest is plentiful but the workers are few. Ask the Lord of the harvest, therefore, to send out workers into his harvest field'" (9:36–38). The metaphor changes from sheep farming to harvest, as Jesus tries to arouse in his disciples compassion similar to his own. The word *harvest* does not here mean "harvest time," as often in the Gospels, and then associated with judgment (e.g., 13:49; cf. Isa. 17:11; Joel 3:13). Rather, it means "harvest crop," a point made clear by the word *plentiful*. If the "harvest" is "plentiful," it must be the harvest crop that is in view. Stripping the metaphor away, Jesus is saying that there is a large number of people in some sense simply waiting to hear the gospel of the kingdom. The fields of people are ready, waiting to be harvested. They are urgently in need of workers to go and proclaim the good news to them.

What, then, should be done? Should we begin with training sessions to enable us to multiply the evangelizing force? Should we plot a major strategy of recruitment? Should we found a few strategically placed seminaries? Or perhaps we should begin by establishing two or three international foundations to help pay for these plans?

At some point or another, all of these may be good steps to take. But they are secondary steps, not to be attempted until considerable energy is poured into the first step. And the first step is to pray—to pray to the Lord of the harvest, that *he* would send out workers into *his* harvest field. One commentator puts it this way: "As no man will himself become a sincere and faithful minister of gospel, and as none discharges in a proper manner the office of teacher, but those whom the Lord raises up and endows with the gifts of his Spirit, whenever we observe a scarcity of pastors, we must raise our eyes to him to afford the remedy."

The world is full of wickedness, whether in the first world or the third, the second or the fourth; whether in "civilized" areas or more primitive situations; whether in the democracies or under totalitarian regimes; whether in countries where there is a great deal of "churchianity" or in countries where raw animism still dominates. Who is sufficient to meet such needs? Shall lives and whole societies be transformed by mere oratory, or merely by the power of doing good deeds? Nothing will suffice but the power of God; and therefore we must entreat him to work.

Nevertheless, the work we are to entreat him to perform, according to Jesus, is that he raise up workers! Doubtless we could have asked him to save a lot of people; doubtless that is a fine prayer. But it is not the focus here. God *normally* works through *means;* and that is why we are to pray to God, asking him to raise up the workers, the means, to spread the gospel and to display the power of the kingdom. This is *not* the same as mere recruitment and training; for the workers *God* raises up will be endowed by him with the gifts and graces necessary to meet this enormous challenge. The workers we commission who do not enjoy this divine endowment will not be much more than functionaries, and may actually do considerable damage by confusing thousands and thousands of people as to what Christian work is really all about.

The centrality of prayer in the purposes of God surfaces at many crucial places in the Bible. One of them was instrumental in my own sense of call to the ministry. While working in a Canadian government chemistry laboratory, trying to tackle a certain problem in air pollution, I gradually became more concerned with moral pollution than with air pollution, more interested in biblical truth and its application to men and women than in the application of scientific discoveries to our daily lives. I am not for one moment suggesting that Christians cannot serve the Lord in the context of the natural sciences. On the contrary, this is my Father's world, and Christians need to be involved in every part of it. But for me, the focus of interest and compulsion began to change. Doubtless God was quietly working in my life, through reflection, the counsel of friends, early opportunities for ministry that came my way, and other means. Toward the end of this period of uncertainty, I heard someone preach a sermon on Ezekiel 22. I remember very little of that sermon; I remember the text vividly. There God lists the gross corruptions of ancient Israel, especially of the aristocracy, of the merchants and of the prophets. Toward the end of the catalog we read, "Her officials within her are like wolves tearing their prey; they shed blood and kill people to make unjust gain. Her prophets whitewash these deeds for them by false visions and lying divinations. They say, 'This is what the Sovereign LORD says'—when the LORD has not spoken. The people of the land practice extortion and commit robbery; they oppress the poor and needy and mistreat the alien, denying them justice" (Ezek. 22:27–29).

But the most searing indictment of all comes in the final words of the chapter. God says, in what appears to be a combination of profound sorrow, deep disgust, and holy indignation, "I looked for a man among them who would build up the wall and stand before me in the gap on behalf of the land so I would not have to destroy it, *but I found none.* So I will pour out my wrath on them and consume them with my fiery anger, bringing down on their own heads all they have done" (22:30–31; emphasis added). Clearly, the man the Lord looked for was not in the first place a candidate to prophetic or priestly ministry; he was someone who would "stand before *me*"—that is, someone who would stand before the Lord as an intercessor. The account of Moses comes to mind in the episode of the golden calf: he intervened on behalf of the people, begging God not to wipe them out, beseeching God to have mercy on them. But when God looked at his people this time, he could not find anyone who would exercise that role. Not one.

I wish I could say that I have always been faithful to that calling. To my great shame, I have not. But I am convinced that the really great issues before us will be settled on our knees. This does not mean (I repeat) that we should do nothing but pray; it does mean we should do nothing without praying. If it is true that God customarily uses means, it is no less true that we so often focus on the means that we forget that the really significant work must be God's, or the whole is to little avail. It may be that there are some Christians around who are so heavenly minded they are no earthly good; but I have met few of them. I know far more who are so earthly minded they are good for neither heaven nor earth.

Jesus' compassion issues in prayer, and in a call to pray. It may be that if we fail to pray, it is because our compassion is defective. Or it may be that our compassion is engaged, but our diagnosis of the problems and their remedies is faulty, prompting us to devote all our energies to what are at best secondary solutions. But if we align ourselves with the compassion of the Lord Jesus, and his analysis of the most urgent needs and their solution, we shall learn to pray to the Lord of the harvest that he will send forth laborers into his harvest field.

3. The compassion of Jesus issues in mission carried out by his disciples (10:1ff.). The call to prayer is central, but it is not everything. As faith without works is dead, so also is prayer without mission.

In some ways, of course, this mission was a training mission, and only in that sense was it a pattern for the continuing mission of the church. Luke reports a later mission that sent out seventy-two disciples (Luke 10:1–24)—apparently a growing group of trainees. The particular commission that Jesus delivers to the twelve apostles here in Matthew 10 preserves a number of features of relevance only during this pre-Passion, pre-Pentecost phase of outreach.[1] In particular, he tells them, "Do not go among the Gentiles or enter any town of the Samaritans. Go rather to the lost sheep of Israel" (10:5–6). This restriction was probably advanced for several quite different reasons. Normally Jews and Samaritans did not get on very well; Jews and Gentiles could not be expected to get on any better. If (as I think likely) the foray Jesus makes into Samaritan territory, reported in John 4, had already taken place by this time, it may be that some of the disciples naively thought that everything would go swimmingly if they returned to Samaria. If so, they were unaware of the depth of their prejudices, or how difficult the task of proclaiming the kingdom could be; for a short while later, when some of the Samaritans reject Jesus and his followers, James and John at least are ready to call fire down from heaven on them (Luke 9:52–56), thereby demonstrating they are in no fit state to exercise a ministry in that region. Even after Pentecost, most of the believers, including the apostles, need some time before they are able to integrate a Gentile mission into their thinking.

Another reason for this temporary restriction may have been Jesus' understanding of his own place in redemptive history. He was sent as a Jew among Jews; he himself obeyed the law of Moses, and lived and died under it. When he ministered outside this framework, he himself seems to have seen it as something of an exception (e.g., see Matt. 15:21–28). This was a stage in the drama of redemption, a stage to be superseded in the great commission he himself would one day leave with his followers, commanding them to make disciples of all the nations (28:18–20).

Training mission or not, however, the first fifteen verses of this chapter nicely preserve a number of features endemic to all genuine Christian mission; and thus they contribute to our grasp of what Jesus' compassion really means. If Jesus' compassion issues in mission, we need to know something of the kind of mission we are talking about; and when we find that out, we shall learn something more about the nature of the compassion that prompted the mission.

(a) This mission is itself an extension of the saving reign of God. In the context of expressing his compassion, Jesus "called his twelve disciples to him and gave them authority to drive out evil spirits and to heal every disease and sickness" (10:1). More explicitly, he told them, "As you go, preach this message: 'The kingdom of heaven is near.' Heal the sick, raise the dead, cleanse those who have leprosy, drive out demons" (10:7–8a). Their *verbal* message was the proclamation of the nearness of the kingdom; their *deeds* were to display the power of that kingdom, delegated to them by Jesus, in powerful acts of healing, exorcism, and even raising some from the dead.

In short, then, their mission was to multiply the activity of their Master. The new age of his reign was being inaugurated. He himself was proclaiming the nearness of the kingdom (4:17); so would they. He himself was displaying the kingdom's power and anticipating what the consummated kingdom would be like (chaps. 8–9); so would they. He himself was rolling back the frontiers of suffering and making public connections between sin and sickness; so would they. He himself was confronting the powers of darkness and throwing evil spirits out of their human dwelling places; so would they. And they would do these things because he would delegate to them the authority they would need.

A few years ago that might have been all I would say on this passage, save that I would seek to apply it a little to the modern setting. As I prepare this today, however, the Western church is feeling the impact of the so-called signs-and-wonders movement, usually identified with John Wimber and his associates in the various "Vineyard" organizations. In brief, this movement holds that when the gospel is properly proclaimed, it should be accompanied by signs and wonders—that is, by an observable display of divine power in healing and other supernatural manifestations that attest and confirm the truth of the message that the kingdom is actually invading this world. This outbreak of power is often combined with "words of authority" that seem to be a kind of subset of what older charismatics would have called the gift of prophecy.

It is not the place to assess so large and diverse a movement here, or to attempt an interpretation of the key passages on which the movement largely relies. In any case I have attempted something of the sort elsewhere.[2] My purpose in raising the subject here is to acknowledge that the subject can scarcely be avoided in a context that plainly talks about Jesus' delegation of authority to his disciples, in the days of his flesh, in terms largely congruent with the categories used by the signs-and-wonders movement. At least some sort of brief reflection about the movement seems called for.

In fact, I find myself in large agreement with a lot of the statements that Wimber makes; and I have no desire to tear down another's work, especially where large parts of it seem wholesome, biblical, and on the whole helpful. If I must articulate a few cautions (which are better grounded in the book to which I have just referred), I would make the following four points.

First, although after Pentecost signs and wonders are performed by a wide variety of believers, they are rather frequently associated with the apostles (Acts 2:43; 4:30; 5:12, 16; 8:18; 2 Cor. 12:12), sometimes as attesting acts. Of course, some today argue that the gift of apostleship has never been withdrawn; and so if apostles in the first century were in part attested by signs and wonders, their modern counterparts may be similarly endowed. This view does not adequately recognize the diversity of meanings that are subsumed under the word *apostle*. In one sense, Jesus alone is "the apostle and high priest whom we confess" (Heb. 3:1): presumably no one claims to be an apostle in exactly the same way as Jesus is an apostle. Then there are the Twelve, who according to Acts 1 had to meet the condition of being with the other disciples of Jesus throughout his earthly ministry, and who were appointed to the task by Jesus himself (or in the case of the replacement of Judas Iscariot, by the church in solemn deduction from Scripture and drawing of lots). Again, there can be no modern counterparts to apostles in this sense, unless someone turns up who is at least a couple of thousand years old. Then there is Paul, who insists that among his qualifications is the fact that he saw the resurrected Jesus on the Damascus road and received his commission directly from him (especially 1 Corinthians 9 and 15). Paul does not think of his experience on the Damascus road as one of many visions, but as qualitatively different: a special, final ("last of all," he says, 1 Cor. 15:8) appearance of Jesus, in his resurrected form, an event not to recur until Jesus comes again at the end of the age. And further, there are apostles in a still broader sense: missionaries, envoys, messengers of the churches. In this broader sense, we may speak (as one book title does) of *Adoniram Judson, Apostle to Burma*. But the frequent association of signs and wonders, I would argue, is with "apostles" in the narrower senses. This does not mean that there is no valid display of signs and wonders today, nor that others than apostles (in this narrower sense) will inevitably find it impossible to display God's power. It does mean, however, that the frequent, biblical association of apostles with supernatural displays of kingdom power must not be denied, or cavalierly warped by identifying certain contemporaries as "apostles" without carefully sorting out *in what sense* they are apostles.

Second, the emphasis on the inbreaking power of the kingdom of God must be balanced against other equally biblical emphases, including the prevalence of suffering in this fallen world. Not all deaths end in immediate resurrection: if the command to raise the dead (Matt. 10:8) were a universal mandate, it is rather surprising that none of the early Christians has survived to the present day. We have already noted that Paul first preached the gospel in Galatia because of an illness; he had to leave Trophimus behind in one mission, owing to a protracted illness; and Timothy had ongoing problems with his health. Even so-called natural disasters function, according to Jesus, as warnings to encourage people to repent (Luke 13:1–5). To this we must add the special emphasis in the New Testament on the inevitability of Christian suffering that stems from the world's opposition (about which I'll say more in the next chapter). To put the matter another way, to have no theology of the power of the gospel in our contemporary world is to relegate virtually all kingdom blessings to the return of Jesus—that is, it is to have an overemphasis on futurist eschatology. On the other hand, to place too much stress on the transforming power of the kingdom today, divorced from other competing and qualifying themes, is to depreciate what we are still waiting for, what the entire created order still groans for, the final redemption. It is to have an overemphasis on realized eschatology. After the cross and the resurrection, New Testament writers can say, in various words, that whoever calls on the name of the Lord will be saved; they do not say that everyone who calls on the name of the Lord will be healed from every physical illness. The church will remain in tension over how much power and how much weakness should characterize her until the consummation of all things.

Third, moreover, if this signs-and-wonders theology is treated as a kind of key to evangelism and mission, we are in for some weighty disappointments. With time, virtually all keys—whether the four spiritual laws, a certain style of evangelism (e.g., with altar calls), a particular theological emphasis—tend to become fetishes, the necessary means exploited by the faithful to produce inevitable results. Somehow God's work in regeneration becomes hostage to the particular key. Exercising the specified means becomes a test of orthodoxy. What begins as a salutary correction easily degenerates into a party position, with disproportionate energy devoted to the key and precious little to God or to people.

Fourth, perhaps most serious in this particular instance is the failure of the leadership to dissociate itself from some of the worst extremes of its followers. Obviously no leader can be permanently responsible for everything one of his students says or does; but in this instance there have been such remarkable excesses and abuses that some kind of clarification is urgently needed from the principal leadership. Historical examples flock to mind. During the Evangelical Awakening, for instance, George Whitefield, the Wesleys, and other leaders were at first openly sympathetic to a group known to historians as the French Prophets. The French Prophets cherished supernatural phenomena, wild displays of emotional frenzy, utterances they claimed were from God, and so forth. The principal leaders of the Awakening wanted to be open to all that God might in fact be doing among them. But as the French Prophets became more and more extreme, cherishing their experiences and orientation more than the biblical framework and balance (even though they doubtless thought themselves to be biblical), Whitefield and the others eventually dissociated themselves increasingly from representatives of that movement, even on occasion administering public rebukes when the Prophets tried to take over the direction of a meeting. In short, there is ample evidence that the love of the spectacular can never be satisfied, and will issue in progressively serious distortions of biblical Christianity. When reports hit the media of Wimber protégés holding a gruesome vigil to bring back from the dead a believer who had been a cripple most of his life (Why wasn't he healed before he died?), it is time for some public dissociation.

Having said so many negative things, it is the more important for me to stress that not only this initial trainee mission of the Twelve, but also the entire mission of the church, is an expression of the compassion of Jesus Christ. The saving reign of God is being extended, sometimes in strange ways difficult to understand, sometimes in dramatic displays of life-transforming power, sometimes in the context of persecution and suffering, "famine or nakedness or danger or sword" (Rom. 8:35). As Jesus' compassion moved him to incite his disciples to prayer, so his compassion moved him to train them for ministry, and to delegate some of his authority so that they too might preach the message of the nearness of the kingdom and display its power among the lost sheep of Israel.

(b) The discharge of this mission must never be for personal financial advantage. Jesus tells his followers, "Freely you have received, freely give" (10:8b). The word *freely* does not here mean "bountifully," that is, "You have received a bountiful supply, so give bountifully" or the like, even though that would have been true. Rather, it means gratis: that is, "You have received without paying for anything, *freely;* therefore you must give *freely* as well, without charging for anything."

Yet this does not mean Jesus' emissaries are not to be supported by those to whom they minister; for Jesus adds, "Do not take along any gold or silver or copper in your belts; take no bag for the journey, or extra tunic, or sandals or a staff; for the worker is worth his keep" (10:9–10). Whatever the precise significance of this list, it is clear that the Twelve are to go stripped to essentials. The "sandals," for instance, may well be an extra pair that they are prohibited from carrying: such basic necessities they should expect to be provided for them along the way, along with the food and shelter that the gold and silver would otherwise purchase.

At first glance this might seem like a contradiction. On the one hand, the disciples are to give "freely," that is, without charging; on the other hand, they are to remember that "the worker is worth his keep," and travel lightly in the full expectation that their needs will be met by those to whom they minister. Why this tension between what appear to be competing or even mutually contradictory principles?

This strange arrangement makes good sense once it is clear what values are preserved by it. On both sides of the arrangement, we must consider the effect on those whom Jesus sends and those who receive them. That the disciples do not charge for their ministry forces them to remember that they, too, are the recipients of grace, and that spiritual treasures are not to be marketed in anticipation of the greed of Simon Magus (Acts 8). Those who charge for spiritual ministry are dabbling in simony. Meanwhile, those who receive the benefits from ministry freely bestowed are forced to consider that even by these strange means God makes it clear that his forgiveness and power cannot be earned, bought, or sold. The kingdom comes as he sees fit, when he sees fit; and when he displays his power in forgiveness, healing, and transformation, it is never because he has been coerced, bought, or domesticated.

Yet these people who receive the gospel of the kingdom want to respond in tangible ways; and so they provide food, shelter, and support for those who are primarily engaged in spreading the gospel. They recognize that considerable labor goes into the task the disciples have taken on. They reason that, although the gospel came to them freely, there is a profound sense in which they *ought* to pay for the work of those who brought them the good news of the kingdom. The worker is worth his keep. Meanwhile, those who are busy primarily in proclamation and ministry are reminded by the generosity of others that they do not stand alone, isolated heroes completely independent from the common herd. They may not be sure where their next meal or bed is coming from; they therefore trust God to provide what is needed, and learn that God in his mercy supplies their needs through other of his servants.

If we apply this to the modern setting, we would phrase it something like this. The church should not *pay* its clergy for services rendered, as if somehow ministers and others live by *earning* their keep. Pushed to the limit, this might also suggest that a servant of the Lord is paid so much per prayer, so much per sermon, so much per hour of preparation, so much per counseling session with a distraught widow who has just lost her son, and so on. No, the church does not *pay* its ministers; rather, it provides them with resources so that they are able to serve freely. The church recognizes that those who serve in this way must be "kept," and are worthy of it. In practice, this means that the ideal situation occurs when the church is as generous as possible, the ministers do not concern themselves with material matters and are above selfish material interest. The worst situation occurs when the ministers are grasping and covetous, constantly comparing themselves with other "professionals," while the church adopts the attitude, "You keep him humble, Lord, and we'll keep him poor."

The particular side that needs special emphasis in any setting is the one the people of that setting are most trying to avoid. In general terms, the church needs to hear verse 10b ("for the worker is worth his keep") to be reminded of its responsibility, its debt; and the serving disciple needs to hear the same verse to be reminded of how the Lord will provide for him. The minister needs to reflect on verse 8b ("Freely you have received, freely give") to bear in mind that grace is always free, and that the service rendered must not be bought or sold, but distributed as freely and as widely as possible.

This particular arrangement continues, I would be prepared to argue, in the letters of Paul—although he adds some important wrin-

kles of his own that cannot be discussed here. The values embraced
by this tension not only make the immediate mission possible, but
also lay the groundwork for a view of Christian witness and an understanding of the nature of grace that belong to the very heart of the
gospel. In the context of Matthew 10, they are an expression of the
compassion of Jesus Christ, a reflection of what he understood the
mission of the church should be.

But more, there is in these arrangements a wise reflection of the
relationship between Jesus and his disciples. Jesus' attitude to his
own disciples is full of grace, abundant in compassion. If they are
peculiarly his, it is because, like Matthew, they have been called by
him; if they are in some sense more whole than others, it is because
Jesus has come to them in their sickness and transformed them. They
did not earn his favor; they did not deserve his compassion. Can compassion ever be deserved? It may be desperately needed; but it cannot be deserved without destroying its essence. Yet at the same time
Jesus makes *demands* on his disciples. That he is compassionate does
not mean there are no demands on his followers; that he wins people by his grace does not mean they can simultaneously be his and
unchanged. For although Jesus has not come to call the healthy, but
the sick (9:12), it does not follow that he permits them to remain sick.
What kind of compassion would it have been if, in the days of his
flesh, Jesus had "felt compassion" on the sick and then cured none
of them? What kind of compassion would it have been if he came to
call not the righteous but the sinners, and then left them to wallow
in their sin? The truth is that the exercise of his compassion results
in the *transformation* of individuals. If his compassion is not effective, it may be morally commendable sentiment; but it is totally useless, save as self-serving catharsis. Jesus' expenditure of compassion,
of grace, issues in transformed people who *will* increasingly meet his
demands and follow in steps of obedient discipleship. And if so-called
disciples fail to change at least the *direction* of their lives, they are no
disciples at all.

Thus, Jesus' insistence on a certain tension between the free dis-
pensing of kingdom benefits and the obligation of the recipients of
those benefits to provide for the kingdom's messengers is far from
being an arbitrary decision. It is a reflection of the deepest realities
of the gospel.

(c) This mission results in a divided response (10:11–16). Just
because this mission is to be motivated by compassion does not mean

everyone exposed to its message will be won over. Far from it: it divides people.

The division, Jesus says, will begin when the disciples arrive in any village and make arrangements to stay at someone's home. "Whatever town or village you enter," Jesus says, "search for some worthy person there and stay at his house until you leave" (10:11). The worthiness of the person, in this context, is not measured by wealth, personal charm, multiplied gifts, or moral superiority, but by his or her reputation for being open to the ministry and emissaries of Jesus. The disciples are to find out who is interested in supporting Jesus' outreach in this way; such a person is worthy, and Jesus' followers should go and stay there, without going from place to place trying, perhaps, to secure "superior" lodgings. They are already superior if they are provided by someone who is worthy in this way.

And so the disciples arrive on this worthy's doorstep. There they will find out if genuine worth abides here or not. It may be, of course, that the disciples have been misinformed: perhaps no worthy person lives there. In his instructions Jesus allows for both possibilities: "As you enter the home, give it your greeting. If the home is deserving, let your peace rest on it; if it is not, let your peace return to you" (10:12–13). The greeting *peace to this house* (Luke 10:5) or the like was common in Jesus' day. In itself it conveys nothing special in this context; but because it is uttered by an emissary of Jesus to someone who is allegedly interested in nurturing his cause, the response to the greeting turns out to be critical. If the householder turns out to be unworthy (i.e., not interested in following Jesus or giving aid to his disciples), then the disciples should let their peace return to them— that is, they shouldn't stay. But the loss is not theirs. Those who receive Jesus' disciples receive him (10:40). The unworthy person is not simply rejecting a few disciples; he is rejecting the Jesus they represent. Their greeting of peace is of special value because of their relationship with him; and if they leave, taking their greeting with them, the home they thus abandon is impoverished incalculably. Potiphar's home was blessed because of Joseph's presence (Gen. 39:3–5): how much more the home that harbors the apostles of Jesus the Messiah!

Rejection of the disciples of Jesus, *because they are his disciples,* therefore ultimately invites judgment, and that is true not only of the individual or home but even of entire towns: "If anyone will not welcome you or listen to your words, shake the dust off your feet when you leave that home or town" (10:14). Pious Jews leaving Gentile territory and returning to the Promised Land might shake the dust of the pagan territory from their clothes and feet, a symbolic way not only of expressing thanks for a safe return home, but also of rejecting all that was seen to be pagan. For Jesus to apply this custom to Jews must have been deeply shocking. The emissaries of Jesus the Messiah are now treating certain Jewish homes and towns as essentially pagan, ignorant of God, threatened with judgment.

The judgment theme becomes explicit in the final verse of the section: "I tell you the truth," Jesus says, "it will be more bearable for Sodom and Gomorrah on the day of judgment than for that town" (10:15). Sodom and Gomorrah, proverbial for wickedness (Genesis 19; Isa. 1:9; cf. Matt. 11:22–24; Rom. 9:29; Jude 7), suffered catastrophic judgment on account of their sin; but on the final day, Jesus insists, as much as they will be condemned, the homes and towns that rejected Jesus and his emissaries will face more fearsome judgment yet. The point is made in greater detail in the next chapter (11:20–24), and presupposes that our responsibility before God is related to the advantages and opportunities we have enjoyed. That is a perennially sobering perspective that stands over the Western world, a threat that looms larger when self-interest and materialism squeeze out what we know to be a better way.

"But," you say, "I thought you were going to talk about the compassion of Jesus. Yet here you are threatening judgment and hell."

The truth of the matter is that it is common in Scripture to find the love of God and the threat of judgment side by side. God so loves the world that he sends his unique Son, we are told (John 3:16); but a few verses on we are told that "whoever rejects the Son will not see life, for God's wrath remains on him" (John 3:36). "God demonstrates his own love for us in this: While we were still sinners, Christ died for us" (Rom. 5:8), Paul writes; but it is only this that guarantees we shall "be saved from God's wrath through him" (Rom. 5:9). Elsewhere, John delights us with the words *God is love* (1 John 4:8, 16); but he is quick to add, "We love because he first loved us. If anyone says, 'I love God,' yet hates his brother, he is a liar. . . . He who has the Son has life; he who does not have the Son of God does not have life" (1 John 4:19–20; 5:12).

It appears, then, that if we are to be faithful to Scripture, it is difficult to deal at length with the love of God without saying something about God's wrath. This is not because God's love and God's wrath are entirely symmetrical. Rather, it is because God's wrath, a function of his holiness when it confronts rebellion, is the environment in which we live and breathe: we are all by nature "objects of wrath," the apostle tells us (Eph. 2:3). What is marvelous is that this same

God, who has every just cause to be angry, is nevertheless the God of love; and it is that love that sent his Son, that love that sent the disciples, that same love toward us today that "compels us" (2 Cor. 5:14) to bear witness.

The exercise of Christian compassion in a lost, harassed, and rebellious world leaves behind a transformed people or an increasingly guilty people. Everyone who reads these lines will either be drawn more closely to Christ, or become increasingly guilty before him. There is no middle ground; for the mission of Jesus results in a divided response. But those who have tasted and seen that the Lord is good cannot but rise and sing:

> *High beyond imagination*
> *Is the love of God to man;*
> *Far too deep for human reason;*
> *Fathom that it never can;*
> *Love eternal*
> *Richly dwells in Christ the Lamb.*
>
> *Love like Jesus' none can measure,*
> *Nor can its dimensions know;*
> *'Tis a boundless, endless river,*
> *And its waters freely flow.*
> *O ye thirsty,*
> *Come and taste its streams below.*
>
> *Jesus loved, and loves for ever;*
> *Zion on his heart does dwell;*
> *He will never, never, never*
> *Leave his church a prey to hell.*
> *All is settled,*
> *And my soul approves it well.*

William Gadsby (1773–1844)

---

[1]Matthew 10 is a hotly disputed passage in New Testament research. In my larger commentary on Matthew (in *The Expositor's Bible Commentary*, edited by Frank E. Gaebelein, vol. 8 [Grand Rapids: Zondervan, 1984]), I have discussed at some length the literary, source, and theological questions surrounding this chapter, and I shall not repeat myself here. I shall also omit all mention of the individual apostles named in verses 2-4: these too are discussed in the commentary.

[2]D. A. Carson, *Showing the Spirit: A Theological Exposition of 1 Corinthians 12–14* (Sydney: Anzea; Grand Rapids: Baker; Exeter: Paternoster, 1987).

12

The Divisiveness of Jesus

(10:16-42)

[16]"I am sending you out like sheep among wolves. Therefore be as shrewd as snakes and as innocent as doves.

[17]"Be on your guard against men; they will hand you over to the local councils and flog you in their synagogues. [18]On my account you will be brought before governors and kings as witnesses to them and to the Gentiles. [19]But when they arrest you, do not worry about what to say or how to say it. At that time you will be given what to say, [20]for it will not be you speaking, but the Spirit of your Father speaking through you.

[21]"Brother will betray brother to death, and a father his child; children will rebel against their parents and have them put to death. [22]All men will hate you because of me, but he who stands firm to the end will be saved. [23]When you are persecuted in one place, flee to another. I tell you the truth, you will not finish going through the cities of Israel before the Son of Man comes.

[24]"A student is not above his teacher, nor a servant above his master. [25]It is enough for the student to be like his teacher, and the servant like his master. If the head of the house has been called Beelzebub, how much more the members of his household!

[26]"So do not be afraid of them. There is nothing concealed that will not be disclosed, or hidden that will not be made known. [27]What I tell you in the dark, speak in the daylight; what is whispered in your ear, proclaim from the roofs. [28]Do not be afraid of those who kill the body but cannot kill the soul. Rather, be afraid of the One who can destroy both soul and body in hell. [29]Are not two sparrows sold for a penny? Yet not one of them will fall to the ground apart from the will of your Father. [30]And even the very

hairs of your head are all numbered. [31]So don't be afraid; you are worth more than many sparrows.

[32]"Whoever acknowledges me before men, I will also acknowledge him before my Father in heaven. [33]But whoever disowns me before men, I will disown him before my Father in heaven.

[34]"Do not suppose that I have come to bring peace to the earth. I did not come to bring peace, but a sword. [35]For I have come to turn

"'a man against his father,
a daughter against her mother,
a daughter-in-law against her mother-in-law—
[36]a man's enemies will be the members of his own household.'

[37]"Anyone who loves his father or mother more than me is not worthy of me; anyone who loves his son or daughter more than me is not worthy of me; [38]and anyone who does not take his cross and follow me is not worthy of me. [39]Whoever finds his life will lose it, and whoever loses his life for my sake will find it.

[40]"He who receives you receives me, and he who receives me receives the one who sent me. [41]Anyone who receives a prophet because he is a prophet will receive a prophet's reward, and anyone who receives a righteous man because he is a righteous man will receive a righteous man's reward. [42]And if anyone gives even a cup of cold water to one of these little ones because he is my disciple, I tell you the truth, he will certainly not lose his reward."

Introduction

In many societies, a polarized or sectarian stance is often considered a sign of maturity, even of manhood. This is true in large sectors of the population in Northern Ireland, Iran, and Nicaragua. This is not to say that in Northern Ireland everyone belongs either to the UDF or the IRA, or that in Nicaragua everyone is profoundly sympathetic to either the Sandanistas or the Contras. Rather, it is to say that in these countries there are many elements of society whose very *raison d'être* is bound up with a polarized stance.

I am not of course referring to mere disagreements over a policy or a political party. Every society knows its disagreements. I refer rather to such polarized and absolute disagreement that each side assumes an almost revelatory stance, treating its own position as transcendental, absolute, and nonnegotiable truth—with all other views seen, correspondingly, as heresy, to be damned or burned out.

It might even be argued that what is distinctive about the "civilized" Western world is our degree of tolerance. Nothing is so important it is worth fighting for, it seems. Or is that really so? Is there *nothing* in our culture to which we attach transcendental importance?

Some might nominate hedonism. Certainly millions of men and women pursue hedonism with reckless energy. In one sense, hedonism is their god. But no one ever dies in support of hedonism—in the practice of it, doubtless, but not in the support of it; that would be a contradiction in terms. Others might argue that materialism or the vague concept of "progress" might be appropriate candidates. But although materialism has taken deep rootage in the soil of Western culture, and sporadically surges forward with new momentum and power, most people treat it as a wonderful goddess worth pursuing but not worth dying for. After all, rising numbers of people are voicing their awareness of the finite resources on our planet. Perhaps "small is beautiful" after all. And insofar as materialism is one form of hedonism, it is hard to imagine suffering for it.

If there is one underlying, deeply rooted position that is treated as of transcendental importance in Western societies, I suspect it is the notion of pluralism. This does not simply adopt the stance that diversity is a good thing, but that in the religious and philosophical arenas no position has the right to declare another position wrong. That is pluralism's position: and that position is the only one exempt from criticism. The power of this stance came home to me a few years ago when I gave some lectures at an Ivy League divinity school. Not a few evangelicals had been attracted to this institution with its history of great learning, on the grounds that evangelicals were tolerated there. Every group represented in the student body, for instance, had its turn to organize and run a chapel service: liberals and conservatives, Roman Catholics (of various stripes) and Protestants (of various stripes), and even a representative from one of the tribes of Plains Indians with their essentially animistic faith. The student paper allowed all the voices to speak, so long as there was no criticism of another position. Only two beliefs, so far as I could see, were so sacrosanct throughout most of the student body that if anyone had the temerity to demur there was invariably a violent reaction. The first was the right of women to be ordained; the second was the moral acceptability of homosexuality. Those two points were not to be questioned; everything else was negotiable, and the diversity itself judged wholesome and enlightened. The great god Pluralism enjoyed praise without ceasing.

All this may seem not only more tolerant but far wiser, far more mature and civilized than, for example, the fanatical commitment found under the Ayatollah Khomeini's regime. But there is a high price to pay, too seldom recognized. First, pluralism, as I have already hinted, is surprisingly *in*tolerant. All positions *except its own* are negotiable. That is the great problem with most forms of liberalism: liberalism can afford to be liberal only to liberals. Others are dismissed as fanatics, bigots, narrow-minded hate-mongers, and so forth. Pluralism turns out to be as intolerant as the intolerant concoctions it condemns. Second, pluralism turns out to be the unwitting stooge of the contemporary social agenda. Because it is rootless in its values (except for the vague but powerful values of pluralism itself), it does not therefore abandon absolute values but tends instead to adopt as absolute those values at the top of the current cultural agenda. Hence my experience at the divinity school. That generation of students did not begin to suspect how much their values will appear to later historians to be the culture-bound hostages of the eighties. They thought they were on the leading edge of Christian truth; in fact they were on the trailing edge of a culture whose god is pluralism. And that brings up the third element in the high price paid by pluralism: it inevitably tends toward the depreciation of truth, even the possibility of knowing truth. The positions it then espouses are informed less by thoughtful criteria than by current fads. A position strongly held by those judged out of step with pluralism will be dismissed not on the basis of careful assessment but on the basis of the fact that it is out of step with pluralism. The truth-claims advanced by the position will never get a hearing.

Well, then, someone might ask, are we to return to the Crusades? Would we be better off with a worldview that could renew the Spanish Inquisition? Should the church, claiming absolute truth, take the power of the sword and put matters to right?

God forbid! In the centuries that spawned the Crusades and the Inquisition, the church, true enough, had some genuine appreciation of the nonnegotiability of truth; and that was commendable. But the church made other crucial errors. It aligned itself with the state—indeed, it declared itself so superior to the state that it utilized the sword of the state to enforce its wishes. It thereby failed to come to grips with the relationships between the old covenant people of God and the new. Under the old covenant the locus of the people was a nation, with a nation's laws; under the new, it is a transnational community, a minority, a frequently suffering fellowship, whose supreme sanction is excommunication. In the Western world today, however, these costly errors are not so prevalent. The church is largely free from the state; and even where in the Western democracies there is a state church, that church is largely free from the *power* of the state. Moreover, the force of circumstances is making it begin to understand, at least in some circles, its calling and role as a suffering community. But by and large the church has not yet grappled very hard with the nonnegotiable character of *truth*, thoughtfully setting out the implications against the backdrop of the prevailing pluralism.

We may ask ourselves: What does the man on the street think of Jesus Christ? Probably rather little; but if pushed, our interviewee will either cite some credal formula learned in childhood ("Jesus is the Son of God," or something similar), or else say something like, "Well, I suppose he was a very good man who said and did a lot of good things. Wasn't he the one who taught the Sermon on the Mount—be kind and love your neighbor and the Golden Rule and that sort of thing?" Such a response betrays not only a rather reductionistic view of Jesus, but a sentimental approach to the Sermon on the Mount; for the latter contains not only the Golden Rule ("In everything, do to others what you would have them do to you, for this sums up the Law and the Prophets" [Matt. 7:12]), but also sweeping claims to authority on the day of judgment: "Not everyone who says to me, 'Lord, Lord,' will enter the kingdom of heaven, not only he who does the will of my Father who is in heaven. Many will say to me on that day, 'Lord, Lord, did we not prophesy in your name, and in your name drive out demons and perform many miracles?' Then I will tell them plainly, 'I never knew you. Away from me, you evildoers!'" (Matt. 7:21–23).

In other words, even the Jesus of the Sermon on the Mount is a Jesus for whom the modern Western world is woefully ill-prepared. How much less prepared is it for the verses before us—indeed, for the entire theme of the divisiveness of Jesus! How often are we likely to meet a man on the street who would define the mission of Jesus in terms of 10:34: "Do not suppose that I have come to bring peace to the earth. I did not come to bring peace, but a sword"? The reason why our world is so unprepared for this theme is because of the pervasive influence of pluralism. So formidable is this influence on the popular mind that even Jesus has been recast as a prophet of this new god. The fact remains that the Jesus of Scripture bears little likeness to this new Jesus. The real Jesus, the authentic Jesus, the authoritative but compassionate Jesus, the Jesus who confronts the world, is quite frankly a divisive Jesus. This divisiveness is unavoidable, not only because of the unyielding truth-claims he makes for himself, but because at the heart of his message and purpose is his bold insistence that men and women can be rightly related to God only if they know him and come to him on his terms. This unabashed, exclusivistic, either/or mentality lies at the heart of the New Testament, and can be removed only by radical surgery on the documents. To resort to such devices because we are uncomfortable with the historical Jesus is merely another way of saying that we reject him in favor of a tame Jesus, a domesticated Jesus who will not challenge us or tell us we are wrong, force us to rethink our most fundamental assumptions, or question our most cherished priorities.

Four Features of the Divisiveness of Jesus

1. The divisiveness of Jesus leads to outright opposition from the world, and sometimes to persecution by it. When we remember what happened to Jesus, this first point should not be surprising. After all, as he reminds us, "A student is not above his teacher, nor a servant above his master. It is enough for the student to be like his teacher, and the servant like his master. If the head of the house has been called Beelzebub, how much more the members of his household!" (Matt. 10:24–25). Beelzebub, or perhaps Beelzeboul, has an uncertain derivation. It may mean "lord of flies," a kind of god of filth, developed as a pun on "Prince Baal." Whatever the derivation, some pious Jews applied the word to the devil himself. Now the sobriquet is being applied to Jesus. If the matchless Son of God himself can be aligned in the minds of many with the devil himself, why should his followers think they will escape all opprobrium? Indeed, according to these verses the genuine disciples of Jesus will so attach themselves to the Master that they will be satisfied to be treated as he was. In that light it is not surprising that when the apostles first began to feel the heat of serious persecution, in the early years of the Christian church, they rejoiced "because they had been counted worthy of suffering disgrace for the Name" (Acts 5:41).

This is of course nothing more than a reflection of the cosmic conflict between God and the order he has created but which now stands in rebellion against him. Sometimes those whose zeal for mission is informed less by knowledge than by enthusiasm tell us that there is a whole world out there waiting to hear the gospel. If by "waiting to hear the gospel" they really mean "needing to hear the gospel," then of course they are right. But only rarely are people "waiting to hear the gospel" in the sense that they are "eager to hear the gospel." When it happens there has invariably been some antecedent work of the Spirit of God, often through cultural and other pressures, that opens up a window of opportunity. Far more common is it to find genuine receptivity among a subset of the broader society, coupled with indifference or opposition from the masses.

In one sense, of course, Jesus was as concerned to prepare his disciples for ministry beyond the immediate mission as he was for this trainee mission itself. He was sending them out for this brief tour; but this mission was paradigmatic of their lifelong calling, and of the perpetual mission of the church. The opposition the apostles might face in the first instance was being shut out of someone's home, as we saw in the last chapter (on 10:11–15); but principially, Jesus was sending his followers out "like sheep among wolves" (10:16). Down the road, they would face more vigorous attack; so Jesus warns them, "But be on your guard against men; they will hand you over to the local councils and flog you in their synagogues" (10:17). What is in view is not the first mission—there is no evidence that the apostles faced flogging at this point—but the earliest years of the Christian church, before the irrevocable split with the synagogue had occurred. Synagogues often wielded discipline over their own members, and this included flogging with thirty-nine stripes. Once Christians had entirely withdrawn from the synagogue, of course, this punishment could no longer be meted out on them. But in many centers that breach was a long time coming. Paul himself suffered this flogging five times within the first two decades of his ministry (2 Cor. 11:24)— eloquent testimony to the persistence with which he himself practiced the principle that the gospel was "first for the Jew, then for the Gentile" (Rom. 1:16).

But the Christian mission would not stop there. As Christian witness would one day extend beyond Judea and Galilee, and beyond the Jewish race, so too would the opposition: "On my account you will be brought before governors and kings as witnesses to them and to the Gentiles" (Matt. 10:18). The words *governors* and *kings* indicate a non-Jewish environment; and the final phrase, "and to the Gentiles," makes this explicit. Over the centuries, these simple words have been fulfilled in vast arenas of persecution. Christians have been flogged, drowned, burned alive, racked, as well as suffering more esoteric punishments like having boiling oil poured down their throats, or being covered with pitch and set alight as human candles. Like the heroes of the faith listed at the end of Hebrews 11, "the world was not worthy of them" (Heb. 11:38).

More commonly, Christians have not faced the ultimate trial, but have faced considerable harassment. When I was growing up in Quebec, it was not uncommon for a new believer to lose his clients once word of his conversion spilled out. In totalitarian regimes of the left or the right, Christians are often kept out of the best schools, restricted to certain menial types of employment, physically attacked, or simply shipped off to the local version of the Gulag Archipelago.

But this is part of the Christian's calling. The Master himself has said, "I am sending you out like sheep among wolves" (10:16a). What a metaphor! The shepherd sends his sheep among the wolves! We are often treated to some artist's conception of Jesus the good shepherd rescuing his lost sheep—another use of the sheep/shepherd metaphor that obviously has many resonances for Christians. But I cannot recall having seen any representation of the strange imagery in this verse, even though it is clearly designed to help Jesus' followers get a handle on the nature of the mission to which they have been called. This is part and parcel of what Christian experience normally entails, and the point is repeatedly stressed in the New Testament (e.g., John 15:18–16:4).

How then should Jesus' disciples act? The metaphorical language turns to pick up two other creatures. We are to be "as shrewd as snakes and as innocent as doves" (10:16b). In several ancient Near Eastern cultures, snakes were proverbial for prudence, shrewdness. But this virtue easily degenerates into cheap cunning unless it is married to simplicity, innocence. Doves are retiring but not astute: they can easily be snared by the fowler. Such innocence quickly degenerates into ignorance, even naiveté, unless married to prudence. Jesus' disciples must therefore be shrewd, prudent, avoiding attacks where possible, behaving wisely and with far-sighted realism; but they must also be innocent, open—not so cautious, suspicious, and cunning that they become paranoid, elusive, fearful. Doubtless the balance is difficult; but if we find it hard to articulate in the Western world, it is because we have experienced relatively little opposition.

Clearly, then, the fact that the divisiveness of Jesus leads to opposition by the world, and sometimes to outright persecution, is no cause for either paranoid glee or rough belligerence among the people of God. Instead, it is cause for sober reflection, careful counting of the cost, wise assessment that fully expects trouble and is grateful when it passes us by. We are no better than fellow Christians in parts of the world where being a Christian can exact a high toll. Often we are less mature, because less tested. The *principle* laid down in this passage, however, is that we as disciples of Jesus should *expect* opposition, sometimes of the crudest kind, and view it as part of our calling. That is the way the Master went.

2. The divisiveness of Jesus extends to the disruption of families (10:21, 34–39). In the first century, the words found in verse 21 would have been more shocking than they are to us—and they are shocking enough to us: "Brother will betray brother to death, and a father his child; children will rebel against their parents and have them put to death" (10:21). Where the family unit is stronger than it is in most Western democracies, there is corresponding horror at the thought of disruption. Ironically, it is often that very cohesiveness that can generate the betrayal of which Jesus speaks. In cultures with tight social units—Japan, or some Muslim countries—it is considered an extraordinary offense to do something that brings *shame* on the family. In such "shame" cultures (as the cultural anthropologists refer to them), it can actually become a point of honor to take drastic action to remove the shame. Thus in some tightly controlled countries where Islam reigns uncontested, a family member who becomes a Christian brings shame on the entire family, and is therefore in serious jeopardy of being killed *by his own family*. It does not take much knowledge of Christianity in many non-North Atlantic countries to know how often conversion generates, as a by-product, the horrible betrayals and brutal violence of which Jesus warns us.

But let us not deceive ourselves. Although in the West we may not condone that degree of violence, we do not have to witness many conversions within our own culture before we discover painful examples of the family breaches that may ensue. Among personal acquaintances during the last few years who became Christians, three or four stand out for the price they paid in family relationships. A young Irishwoman placed her faith in Christ, and generated consternation among the members of her family when she shifted allegiance from the church of her birth. A Canadian university student, a Jew, became a Christian; his parents not only disinherited him, but held a funeral for him to symbolize how radically they were disowning him. An Englishwoman closed with Christ at a British university, and her middle-class family felt deeply wounded—as if she were telling them that they were not good enough, or that they had not reared her properly. Several years elapsed before the breaches were healed. An American high-school student became a Christian, and went on to become a well-trained psychiatrist. When he decided to devote his life to training Christian ministers and missionaries, instead of pursuing one of the lucrative and prestigious practices or research posts he was offered, his wealthy father completely disinherited him.

Of course, these are more extreme cases; but few people who have become Christians as adults, and who come from homes with little sympathy for the gospel, have not faced some sense of serious dislocation. The truth is that we should not be surprised by this outcome. Jesus himself could define his mission in terms of such family disruption: "Do not suppose that I have come to bring peace to the earth. I did not come to bring peace, but a sword" (10:34). Of course, he does not mean that his *primary* objective was division within families and larger units in society. He means, rather, that his firm commitment to his *primary* purpose, calling sinners to repentance (1:21; 9:13), inevitably results in lives so transformed in their direction and values that they will clash with the society from which they have emerged. Nor does Jesus mean that the consummation of the kingdom will bring perpetual strife and no tranquility. Rather, against many Jewish expectations that the kingdom would come in one climactic burst, Jesus insists that the kingdom comes in stages. The final climactic burst, the consummation, lies ahead; meanwhile, the inauguration of the kingdom brings stresses and division to a sinful world that cherishes its own self-centeredness. Such a world may pride itself on its high-sounding religious and ethical formulations; but in practice it is little prepared for the righteousness, forgiveness, and transformation of character the kingdom introduces.

The Old Testament analogy to which Jesus likens this situation is drawn from Micah 7:6: Jesus has come to turn "'a man against his father, a daughter against her mother, a daughter-in-law against her mother-in-law—a man's enemies will be the members of his own household'" (Matt. 10:34–35). In using words like these, Micah the prophet was describing the gross sinfulness and rebellion in the days of King Ahaz. As Jesus cites the words, however, he claims he will actually *bring about* these conditions: he has come *to turn* a man against his father, a daughter against her mother. He does not mean that those he wins as his disciples will turn against their family members, but that by winning men and women to himself their family members will turn against *them*. Since that is the inevitable effect of his mission, and he knows it, then in a sense he can say he has come to bring it about. Moreover, since the disciples by following Jesus and thereby attracting opposition actually align themselves with the prophets who were persecuted before them (5:10–12), the disruptive wickedness in the time of Micah the prophet points to the wickedness that erupts with similar malice against Jesus' disciples.

But why must the gospel have such negative effects? The reason is spelled out for us in the next verse: "Anyone who loves his father or mother more than me is not worthy of me; anyone who loves his son or daughter more than me is not worthy of me" (10:37). Of course, anyone who dares say such a thing is either a maniac or the Messiah. But even if we grant that Jesus really is the unique Savior, Emmanuel ("God with us"), the virgin-born Son of God Matthew presents to us, at first sight it is still hard to make sense of this text. Why should Jesus do something that is likely to weaken family ties? Isn't he the one who elsewhere excoriates opponents for *not* honoring their parents as they ought?

In fact, the text makes sense only if we have already grasped two perspectives frequently found in the Scripture. The first is that the entire world order is given over to rebellion against God. Even the best of our social institutions—our families, the best of our governments—are weighed down with self-interest that leaves no time for God, or only for a domesticated God. God's grace restrains such institutions and enables them to produce many wonderful things, to serve in many good ways; but so far as their orientation is concerned, they are not principially pledged to serve God our Maker, to please him in heart and in deed. Even when fairly high motives operate in these institutions, the *reason* for the motive is frequently not much more than mere utilitarianism. The second perspective is that the only way out of this dilemma, the only solution to our deeply ingrained self-interest, is conversion to Jesus Christ.

Within this context, the text makes sense; and indeed it can be applied beyond the family. Even when Caesar represents fairly good government, the new Christian finds his or her goals, priorities, and allegiances different from those of Caesar. If Caesar demands ultimate loyalty, the Christian must demur: he or she is sworn to another. Ideally, the Christian will still be, in many ways, an ideal citizen: honest, industrious, generous, law-abiding. But the Christian cannot focus all hope and expectation on the state, or a ruler, or a political party; and even if the Christian shares some of the hopes and aspirations of that party, final allegiance, ultimate confidence, and heart loyalty are devoted only to Jesus and his gospel. Exactly the same priorities are applied to family relationships. As warm, noble, and endearing a family as we may have enjoyed, unless it is profoundly *Christian* in its values it will primarily cherish things which, in their own way, are marks of rebellion against God: material prosperity, self-interested pursuit of status or reputation, dignity, cohesiveness. Some of these values are good, *provided* they do not become absolute, the organizing point around which life revolves. At that point, the family member who becomes a Christian must demur. Ideally, a Christian will do all that is possible to strengthen family ties and nurture this God-given institution; but a Christian will not yield top devotion, princial service, to the family or its values. Non-Christian members of the family sense this, and resent the conversion of the new Christian. The pressure is turned on; fundamental choices are demanded.

Sadly, it must be frankly acknowledged that some family problems experienced by new Christians owe a great deal to the spiritual immaturity of the convert. This Christian can cause needless offense. Even zeal for the conversion of family members can become a dreadfully insensitive triumphalism that breeds hurt feelings and deep resentments. But the naive zeal of a new convert is one thing; the sustained malice, suspicion, and even hatred of the rest of the family quite another thing.

Indeed, Christian conversion brings the new convert into conflict not only with the institutions of which he is a part, but with himself. For Jesus goes on to say, ". . . and anyone who does not take his cross and follow me is not worthy of me. Whoever finds his life will lose it, and whoever loses his life for my sake will find it" (10:38–39). The cross we are called to bear is not an individual affliction: migraine headaches, a bad marriage, difficult financial circumstances, a wayward child—all of them criticized under the frequently heard lament, "We all have our crosses to bear." We may all have individual burdens and difficulties to undergo; but that is not Jesus' point. Christians all have the *same* cross to bear: death to self-interest. In the Roman world, the person who picked up the cross-member and lugged it out to the place of execution had come to the end of hope. Only death was left. It was futile to plot new schemes larded with self-interest. And that is what Jesus means: he is talking about principial death to self-interest, and a new and principial commitment to himself.

The church needs to hear and proclaim this message afresh. Today we are bombarded with endless pseudo-Christian books to help us to become happy, content, resourceful, spiritual, successful, effective, creative. Even when these works convey considerable insight, the basic appeal is far too often, and far too deeply, to self-interest, covered over with the garnish of "spiritual" language. The core truth is far simpler: "Whoever finds his life will lose it, and whoever loses his life for my sake will find it" (10:39). That is why this message is not full of gloom. The point is that, precisely because we were made *for* God, pursuit of *self*-interest is ultimately death-dealing; and for the same reason, when self-interest dies for Jesus' sake and is replaced by enthusiastic loyalty to him, the greatest spiritual irony occurs and we "find" ourselves again.

That is why the happiest, most "fulfilled" Christians are not those who know the most, or who criticize the most, or who analyze the most, but those who with right motives serve the most. If you seek fulfillment, you will not find it; if you seek to serve Christ, often in the countless loving deeds to others that are universally unacknowledged except in the ledgers of heaven, you will find yourself.

But all this goes against the grain of what Paul calls the "natural man," human nature devoid of transforming grace. We live in a world full of self-interest, some of it crude (rape, robbery, embezzlement, gossip, alcoholism), some of it sophisticated (climbing various social ladders, profound commitment to comfort, self-identification with parties and philosophies [whether good or evil] such that our identity is bound up with the party's progress). But Jesus Christ insists our only hope of escaping this morass, for now and for eternity, is to become his disciple, with supreme allegiance only to him. When that sort of conversion takes place, we are on a path quite at odds with our past, and even with our families. That is why the divisiveness of Jesus is inevitable where genuine conversions take place; that is why the divisiveness of Jesus extends even to the disruption of families.

3. The divisiveness of Jesus, and all the malice released because of it, are not to be feared. The passage before us offers five reasons to encourage us to overcome our fears.

First, persecution is not unexpected. All that I have said so far contributes to this point. Indeed, it becomes explicit in verse 26a. After telling us that the servant is not above his master, nor the student above his teacher, and therefore we ought to expect opposition from those who oppose our Teacher and Master (10:24–25), Jesus concludes, "So do not be afraid of them" (10:26a). Fear is often stimulated by the unknown. But his followers, Jesus says, should *expect* opposition and persecution. Therefore if it breaks out, we should never be surprised; and by the same token we shall not live in dread of the possibility. If by God's grace we are spared serious difficulty, then we shall have all the more incentive to lift our voices to God in gratitude and praise.

This presupposes, of course, that part of the process of becoming a follower of Jesus has been the careful counting of the cost. If someone professes faith in Jesus, anticipating a life of uninterrupted bliss, spiritual victory, and considerable popularity, that person may become like the rocky ground in the parable of the sower (Matthew 13): "But since he has no root, he lasts only a short time. When trouble or persecution comes because of the word, he quickly falls away" (13:21). But where there has been a careful evaluation of the cost, there can be little surprise "when trouble or persecution comes because of the word." Knowledge of this possibility largely reduces the fear.

Second, at crucial points we shall be granted special help. This is particularly true when the opposition takes on the cruder forms of persecution. "But when they arrest you," Jesus says, "do not worry about what to say or how to say it. At that time you will be given what to say, for it will not be you speaking, but the Spirit of your Father speaking through you" (10:19–20). Gnawing fear can be more destructive than persecution itself; and in a totalitarian regime, high officials are likely to evoke far more terror than a corresponding official in a democracy where there is at least some possibility of redress. But Christians are not without unseen resources. Although Matthew does not major on the Spirit (unlike Luke), he elsewhere associates the Spirit with the kingdom's dawning (3:11; 12:28, 31) and witness (28:18–20). The assumption here is that Christians, by virtue of the fact that they are Christians, will have been baptized in the Holy Spirit (3:11); and therefore if they face persecution they are to trust the gracious providence of a heavenly Father to provide through that indwelling Spirit just what needs to be said at that time.

This is not a text on which lazy preachers should rely, in the hope that inspiration will come as they enter the pulpit. They are not standing before persecuting tribunals (although they deserve to be!). Rather, this is the promise of direct help in the specific context of overt persecution; and because of this assurance, at least one of the fears associated with persecution may be laid to rest.

Moreover, the text does not absolve us from the obligation always to "be prepared to give an answer to everyone who asks you to give the reason for the hope that you have" (1 Peter 3:15). That should be part of the sustained commitment of every thoughtful Christian witness; and the older we get, the more we learn. Yet there is considerable comfort in knowing that the Spirit of God is with us even in our witness (cf. John 15:26–27)—the same Spirit of God who provides special assistance when our witness places us in serious jeopardy with the authorities.

Third, although opposition and persecution often occur in hidden ways not open to public scrutiny—not only the secrets of the torture chamber, but the candidate passed over, the quiet snubs, the backroom decisions—nevertheless all this takes place under the eyes of a God of whom it is said, "Nothing in all creation is hidden from God's sight. Everything is uncovered and laid bare before the eyes of him to whom we must give account" (Heb. 4:13). That is why Jesus here says, "So do not be afraid of them. There is nothing concealed that will not be disclosed, or hidden that will not be made known" (Matt. 10:26). Christians will be more willing to be despised for a time, if they consciously live in the light of eternity and what the judgment will reveal. The truth will not be concealed; all will come out.

In the same way, because this gospel we enjoy is destined to be known, we are bound to proclaim it: "What I tell you in the dark, speak in the daylight; what is whispered in your ear, proclaim from the roofs" (10:27). The flat roofs of first-century Judea and Galilee made excellent platforms for orators. Jesus' point is that in certain ways his followers would have a more public ministry than he. There were certain things that he told only to them; in due course they would become responsible for making his teaching known as widely as possible. That obligation continues (28:18–20).

The truth must emerge; it will emerge. That includes both the hard realities of secret opposition and animus, and the glories of the gospel message: the truth will be made known. Living in the light of the end simultaneously encourages bold witness (because the truth of the gospel will prevail and will be recognized as God's truth), and quiet confidence in the face of opposition (because every facet of opposition to the gospel will one day be exposed).

Fourth, the wrath of God is more to be feared than the wrath of men. "Do not be afraid of those who kill the body but cannot kill the soul," Jesus says. "Rather, be afraid of the One who can destroy both soul and body in hell" (10:28). The opposition's worst cannot be compared to God's worst. This is not so much an incentive to avoid all fear, as to ensure that fear is of the right kind, rightly directed. Doubtless Satan and his minions have great power (6:13; 24:22); but only God can destroy soul and body in hell. Small wonder, then, that "the fear of the LORD is the beginning of wisdom" (Prov. 9:10), whereas the fear of men so often proves to be a snare (Prov. 29:25). If you fear God, you need fear no one else.

This is especially true because of the fifth reason put forward to calm our fears: God carefully watches over every detail of our life, not least when we are being vilely persecuted. God is not just to be feared; he is to be trusted. "Are not two sparrows sold for a penny? Yet not one of them will fall to the ground apart from the will of your Father. And even the very hairs of your head are all numbered. So don't be afraid; you are worth more than many sparrows" (Matt. 10:29–31).

Jesus' argument is rather different from that put forward by many people today. They think that perhaps God is interested in the big issues, but find it difficult to believe that his sovereignty can extend to the tiny details of our lives. Jesus approaches the question of God's sovereignty by assuming that God's control over even the tiniest detail of the universe is absolute, and then draws comfort from the deduction that his care for larger matters must be correspondingly greater. If not a sparrow falls to the ground without his consent, should we suppose that his elect, redeemed at the cost of his Son's life, shall be of little concern to him?

This does not mean that we can rely on God's sovereignty to keep us out of persecution and difficulty. After all, Jesus has just told us that we should expect to face some opposition. The appeal to God's sovereignty is not to foster hope that we will be spared all difficulty, but to foster confidence that when those difficulties come we are not abandoned. Things have not fallen out of hand. We can still rely on the God who has permitted us to face these things to supply us with the grace and help we need to be faithful under such circumstances. Indeed, even beyond the question of persecution, it is the sovereignty of God, and the reliability of his covenanted love toward his own people, that enable Paul to assure the Corinthians: "No temptation has seized you except what is common to man. And God is faithful; he will not let you be tempted beyond what you can bear. But when you are tempted, he will also provide a way out so that you can stand up under it" (1 Cor. 10:13).

These five reasons provide powerful incentive for allaying our fears when we contemplate the divisiveness of Jesus. Together they point to two further lessons that must not be missed.

First, our willingness to face opposition, and the cogency of the reasons advanced for not fearing it, depend utterly on a biblical Christianity that weighs everything from the perspective of eternity. If there is no heaven to be gained or hell to be shunned, if the forgiveness of our sins and reconciliation to God are not the most important things both for this world and for the world to come, then none of the arguments makes sense. Conversely, if these biblical perspectives constitute the fundamental realities of our existence, whether they are widely recognized in fallen human society or not, then it is folly to ignore them. What is said to find is that form of belief that nominally assents to the existence of eternal realities, but does not act on that voiced assent. Such a tragedy is not merely inconsistent; it is dangerous. To put the matter another way: we cannot really see what biblical Christianity is all about until we live in the light of eternity. Only then do our responsibilities in *this* world come into sharp focus.

Second, in the light of these verses it is important to count the cost *both ways*. The expression *to count the cost* is regularly applied to the obligation would-be disciples have to weigh the nature of the potential opposition before forming a commitment. That is wise and right. But in the light of the blessings promised, and in the light of him who can destroy both soul and body in hell, would-be disciples are equally obligated to weigh the cost *if they ignore* so great a salvation. The calculation cannot be rightly made without considering eternity; it cannot be wrongly made if we are concerned to please him to whom we must still give an account fifty billion years from now.

4. The divisiveness of Jesus characterizes Christian mission, but certain elementary truths soften the prospect and keep that divisiveness in perspective. It is not just while *becoming* a Christian that painful opposition is sometimes experienced; it is also when *witnessing as a Christian*—that is, when engaged in Christian mission. In one sense, this is obvious; and it has already been made clear by a Lord who tells his followers quite frankly that he is sending them out like sheep among wolves (Matt. 10:16). But if we focus on this point without keeping several elementary truths in mind, we are likely to become paranoid, gloomy, pessimistic, even (God help us!) masochistic—like certain cult missionaries who seem to extract a gloomy glee out of being told that they are not invited into our home.

What, then, are those elementary truths?

First, the need will always exceed the persecution. On the one hand, Jesus can say, "All men will hate you because of me, but he who stands firm to the end will be saved" (10:22). "All men," of course, does not mean "all men without exception," or there would be no converts; rather, it means something like "all men without distinction," "all men commonly" or the like. Even so, the prospect is daunting. But on the other hand, Jesus then hastens to add, "When you are persecuted in one place, flee to another. I tell you the truth, you will not finish going through the cities of Israel before the Son of Man comes" (10:23).

Some of the details in this verse make it extremely difficult to comprehend. For reasons I have discussed at length elsewhere,[1] I think it is likely that the coming of the Son of man here refers to the destruction of Israel in A.D. 70. "The coming of the Son of Man" and "the coming of the kingdom" refer to the same *event*, though of course the first expression puts more emphasis on Jesus himself. But both expressions are ambiguous precisely because the kingdom comes in stages and the Son of man comes repeatedly. In one sense, Jesus is born a king (2:2); in another, the kingdom draws near when Jesus begins to preach (4:17). It has dawned when he casts out demons by the power of the Spirit (12:28); yet Jesus gains its full authority only after the resurrection—and even then, his reign is contested until he comes at the end and the kingdom is consummated (24:30–31). Even during the course of Jesus' ministry, the kingdom was dawning in both blessing and wrath (8:11–12; 21:31–32). Here in 10:23, the coming of the Son of man is that coming which makes it no longer possible to preach through the cities of Israel. It is that coming in which the judgment on Israel repeatedly foretold finally falls; and with it the temple cultus disappears, and the new wine necessarily takes to new wineskins (9:16–17). The new age comes into its own; the structured institutions that foreshadowed it are forced into oblivion.

In the immediate context of the disciples, that meant that as long as the nation existed they were not to permit persecution to engender defeatism or despair. If things became too explosive in one town— well, there were plenty of others that needed the gospel. The need would always be greater than the persecution.

The same principle has been invoked in various ways throughout the history of the church. Persecution may shut down one avenue of witness, but there are always others. Missionaries may be expelled from a country, many of the local leaders imprisoned or killed. But that does not necessarily spell defeat. The church may go underground, prosper, and multiply (as did the church in Ethiopia during World War II, or as has the church in China since the Revolution). Missionaries to China were reassigned all over the world, sometimes among large segments of the Chinese diaspora, carrying on fruitful work. The need will always exceed the persecution.

Second, our faithfulness in this mission is bound up with heaven and hell. Jesus insists, "Whoever acknowledges me before men, I will also acknowledge him before my Father in heaven. But whoever disowns me before men, I will disown him before my Father in heaven" (10:32–33). Paul similarly insists that a necessary criterion for being a disciple of Jesus is to acknowledge him publicly (Rom. 1:16; 10:9).

Of course, such acknowledgment will vary enormously from person to person. More may be demanded from a teacher or evangelist than from some others. Not all Christians are endowed with the same depth and maturity of faith. But after all the caveats have been entered, there is no Christian whom Jesus does not require to be a witness. In other words, it is impossible to forge an absolute disjunction between being a Christian and Christian witness. One cannot be the former without engaging in the latter.

Third, Christian truth is so crucial to the well-being of men and women that even how people receive Christian witnesses assumes a transcendental importance. That is the point of 10:40–42: "He who receives you receives me, and he who receives me receives the one who sent me. Anyone who receives a prophet because he is a prophet will receive a prophet's reward, and anyone who receives a righteous man because he is a righteous man will receive a righteous man's reward. And if anyone gives even a cup of cold water to one of these little ones because he is my disciple, I tell you the truth, he will certainly not lose his reward."

The same point is repeated several times in these verses to make it very clear. In verse 40, the apostles are in view: to receive them is to receive Jesus, and to receive Jesus is to receive God. In verse 41, the prophet and the righteous man are in view: the combination of the two terms elsewhere in Matthew (13:17; 23:29) points to Old Testament prophets, and the principle is again spelled out. If hospitality and help and general receptivity are extended to prophets and righteous men, not merely out of common courtesy but because of who these people are, there is a profound self-identity with what they stand for, a sharing in their commitments *and rewards*. John lays out the same principle, both negatively ("Anyone who welcomes him [the false teacher] *shares in his wicked work*" (2 John 11; emphasis added]) and positively ("Dear friend, you are faithful in what you are doing for the brothers, even though they are strangers to you. They have told the church about your love. . . . We ought therefore to show hospitality to such men *so that we may work together for the truth"* [3 John 5–6, 8; emphasis added]). We may not all be missionaries or pastors; however, if we receive such people, support them, identify with them, not because of ecclesiastical obligation, social pressure, or courtesy but because we are deeply identifying ourselves with what they are and do, we are sharing in their labors—and we will share in their rewards. The principle is so fundamental that it is extended to the ordinary Christian, "one of these little ones" (to use the language of verse 42). If the courtesy of providing a drink is shown toward a Christian *just because he or she is a Christian, because he or she is a disciple of Jesus Christ,* the one who extends the courtesy is making an identification that will not lose its reward.

This, then, is the complementary truth to 10:11–15, which we examined at the end of the last chapter. If people receive us because we are Christ's, they are blessed; if they reject us because we are Christ's, they are in terrible jeopardy. That, too, is part of the divisiveness of Christ. But while we have been thinking all along of the difficulties aroused by Christian witness, of the opposition and even the persecution that may dog Christians' heels, it now transpires that those who oppose us are in far more danger than we. Just when some of us might have been feeling sorry for ourselves because of what might happen to us, we are now called upon to feel sorry for others precisely *because* of what they might do to us. That is the attitude that Jesus reflects when he cries from the cross, "Father, forgive them, for they do not know what they are doing" (Luke 23:34)—an attitude Stephen, the first Christian martyr, adopted as well (Acts 7:60). Christian truth is so crucial that how others accept Christian witness assumes a fundamental importance. If this is borne in mind, our witness will be both bold and compassionate, and far less interested in our own welfare than in the welfare of those to whom we bear witness.

Conclusion

When Jesus confronts the world, division takes place. That is inevitable.

And when we think of the divisiveness of Jesus in the broader context of the nature of the world and the power of the gospel, we shall not be surprised—except perhaps by how little our faith has cost most of us. When we contemplate how much it cost Jesus, what eternal issues hang on the gospel, and how good and sovereign is the God who watches over our steps, we shall be the more willing to insist on the power and truthfulness of the gospel over against the prevalent pluralism. This insistence will not be sparked by spiritual pride, but by our knowledge of the Father through the Son. Because of him, we have found our sins forgiven and have learned to rest in the wisdom, grace, and power of God, both for our salvation and for protection and strength in the context of our growing discipleship and witness.

We rest on Thee our Shield and our Defender!
We go not forth alone against the foe;
Strong in Thy strength, safe in Thy keeping tender,
We rest on Thee, and in Thy Name we go.

Yes, in Thy name, O Captain of salvation!
In Thy dear name, all other names above:
Jesus our Righteousness, our sure Foundation,
Our Prince of glory and our King of love.

We go in faith, our own great weakness feeling,
And needing more each day Thy grace to know:
Yet from our hearts a song of triumph pealing;
We rest on Thee, and in Thy name we go.

We rest on Thee our Shield and our Defender!
Thine is the battle, Thine shall be the praise;
When passing through the gates of pearly splendour,
Victors we rest with Thee, through endless days.

Edith G. Cherry (d. 1897)

---

[1]D. A. Carson, *Matthew,* in *The Expositor's Bible Commentary,* ed. Frank E. Gaebelein, 12 vols. (Grand Rapids: Zondervan, 1984), 8:250ff.

Appendixes

Appendix A

Reflections on Critical Approaches to the Sermon on the Mount

MANY READERS OF the Christian Bible pore over its pages for no other reason than to discover theological truth and to be spiritually refreshed. Well and good; if we do not read this book with such ends in view, we are mistreating it. Nevertheless, a closer reading of the New Testament prompts a host of critical questions as well. By "critical" I do not refer to negative judgments or a critical (i.e., judgmental) spirit. Rather, I use the expression "critical questions" in a technical sense, to refer to such considerations as authorship, date, destination, sources (if any), and literary relationships to other works. To ask such questions of the documents which make up the Bible is neither a necessary mark of piety, nor a necessary mark of impiety. For the most part, they are questions which arise because the material is there.

Often when I have taken a passage of Scripture like Matthew's account of the Sermon on the Mount, and expounded it to laymen, someone has come up to me after a few sessions and asked questions like these: Isn't Luke 6:20–49 Luke's account of the Sermon on the Mount? Why then does he say it took place on a plain, a level place (Luke 6:17), and not on a mountain? Why is his account much shorter than Matthew's? Why does Matthew record eight positive beatitudes (Matt. 5:3–12), whereas Luke records only four positive beatitudes and four corresponding "woes" (Luke 6:20–26)? Why isn't the wording the same in other passages, where Matthew and Luke are recording the same teaching but in slightly different vocabulary? Why does Matthew put the so-called "golden rule" toward the end of his account (7:12), while Luke puts it in the middle (Luke 6:31)? And why does Luke leave out the words, "for this sums up the Law and the Prophets"? Why doesn't Luke record the

280

Lord's model prayer? Or rather, why, when he does record it, does he put it in an entirely different context, where it appears as Jesus' response to his disciples' request to be taught to pray (Luke 11:1ff.)? Why are many of the verses in Matthew 5–7 not found in Luke 6:20–49 at all, but are scattered throughout Luke's Gospel? If the Sermon on the Mount is so significant, why don't Mark and John record it as well? Did Matthew read Luke's Gospel before writing his own? Or vice versa? Or neither? Just who is Matthew?

I do not intend to give detailed answers to these questions. To even begin to do so would double the length of this book. In this brief appendix I intend simply to outline some of the principles that lie behind the answers. Also, I want to sketch in some of the developments in contemporary New Testament scholarship, including some approaches and some conclusions which I judge invalid and which will not, in my opinion, stand the test of time.

I shall start by providing two charts. The first begins with the Sermon on the Mount recorded by Matthew, and shows the distribution of that material (or very similar material) in Luke's Gospel. The second begins with the Sermon as it appears in Luke's Gospel, and shows how his material is distributed in Matthew's Gospel.

Chart One

Matthew 5–7	Luke
5:3–12	6:20–26
5:13	14:34f.
5:14–16	8:16
5:17–20	16:16f.
5:21–26	12:57–59
5:27–32	(16:18)
5:33–37	—
5:38–42	6:29f.
5:43–48	6:27f., 32–36
6:1–4	—
6:5f.	—
6:7–15	11:1–4
6:16–18	—
6:19–21	12:33f.
6:22f.	11:34–36

6:24	16:13
6:25–34	12:22–32
7:1–5	6:37–42
7:6	—
7:7–11	11:19–13
7:12	6:31
7:13f.	13:23f.
7:15–20 (cf. 12:33–35)	6:43–45
7:21–23	6:46; 13:25–27
7:24–27	6:47–49

Chart Two

Luke 6:20–49	Matthew
6:20–23	5:3–6, 11f.
6:27–30	5:39b–42
6:31	7:12
6:32–36	5:44–48
6:37f.	—
6:39f.	7:1f.
6:41f.	7:3–5
6:43–45	7:16–20
6:46	7:21
6:47–49	7:24–27

It is worthwhile pausing to pick up a copy of the New Testament and to examine each of these pairs. You will quickly discover that the charts make the problem simpler than it really is. To take one example: although I have put Luke 11:1–4 beside Matthew 6:7–15, Luke actually omits some of the material in Matthew 6:7–15. His wording in this case is a little different, even though both writers say approximately the same thing. And to top it off, his context is completely different.

For many modern writers, these problems become occasions to engender a profound skepticism. Some contemporary scholars think that Jesus actually did preach a great sermon, which was variously preserved by Matthew and Luke who used common source document(s). Many others, however, think no such sermon was ever preached. It is common to suggest that Matthew 5–7 is largely an amalgam of snippets from perhaps twenty of Jesus' sermons. In this view,

Matthew's setting is a literary fiction. Another popular argument is that most of the material comes from the early church, but not from Jesus at all. This view argues that the so-called "Sermon on the Mount" is simply a collection of church catechetical material, pulled together about A.D. 90 and ascribed to Jesus partly out of popular (but mistaken) belief, and partly to give the material more authority.

A related question must be introduced, namely, the Synoptic Problem. Matthew, Mark, and Luke are the so-called "Synoptic Gospels." Close study of these three Gospels demonstrates that they are close enough to one another in wording and order of events that some sort of literary relationship exists among the three. Consensus holds (rightly, I think) that Mark was written first, and that Matthew and Luke had at least read Mark's Gospel before composing their own. In addition, Matthew and Luke have a great deal of material in common which is not found in Mark. This material, most commonly designated Q (for *Quelle*, a German word meaning "source"), is mostly made up of sayings of Jesus. It is disputed whether there was one written source which both Matthew and Luke used, or whether there were many different sources. The arguments are complex, and I have no desire to repeat them here. But it should be noted that the Sermon on the Mount is Q-material.

To talk of "sources" and "literary dependence" should not be alarming: Luke, at least, records his own dependence both on eyewitness accounts and on literary sources (Luke 4:1–4).

Contemporary New Testament scholarship goes beyond this fundamental question. It observes that different kinds of literary material tend to fall into classifiable literary forms. "Form criticism," as the study of literary forms is called, is in the first instance largely descriptive. Unfortunately, however, in the hands of many form critics, the merely descriptive becomes the prescriptive. These critics start saying that certain forms *ought* to be there. Moreover, if there are two accounts of the Lord's Model Prayer, they begin to ask which is earlier, according to literary form each possesses. Then they take guesses at what the "original" is likely to be. And then they ask what changes Matthew and Luke performed on this original, and on this basis try to deduce how Matthew's theology differs from Luke's, and so forth.

To add to the immensity of the related problems, the force of any scholar's presuppositions needs to be taken into account. Not a few contemporary New Testament scholars have gone on record as denying the possibility of miracles, the existence of angels, the deity of Christ, and much more. They realize the New Testament affirms such things, but they protest that such beliefs are cultural relics of a pre-scientific age, and that the *real* message of Christianity in no way depends on such beliefs.

For my part, I remain convinced that such presuppositions reflect accommodation to contemporary secularism, and are in no way demanded by the evidence. The Bible's own witness to itself is that it is the Word of God; and its own evidence, not to speak of correlative evidence, I find quite overwhelming. It becomes important, then, to try to understand this book in its own terms, and to avoid as many twentieth-century prejudices as possible, lest we get it to say only what we want to hear. I must here avoid the question of how to interpret this Word from God, except to say that the ordinary rules of grammar and philology, and the ordinary canons of historical criticism, may be safely applied to it in order to understand better all that it affirms.

The radical skepticism of certain critics, therefore, I find unacceptable on many grounds. However, this still leaves us with the Synoptic Problem; with the genuine insights of form criticism; with the relationship of Matthew 5–7 to Luke 6:20–49, and with the relationship of both of them to an alleged written *Q*; and so forth. Although the Scripture (not just the men who wrote it) is God-breathed; and although holy men of God spoke as they were carried along by the Holy Spirit (2 Tim. 3:16; 2 Peter 2:20); yet the divine activity was such that Paul wrote in Paul's style, to respond to the needs he saw in the churches. Matthew wrote according to his own interests. And Luke was not exempted from the tiring work of research (Luke 1:1–4).

I propose, therefore, to sketch in some observations which may make it easier for the general reader to come to terms with the disparate data, and yet retain—even reinforce—his confidence in the Word of God. My focus will zero in on the Sermon on the Mount. I must again insist that this is a light sketch. Detailed help can be sought elsewhere.

First: Most likely Jesus preached primarily, if not exclusively, in Aramaic, a dialect of Hebrew. The New Testament documents were written in Greek. As anyone who has done any translation can testify, the probability of variant readings in different translations of the same material is overwhelming. *If* the Q material did indeed stand in several written sources, how many of those sources were written in Aramaic? What effect would this have on the finished Gospels of Matthew and Luke? At least some variations are to be accounted for in this manner.

Second: We usually have preserved for us, not verbatim records of all that Jesus said on any particular occasion, but highly condensed reports. If we may accept that Matthew 5–7 gives us a resume of what

Jesus preached on a certain hillside in Galilee, it needs to be pointed out that these chapters take only fifteen minutes to read—even if one is a slow reader. The occasion pictured in Matthew 5–7 sounds like a full-fledged teach-in. Undoubtedly it went on for hours, with Jesus preaching the equivalent of many of our sermons. I could well believe, for example, that the beatitudes were points of a larger message, or pithy conclusions to major topics. Perhaps there were other points omitted by the condensed reports we have in hand. I have no difficulty theorizing that the woes of Luke's account were embedded in this preaching. In other parts of the Sermon, if Luke leaves out more than Matthew, both leave out much more than was there.

Third: The Synoptic Problem is a desperately complex issue, honeycombed with many uncertainties and speculations. That first-century writers should borrow from one another on such a wholesale scale is no problem; that was customary enough in the ancient world (compare, for example, Jude and 2 Peter 2). The problem is much deeper. The Synoptic Problem has never been "solved," and probably never will be—there are just too many unknowns. It does not in any way vitiate faith; but it does make explanations about literary relationships extremely complicated.[1]

Related to this problem is the question of authorship. Luke's Gospel was not written by an apostle; what of Matthew's Gospel? The Gospel itself does not claim Matthean authorship, so we cannot be sure. External evidence supports a very early belief that the apostle Matthew did in fact write it, and evidence thought to contradict this tradition is not as strong as people think.[2] Others date it late and ascribe it to unknown authors because this would, in their view, reduce its historical credibility. I point these things out, not to offer easy answers to each question, but to indicate that discussion about the relationship between Matthew 5–7 and Luke 6:20–49 touches on some very difficult issues. Glib answers should be avoided.

Fourth: The Evangelists themselves have their own purposes in writing. Although they are describing select parts of the life, ministry, death, and resurrection of one man, Jesus of Nazareth, yet they frame their work in somewhat different vocabularies. They aim at different readerships, and they include material and exclude material according to their own purposes and interests. Moreover, they sometimes arrange their narratives chronologically, and sometimes topically. As a result, a particular miracle may be moved by one Evangelist to a different part of his story, simply because it fits better with the theme with which he is then concerned.

We do the same thing today, although perhaps not to the same extent. I have just finished reading Antonia Fraser's excellent biography, *Cromwell: Our Chief of Men*. Once Cromwell has become Lord Protector, she divides up her next few chapters into a topical arrangement which examines Cromwell's rule from various perspectives. Each of these chapters covers the entire period of that rule; they cannot be read chronologically.

In older liberal commentaries, whenever a particular Evangelist left something out, it was common to read such words as these: "Luke didn't know about that," or, "This saying was not in Matthew's source." Now, however, there is a more sensitive recognition of the fact that an Evangelist might leave out an account or omit certain details simply because it doesn't suit his purposes to put them in. The four Evangelists provide us with four "theologies" which complement one another and provide us with a multiform testimony to the person and work of the Lord Jesus Christ. We ought to be grateful that the Spirit of God has overseen their work in such a way that we have received a series of portraits of inexhaustible richness.

Sadly enough, not a few New Testament scholars, newly aware of the theology of each Evangelist, pit theology against history. Every little difference becomes a clue to wildly speculative theological motifs, whereas the simplest harmonization may be the better route to follow. If Jesus goes *up* on a *mountainside* and *sits* in Matthew, and comes *down* to a *level place* and *stands* in Luke (Matt. 5:1; Luke 6:17) must we hypothesize all sorts of deep symbolism? Perhaps he started off doing the former, but touched by the needs of the crowd that would not let him alone (Luke 6:18f.), he did the latter, and continued his discourse. Half a dozen other possibilities come to mind. It is certain, in any case, that both Matthew and Luke give the impression that the material they present from Jesus' teaching is a fair synopsis of parts of that teaching *as uttered on that particular occasion*. It is both unnecessary and, methodologically speaking, quite improper to suppose that Matthew 5–7 is an amalgam of isolated sayings vaguely remembered by the church and melted together by Matthew and Luke to make up a sort of sample sermon which Jesus never preached. The Evangelists do not tell us this is a sample of Jesus' teaching, even though they sometimes introduce Jesus' parables with the vagueness appropriate to that idea. No, they make the Sermon on the Mount historically specific. This is typical of the fact that the Evangelists were, under God, both historians and theologians.

Fifth: Whatever else he was, Jesus of Nazareth was an itinerant preacher. This is not to deny that he was more; it is simply an emphatic way of underscoring his *modus operandi*. That means he preached the same sorts of messages again and again, in town after town and city after city. Undoubtedly the same themes came up repeatedly, and even many of the same arresting phrases.

I was involved in a part-time itinerant ministry for several years. I know firsthand how the same sermons get honed and adapted, repeated and variously applied, as the itinerant preacher moves from center to center. Entire paragraphs came out exactly the way they did in the last town. Changes may be accidental, or they may be premeditated.

I believe this is one of the most overlooked features of the ministry of Jesus Christ as recorded in our Gospels. (Perhaps this is because too few New Testament scholars have done much itinerant preaching!) If part of the message of Jesus in Matthew's account of the Sermon on the Mount is found in another context in Luke, it may simply mean that Jesus preached the same thing more than once. Sometimes even the discovery of an ordered pair of associated ideas in different contexts in the two Gospels indicates nothing more than that Jesus himself paired off the two ideas in that way.

Consider the Lord's model prayer. Luke definitely associates his version of that prayer with the disciples' request for instruction (Luke 11:1–4). Matthew's version of it places it in the middle of the Sermon on the Mount (Matt. 6:9–13). How are we to account for the difference?

According to what we've seen so far, several possibilities are open to us: (1) Matthew borrowed from Luke (or, less likely, vice versa), or they both borrowed from a common source. This means that the setting in at least one of these two Gospels is artificial. This view is popular enough. However, quite apart from the presuppositions about the nature of Scripture, I must ask if this is the most likely solution, the solution most sensitive to the historical realities of Jesus' itinerant ministry. I would argue strongly to the contrary, especially if, as I think, these two books were written when there were still enough eyewitnesses around to set the record straight.

(2) Luke's setting is historically accurate. Matthew records a resumé of a sermon preached by Jesus in the setting he describes in chapter 5, but includes *some* other material, including the Lord's model prayer, which Jesus did not actually teach on that occasion, but which suited the context well enough. In other words, Matthew adds at least a little material to his resumé, such material being authentic in the sense that it is indeed the teaching of Jesus, but inauthentic in the

sense that it did not originally belong to this historical context. Matthew has introduced it here because of topical considerations typical of his methods. And after all, doesn't my own outline of Matthew 5–7 suggest that 6:9–15 is something of an excursus?

(3) Alternatively, Jesus taught the model prayer in this early sermon; but it was something he needed to teach again. After all, Matthew 5–7 has a good deal to say about humility, yet Jesus' disciples failed to learn much about this lesson the first time around. Jesus had to return to the theme more than once. I have no difficulty believing the disciples were equally slow in learning to pray; and, coming to Jesus for help in Luke 11, he may well have taught the same basic form as he earlier outlined in Matthew 6.

What then shall we say of the internal differences between the Lord's Model Prayer as recorded in Matthew, and as recorded in Luke? It is interesting to observe that scholarly critics who rely heavily on form criticism are divided as to which form came first. Therefore, their criteria cannot be as objective as they would sometimes have us believe. Moreover, if (2), above, is correct, then Luke's form came first; and that possibility cannot simply be dismissed. But if (3) is correct, the question is irrelevant: there remains no reason why both cannot be authentic.

In this connection, it is worth noting that the function to which any particular saying is put helps to define its context. Sometimes the Evangelists appear to be offering detached sayings to illustrate a point; but when they nail down the time and place in which Jesus said such-and-such, I take it they expect the reader to believe their testimony is an accurate reflection of what he said, or of part of what he said, on that occasion. They are telling us that the immediate function of a particular saying, or at least part of that function, has been preserved in its historical setting. Arguments which ignore this observation are tampering with the objective evidence in favor of speculative theories.

Sixth: There is in the Gospels much more internal evidence supporting their general historical reliability than is often recognized. I deeply regret that some books demonstrating this fact have not received the wide distribution they deserve. And even where there is minor difference and no direct literary dependence between two Gospel accounts, we have testimony of increased strength, not contradiction; for the absence of collusion in such instances means there is multiple attestation.

Another factor deserves weighing. In teaching Africans and Asians in a Western setting, I have observed that they excel wherever rote learning is required. But they are not as strong when it comes to understanding and formulating abstract concepts. Of course, I am generalizing; but I have talked over the problem with Asian and African nationals doing graduate work in our seminary, and they acknowledge the basic difference in educational approach. The difference is not genetic; second and third generation Asians do not seem to enjoy any special ability to memorize, nor to labor under any conceptual handicap. (Investigation of these phenomena in depth would be worth pursuing.)

In first-century Palestine, education was heavily oriented toward rote learning. Some have even tried to argue that Jesus trained his disciples to memorize all his teachings in the same way that Jewish rabbis memorized the entire Hebrew Bible (the Old Testament) plus great masses of traditional material. Although this theory goes too far, there can be little doubt that Jesus' disciples were indeed capable of memorizing vast amounts of material quickly, even when they did not understand it all right away. I believe this observation helps sustain the historical credibility of the eyewitnesses on whom Luke, for example, relied. Moreover, the fixity of the oral forms which characterized some of the gospel material before it was reduced to writing is better understood in terms of such an ability to memorize, than in terms of stylized "forms" which would often take many more decades to develop than the evidence will allow.

Finally: The positions held by most scholars, of whatever persuasion, are the result of a tight interlocking of various bits and pieces of hard evidence, deductions, speculations, and presuppositions. Even the wildest bit of theorizing can begin to appear credible if it can be made to cohere with a larger structure.

Because of these interlocking chains, to overturn someone else's theory is a major undertaking. We all need to admit that we are capable of being quite mistaken, and even self-deceived, in our own chains of argument. Such an admission will evoke attention to detail and a return to the hard evidence; and perhaps it will also mitigate arrogance.

Having observed that dangers are built into these interlocking structures, we also derive some benefit from them; for careful work will often reveal how some opposing position, at first sight impregnable, is in reality a tight chain made up of a few solid facts and a large number of highly doubtful links.

For example, one very competent scholar pictures the church putting together the teachings of the Sermon on the Mount in present codified form, largely in reaction to the Council of Jamnia, about A.D. 90, even though Jesus' death, resurrection and ascension took place before

A.D. 30. This Council of Jamnia is alleged to be a turning point in Jewish history, when opposition to Christianity hardened and the decisions were made regarding what books would be admitted to the Hebrew canon. However, although the two councils did convene in Jamnia, it is in my judgment very doubtful if either had much to do with the Old Testament canon (except to air difficulties); and equally, Jamnia merely reflected a long-since established opposition to Christianity. A growing body of evidence now supports these contentions, calling into question the earlier assumptions. We might also ask, why was the church so long (some sixty years!) in formulating its relationship to Old Testament prophecies? What evidence is there that Jesus himself did *not* teach such things as those found in Matthew 5–7?

For a second example, let us follow what another distinguished scholar makes of Matthew 7:7–11 (Luke 11:9–13), concerning asking, seeking, knocking, and the Father's eagerness to give good gifts. He thinks that the Q-material of Matthew and Luke was actually found in one document, Q. He notes that in Luke, this particular passage, Luke 11:9–13, is found in a section on prayer (Luke 11:1–13) following the Lord's Model Prayer (Luke 11:2–4) and the parable of the friend at midnight (Luke 11:5–8). Why, then, does this passage appear where it does in Matthew (7:7–11), quite separated from the model prayer (6:9–13), but following hard after a saying about not giving holy things to dogs (7:6), and just before the "Golden Rule" (7:12)? He acknowledges that no completely satisfactory answer can be given, but offers a conjecture. He thinks the natural place for Matthew (7:7–11) would be right after the Lord's Model Prayer (6:9–13). However, because Matthew puts something else after that prayer, the warning about an unforgiving spirit (6:14f.)—which, admittedly, equally suits that context—Matthew is left with the material of 7:7–11 on his hands and no place to put it. Matthew finally decides to put it in an unsuitable context—where it is now.

At first sight this seems plausible enough; but a few questions weaken the conjecture considerably. If Matthew had this material in hand, and if the obvious place for it was right after the model prayer, why didn't he at least put it after 6:14f., the saying on forgiveness? Wouldn't the context still have been prayer? Is the present context (7:7–11) so very unsuitable? I have tried to show in my exposition that the flow of thought in Matthew 5–7 is remarkably coherent, despite the fact it is only a resumé of a much more extended discourse. And besides, I remain unconvinced that the Q-material came from one document anyway. I confess I remain persuaded that Jesus gave this material in the context of his most famous sermon, and, quite likely, in the context of Luke 11 as well.

In his famous poem, *The Everlasting Mercy*, John Masefield included these lines:

> *For while the Plough tips round the Pole*
> *The trained mind outs the upright soul,*
> *As Jesus said the trained mind might,*
> *Being wiser than the sons of light.*
> *But trained men's minds are stretched so thin*
> *They let all sorts of darkness in;*
> *Whatever light man finds they doubt it;*
> *They love not light, but talk about it.*

This sweeping judgment goes too far: I have met both untrained men and trained men with "upright souls." Behind Masefield's lines, however, there lurks a real danger. That danger is the temptation to make human reason autonomous.

Lest I be accused of pleading for the irrational, I hasten to add that we human beings are responsible to use our reason to the best of our abilities. But if the Bible's presentation of God be true, then no man, and no man's reason, has the right to be autonomous—there is not even the possibility of being genuinely autonomous. In fact, every effort to become so is part and parcel of our rebellion.

This is not the place to defend such a perspective. I simply wish to emphasize that the more years I put into the study of the Scripture, the more I find myself under its authority and judged by it, rather than the authority over it with competence to judge it.

---

[1]The interested reader may proiftably turn to some such book as Donald Guthrie's *New Testament Introduction*.

[2]Compare N. B. Stonehouse, *Origins of the Synoptic Gospels*.

Appendix B

Reflections on Theological Interpretations of the Sermon on the Mount

OVER THE YEARS the Sermon on the Mount has been interpreted in a remarkable number of ways. A rapid sketch of the most significant of these theological interpretations may help to explain why I have proceeded as I have.

Some have argued that the Sermon on the Mount is an "interim ethic." That is, Jesus advocated the radical ethics of these chapters because he expected the consummated eschatological age to begin imminently. This ethical stance was to be adopted by his followers in the very short period that remained before the arrival of the end. The terrible urgency of this expectation demanded utter commitment and superhuman righteousness for this climactic period. However, Jesus was mistaken; the end did not arrive. By the same token, the unyielding demands of this "interim ethic" must be dismissed as quite impossible for people today, whose ordinary conduct is not controlled by this expectation of the end. Literal fulfillment of the Sermon on the Mount is absurd if the world actually continues to plod on for more than a few weeks or months.

This view is not as popular as it once was. Many people have noted its weaknesses. The Sermon on the Mount nowhere limits its ethic to an interim period. More important, Jesus was not a fanatical enthusiast whose moral values were totally determined by his expectation of imminent catastrophe; the tension between the "already" aspects of the kingdom and the "not yet" aspects run right back to Jesus himself. Therefore he expected a community to be formed, a community which lived under the authority of the already in-breaking kingdom, in expectation of the consummation of that kingdom. In fact, the substance of Jesus' ethic is designed not only for the period until his second advent, but for all eternity; for although heaven and earth may pass away, Jesus' words will never pass away.

A second interpretation of the Sermon on the Mount is the existential interpretation. According to this view, the Sermon is not to be taken as an authoritative exposition of concrete ethical principles, but a challenge to personal decision. It orients life to an "eschatological" perspective; but by "eschatological" the theological existentialists do not mean that the age to come must be taken seriously, or that it has already overlapped the present age. In fact, these temporal categories of eschatology are utterly rejected as mythical constructions. Eschatology is reinterpreted; the biblical tension between the present life and the end-time judgment is displaced by a tension between the life and conduct that now is and the life and conduct that ought to be. But what "ought to be" is not formulated in terms of the propositions of the Sermon on the Mount, but in terms of an attitude of openness to the future that brings with it constant self-examination and repentance.

I confess I find it very difficult to be sympathetic to this approach. If theological existentialism wishes to construct its own ethical models, well and good; but it should avoid foisting its models onto the New Testament. According to this view, propositional revelation is in principle impossible—as is the supernatural intervention of a personal/infinite God. Accordingly, the biblical data are filtered through a grid designed to remove all such material and launder it ("demythologize it"). The resulting structure accords nicely with modern existential categories, but very poorly with the biblical texts themselves.

A third approach insists that the Sermon on the Mount is meant for this entire age, and that it is to be rigorously obeyed. Most frequently the adherents to this view divide into two groups. The one argues that the Sermon on the Mount is law and not gospel, and as such is not really compatible with Pauline theology. Jesus and Paul, according to this view, cannot walk together. In fact, Paul is guilty of distorting Jesus' teaching. The other group is often associated with the Anabaptist tradition. It takes the Sermon on the Mount to be an accurate reflection of the divine will, to be obeyed both privately and corporately. It holds that salvation is by grace through faith, but that the necessary manifestation of this salvation is a life lived in con-

formity to the precepts of the Sermon on the Mount. Usually paci-
fism constitutes part of this stance; and therefore, if God has given
the sword to the state (Rom. 13:1ff.), it follows that Christians must
not only refrain from participation in military and police forces, but
must equally avoid all civic positions which would require decisions
in any way associated with such forces.

Both of these perspectives take the Sermon on the Mount seriously.
I find myself differing from the first, however, because it does not take
salvation history sufficiently seriously. To allege antagonism between
the teaching of Jesus and the teaching of Paul is to be insensitive to the
progress of revelation brought about by Christ's cross-work, resurrection, and ascension. Such a view ignores the eschatological dimensions
of Jesus' own preaching, and the heavy stress in the Sermon on the
Mount itself on poverty of spirit, the importance of asking and seeking. It ignores the Sermon's recognition of the need for grace.

The second perspective, the Anabaptist/Mennonite tradition, I find
very attractive. Nevertheless, my own exposition of the Sermon on
the Mount has shown where I must part company with it. I think its
view is insensitive to the antitheical manner in which Jesus often
preaches, and therefore reads more into the text than what either
Jesus or Matthew would defend. The Sermon by itself is not a final
comment on such issues as war and capital punishment—there are
other biblical considerations. Moreover, to make the prohibition of
such things an essential part of moral law seems to argue either for
moral development in God, or a development in what God commands.
This is of fundamental importance, for it suggests that earlier commands by God were actually in contradiction to his real will. If morality is not directly related to what God really approves, but only to
what he commands, a terrible tension is set up in him. Moreover, the
New Testament treatment of the church does not require that Christian people be quite as removed from, say, politics, as this perspective seems to suggest.

A fourth answer to the meaning of the Sermon on the Mount is
that advanced by Lutheran orthodoxy. This claims that the Sermon
is an impossibly high ideal designed to make men aware of their sin
and turn to Christ for forgiveness. The sermon, then, is essentially a
preparation for the gospel. This view does justice to some of the relationships between Jesus and Paul; but it sounds more like the conclusion of systematic theology applied a trifle too soon, than the exegesis of the text.

A fifth approach is that of classic liberalism, popular at the turn of the century. Orthodoxy, which placed emphasis on man's need for redemption, the atoning death of Christ, and a supernatural new birth, was displaced by an optimistic liberalism which saw the Sermon on the Mount as the real gospel, the gospel in a nutshell. The Sermon was thought to be the essential map for building a progressive civilization. But this dream of classic liberalism was shattered by two world wars. Liberalism overlooked the fact that human nature requires forgiveness *and help*. Fed by an optimistic faith in the inevitability of evolutionary development, liberalism actually displaced the real gospel with a secular philosophy of progress. Quite unaware of the subjectivity of its choices, it selected those parts of the biblical revelation conducive to its spirit and theory, and rejected the rest. The result provided man with no Savior, no Redeemer, no divine grace, no empowering Spirit; but only a lovely pattern which men subsequently learned they were not able to copy on their own strength.

A more recent view interprets the Sermon on the Mount as catechetical material prepared by the church, some of which stretches back to the historical Jesus. Because the Sermon was catechetical material, according to this view, it was in every case preceded by the proclamation of the gospel and by personal conversion. The gospel precedes the ethical demands of the Sermon on the Mount. Jesus' call to discipleship is therefore directed only at those for whom the power of Satan has already been destroyed by the gospel and who are already heirs of the kingdom of God.

The chief problem with this interpretation is that it does not treat the Gospel of Matthew as a serious historical (as well as theological) document. If Jesus never preached a Sermon on the Mount, nor even provided the essential content embedded in Matthew 5–7, then it may be legitimate to hypothesize that the Pauline emphasis on grace, salvation, conversion, and transformation precedes the "catechetical" material of the Sermon on the Mount. But if he did, then even if his material has been somewhat framed by the church's concern for the catechizing of new converts, it is illegitimate to explain away the theological relevance of Jesus' preaching in its first historical setting by appealing to such catechesis.

By now it will be fairly clear where my own exposition has agreed with the above interpretations and where it differs, even if the foregoing survey has been painfully brief. I accept the Lutheran position as a partial explanation: the Sermon on the Mount does indeed drive men and women to a sober recognition of their sin and a realistic understanding of their need for grace. But the Sermon does more than that. It portrays the pattern of conduct under kingdom authority, a pattern that demands conformity *now,* even if perfection will not be achieved until the kingdom's consummation. In that sense I agree with the Anabaptist tradition. In my judgment, however, that tradition runs into serious difficulty in its attempt at formulating the relationship between the law in the Old Testament and law in the New. As I indicated in the second chapter, I take it that Jesus sees himself and his teaching as that toward which the Old Testament Scriptures point.

Moreover, I think that the norms of the kingdom, worked out in the lives of the heirs of the kingdom to constitute the witness of the kingdom, touches society a little more trenchantly than the Anabaptist tradition allows. If my view overlaps anywhere with the interpretation of the sermon advanced by classic liberalism, it is in this area—even if I can endorse neither liberalism's naive optimism nor its rejection of supernatural salvation. That men must respond to the probing of the Sermon on the Mount is much stressed by the existentialist approach; and with that stress I concur, although I must divorce myself utterly from the unsubstantiality of the probe as constructed by theological existentialism. The urgency of obedience perceived by the proponents of the "interim ethic" structure is undeniably important; but the urgency depends, not on the false model of eschatology advanced by this position, but on the prospect of coming judgment whose timing is unknown but whose decision and sentence are irrevocable.

There is one more theological interpretation of the Sermon on the Mount that needs to be mentioned, if only because it is so popular, especially in North America. It is the view of dispensationalism. This view rigidly distinguishes the period of law (Sinai to Calvary) from the period of grace (Calvary to the second advent). When Jesus came proclaiming the kingdom of heaven, he was in fact offering a millennial kingdom to Jews. The Sermon on the Mount is seen as the law which pertains to that millennial kingdom. However, because the Jews as a whole did not accept Jesus as their King and Messiah, Jesus went into a second plan, hitherto utterly unforeseen by Old Testament revelation and known only to the secret counsels of God. In pursuit of this secret plan, Jesus delayed the coming of the millennial kingdom and introduced an age of grace, the "kingdom in a mystery." This kingdom may be designated the kingdom of God, not the kingdom of heaven. As a result of this theological structure, the Sermon on the Mount has no *immediate* relevance or application to the Christian. It usually conceded that the Sermon embraces principles of conduct which do apply to us; but its real intent is to serve as law during the coming millennial reign. Of the various entailments of this theological structure, one is the conclusion that Matthew 6:14f. must be taken as a formal legal stipulation which governs the conditions under which forgiveness may be granted. As such, these verses are antithetical to the age of grace.

Dispensationalism is a powerful movement today. It enjoys many godly exponents, and some scholarly ones. It is characterized by a desire to treat the Scriptures seriously, a laudable attitude. However, although it no doubt affords valuable insights, I find myself quite definitely opposed to its overall structure. As this is not the place to enter into prolonged debate, I shall simply offer a short selection of reasons why I cannot accept the dispensationalism interpretation of the Sermon on the Mount.

First: The dispensational interpretation of the Sermon on the Mount depends so heavily on the structure of accepted dispensationalism that it is insensitive to the text itself. In other words, the movement imposes its theological construction onto the biblical data, in a manner quite reminiscent of far less conservative groups. This, I submit, is true in its interpretation of the entire Bible, but it is more particularly true of its approach to Matthew's Gospel. Moreover, this theological construction is so all-embracing that it is extremely difficult for a member of this school of thought to accept a different interpretation of any particular passage without endangering the entire system. As a result, a certain rigidity is frequently observed, the total dispensational package becoming equivalent to orthodoxy itself as far as many of its proponents are concerned.

In dispensationalism, the interpretation of Matthew's Gospel is one of the crucial support pillars of the theological structure. Remove it (or any one of a dozen other pillars), and the structure collapses. Dispensational theologians say that up to Matthew 12, Jesus offers the millennial kingdom (=the kingdom of heaven) to the Jews. Unfortunately, however, they reject him; and so toward the end of Matthew 12, he rejects them. In Matthew 13 Jesus is found unfolding the "secrets of the kingdom," the kingdom hitherto hidden from view, but more or less equivalent to the kingdom that I have expounded.

More recent dispensational writers admit that "kingdom of heaven" and "kingdom of God" are frequently interchangeable, but still insist that there is enough difference between them to sustain the view that the former refers to the millennial kingdom and the later to the hidden, saving reign. This I cannot accept. "Kingdom of heaven" is Matthew's preferred use, "kingdom of God" the preference of other New Testament writers (cf. Matt. 4:17; 10:6f.; Mark 1:15; Luke 9:2). Not only are the two expressions found in synoptic parallels, but there is a broader *historical* consideration. Why is the millennial kingdom = kingdom of heaven concept offered during the early part of Jesus' ministry in only Matthew's Gospel? If, for example, any harmonization between John and Matthew is possible, then John 3 must precede Matthew 5–7; yet John 3 is already talking about the kingdom of God in such categories of salvation as new birth, belief, and the Spirit.

Moreover, to argue that the Sermon on the Mount is law in the sense that it is a legal prescription for the millennium is to confuse certain basic issues. To pit law, righteousness, and peace as kingdom concepts against grace and belief as salvation concepts is to create an antithesis that the New Testament writers will not tolerate. According to Paul, for example, salvation has always been by grace, even when God's people were under the Mosaic legislation. And salvation, however construed, has always demanded the conformity to the will of God portrayed in Matthew 5–7. Hence, to take, say, Matthew 6:14f. as evidence of legal prescription *as opposed to grace* is, biblically speaking, unjustifiable.

Second: A close study of the Sermon on the Mount suggests that Jesus has in view just such a world as our own as the sphere in which to work out his demands. The Sermon presupposes a world in which there is persecution of all followers of Jesus without exception, gross insults, anger, personal litigation, adultery, lying, vengeful attitudes, malice, religious hypocrisy, insincere prayers, love of money, worry, judgmentalism, false prophets, and much more. As Carl F. H. Henry puts it, "An era requiring special principles to govern face-slapping and turning the other cheek (5:39) is hardly one to which the term 'millennium' is aptly applied." Matthew 5–7 envisions *our* world, not a reign of millennial splendor.

Third: A close study of the Sermon on the Mount gives the impression that Jesus Christ is repeatedly emphasizing the lasting validity of his words, rather than indicating that their main concerns may well have to be postponed. The Sermon overflows the present imperatives, with the refrain "But I say unto you," indicating the importance of continued obedience.

Finally: I judge dispensationalism to be particularly insensitive to the ways in which the New Testament uses the Old. This subject is so vast I hesitate even to raise it. Nevertheless I am persuaded that the New Testament writers, whether Matthew or Paul, uniformly see the church as the sole legitimate successor to believing Israel, the people of God in the Old Testament. In so doing they cite many Old Testament passages which they claim *are being fulfilled in Christ's atoning work, resurrection, and the resulting church*. Matthew 5:17–20 fits into this pattern quite easily; it does not fit easily into any other pattern.

None of these points is offered as an argument which demolishes dispensational theology once and for all. I am well aware of the responses which my dispensational friends and colleagues would advance—and of my counter-arguments, and so forth. But I would like to think that these few paragraphs will challenge some exponents from each position, including my own, to study the texts again, and try to listen to them from a perspective other than his customary one, the goal being to free oneself from the shackles (but not the advice) of well-worn tradition and to learn afresh from the Word of God.